Revival sent from God

For my children:
Eric, Krista, Dane and Gavin
God grant you to be a force for revival in your generation.

Raymond C. Ortlund Jr serves as senior minister of First Presbyterian Church in Augusta, Georgia. He received his PhD from the University of Aberdeen, Scotland, and taught Old Testament for nine years at Trinity Evangelical Divinity School in Deerfield, Illinois.

Revival sent from God

What the Bible teaches for the church today

Raymond C. Ortlund Jr

Inter-Varsity Press

INTER-VARSITY PRESS
38 De Montfort Street, Leicester LE1 7GP, England

First UK edition 2000

British Library Cataloguing in Publication Data
A catalogue record for this book is available from the British Library.

ISBN 0–85111–534–9

Set in Garamond

Typeset in Great Britain by The Midlands Book Typesetting Company
Printed and bound in Great Britain by Creative Print and Design (Wales), Ebbw Vale

Published by Baker Books, a division of Baker Book House Company, P.O. Box 6287, Grand Rapids, MI 49516-6287, USA.
This edition published by arrangement with Baker Book House Company.

Inter-Varsity Press is the book-publishing division of the Universities and Colleges Christian Fellowship (formerly the Inter-Varsity Fellowship), a student movement linking Christian Unions in universities and colleges throughout the United Kingdom and the Republic of Ireland, and a member movement of the International Fellowship of Evangelical Students. For more information about local and national activities write to UCCF, 38 De Montfort Street, Leicester LE1 7GP.

Contents

Preface

Revival is a season in the life of the church when God causes the normal ministry of the gospel to surge forward with extraordinary spiritual power.

Revival is seasonal, not perennial. God causes it; we do not. It is the normal ministry of the gospel, not something eccentric or even different from what the church is always charged to do.[1] What sets revival apart is simply that our usual efforts greatly accelerate in their spiritual effects. God hits the fast-forward button. And this blessing spills out from the church to wash over the nations with an ingathering of many new converts to Christ.[2]

But does the Bible teach this, or is this just my brainstorm? The noun *revival* doesn't even appear in the Bible. Although the verb *revive* does appear in our English Bibles, it does not convey the special meaning we think of today. The Authorized Version of 1611 translates Psalm 85:6 this way: 'Wilt thou not *revive* us again, that thy people may rejoice in thee?'[3] But the King James translators were probably using the verb *revive* in a more general sense, meaning something like 'reinvigorate with fresh life', which is what the underlying Hebrew text suggests.[4] They did not have in mind the more technical sense we often have when we speak of God reviving the church.

Iain Murray reminds us that the word *revival*, in its special sense, first appears in the usage of Cotton Mather (1663–1728), well after the translation of the Authorized Version.[5] So even though the verb *revive* appears within the tradition of the English Bible, that fact in itself does not validate what we mean by the word *revival* today.

7

But the teachings of Scripture go beyond its words. The Bible's *ideas* are full of revival theology, even though we cannot claim a certain biblical *word* as our warrant for a biblical concept of revival. After all, do you believe in the Holy Trinity? The word *Trinity* does not appear in the Bible. But the idea does (Matt. 28:19; 2 Cor. 13:14). Do you want to be Christlike? That word does not appear in the Bible. But the idea does (Phil. 2:5; 1 Pet. 2:21). We cherish many convictions that are not localized in certain biblical words but are set forth broadly in biblical ideas. And revival is a biblical idea.

The Scripture is clear. God is able to rend the heavens and come down with unexpected demonstrations of his saving power (Isa. 64). God is able to reinvigorate us (Ps. 85). God is able to heal us (Hos. 14). God is able to pour out his Spirit on us (Joel 2), and more. The definition of revival I propose in my first paragraph on the preceding page distils the essence of what I understand the Bible to teach about revival. When we see that God is the great Life-giver and that we sinners are by nature the living dead, the whole biblical story stands forth as a thrilling account of his reviving mercies. Revival theology is pervasive in the Bible.

And revival yearnings are widespread in the church today. Sermons, concerts of prayer, conferences, songs, books: expressions of revival concern are erupting with encouraging frequency. May the Lord himself be in it all and bring his work to brilliant clarity and power in this day.

But it does seem to me that we need more biblical work on revival. We have many excellent books in this area: histories of revivals, calls to pray for revival, controversial works, and others. But we need to give more attention to the biblical text itself. After all, what God says is both more important and more helpful. So in this book I want to taste with you the feast of revival truth spread before us in the Bible.

One reason we want to think scripturally about revival is, obviously, we don't want to be fooled. If it pleases the Lord to visit us with an awakening, may we welcome it and give ourselves over completely to the Holy Spirit. But may we yield to no other spirit, exposing ourselves to deception. Shel Silverstein illustrates the folly of assessing things at a surface level in his poem 'Smart':

My dad gave me one dollar bill
'Cause I'm his smartest son,
And I swapped it for two shiny quarters
'Cause two is more than one!

And then I took the quarters
And traded them to Lou
For three dimes: I guess he don't know
That three is more than two!

Just then, along came old blind Bates
And just 'cause he can't see
He gave me four nickels for my three dimes,
And four is more than three!

And I took the nickels to Hiram Coombs
Down at the seed-feed store,
And the fool gave me five pennies for them,
And five is more than four!

And then I went and showed my dad,
And he got red in the cheeks
And closed his eyes and shook his head:
Too proud of me to speak![6]

Let's not trade down. Let's not squander our Father's good gifts. We need the discernment that only the Bible can give us, to tell the difference between what's valuable and what's cheap.

Another reason we need to look carefully into the Bible is that our expectations of God may be too small, our desires too flat. We may be so hypercautious that anything taking us out of our usual way automatically becomes suspicious. But the Scripture boldly insists that 'God does whatever he pleases' (Ps. 115:3 RSV). He does not limit himself to our routines, methods, and traditions. Revival is, by definition, an *extraordinary* work of God. The biblical vision of our reviving God is breathtaking. So if we accept the authority of Scripture, we will have to enlarge our concept of what God can do for us. The Bible refuses to give aid or comfort to the impulse that would strangle authentic revival. It challenges us all to get rid of our threadbare ideas of God and think larger, bolder thoughts of him than we have dared to before. Isn't it pretty obvious that with our present performances we'll keep on getting our present results? Who could rest content with that? We need to be stretched in our thinking and in our praying.

I will focus here on the Old Testament, primarily because that's where I've spent most of my life's effort in Bible study. Even within the Old Testament, I will not cover all the passages that deserve attention. This book offers only a small sample. But what I give you here is representative of what the Bible teaches.

I do hope that my writing will not muffle the prophetic power of the Scriptures. It is so hard not to be dull. C. S. Lewis wrote that 'when the old poets made some virtue their theme, they were not teaching but adoring, and ... what we take for the didactic is often the enchanted'.[7] As I write, I am not merely teaching; I am adoring. Please do not take the enchanted as merely the didactic.

My ultimate aim is to persuade you that revival is a valid biblical expectation, so that you join me in praying that God would rend the heavens and come down in our generation. We cannot trigger revival, but we can turn away from all that clogs up God's work. We can devote ourselves to the normal ministry of the gospel in such a way that we give him no reason *not* to empower it mightily. Above all, I want you to be encouraged in God. We must never give up and give in. *He is able.*

I owe so so much to so many. Thanks, Jani, for being my dearest partner in the gospel. Thanks, beloved friends at First Presbyterian Church, for praying me through this project. Thanks, fellow elders, for giving me this month to finish the task. Thanks, Jane and Iris, for your keen eyes on the text.

Edith Schaeffer has been kind to grant permission for a chapter from her husband's book *Death in the City* to be reprinted here as an appendix. Thank you, Mrs Schaeffer.

Dr Don Carson deserves special thanks for reading my manuscript and giving his critique, in the midst of his busy schedule. Thanks, Don, for your wisdom.

I also thank my friends at Baker Book House for their expertise and kindness in this project.

Soli Deo gloria!

Introduction

As a seminary student years ago, I had the privilege of attending lectures by Dr J. I. Packer. His reflections were stimulating in many ways. But over the years one simple sentence has echoed in my mind with almost haunting persistence: 'Do not neglect the revival dimension in your ministry.' And his counsel is even more weighty now than it was at that time.

We live in strange times. While the Bible-believing church is polarized on a wide range of hot-button 'issues', it neglects the powerful truths lying at the centre of our faith. The atmosphere of contemporary evangelicalism is too often overreaction and misplaced enthusiasm. We are not as biblical as we think we are.

For example, some earnest Christians seem afraid of experiential Christianity. They see that the church today is awash in experience-seeking. And as doctrinal and moral standards are also eroding, they connect the dots in such a way as to blame our problems on this yearning for a deeper experience of the immediacy of God.

In a way, their alarm is understandable. As never before, our world is glutted with *experience*: considered as mere sensation, anyway. We are a visceral generation. Bludgeoned into near stupefaction by an entertainment-driven culture, we drag ourselves from one thrill to the next, each one promising to outperform the last. And the quietness of communion with God, the heroism of Christian obedience, the delights of Christian thought are holy privileges not encouraged by the mood of our times. We are deprived of the very experience for which we were made: sublimity and purity with

11

God through Christ. We drink down the ethos of modernity to the point of a caffeine high, but too many of us know little of the profound satisfaction of being 'lost in wonder, love, and praise' at the feet of Jesus in authentic gospel experience.

We should recoil from the moonscape of modern human existence and all false remedies offered in the name of God. But it would be foolish to identify our problem as an overdose on experience. It would be foolish to retreat into a merely cerebral religion out of alarm over the eccentricities sadly evident within the church. C. S. Lewis counsels us wisely when he writes:

> The task of the modern educator is not to cut down jungles but to irrigate deserts. The right defence against false sentiments is to inculcate just sentiments. By starving the sensibility of our pupils we only make them easier prey to the propagandist when he comes. For famished nature will be avenged, and a hard heart is no infallible protection against a soft head.[1]

Change 'educator' to 'preacher' and 'pupils' to 'congregations', and it all fits. The modern world may be flooded with vulgar sensationalism and hyper-spectacularization and mawkish sentimentality. But as far as true gospel experience is concerned, our world is a desert. Therefore the church's answer cannot be a starvation diet of doctrine only. The church's answer is to irrigate the desert with authentic, biblical Christianity. God created us with a craving for himself, and famished nature will be avenged. If we are deprived of true experience of God, we are by nature spring-loaded to overreact in favour of error and distortion.

Do we want to guarantee that our children will run in the opposite direction of our most cherished biblical convictions? All we have to do is sterilize our churches. Make them rigid, unresponsive, grim. Require of our ministers that they play the role of scolding, scowling Reverend Eat-Your-Peas. Treat the gospel as a theological system only, rather than also as a personal remedy. Use the Bible as ammunition for 'culture wars' rather than as food for life. Withdraw from the historical situation in which God has placed us. Build up the walls, reinforce the barriers, and make certain that no experience gets in *here*. Ignore the fact that 'doctrine only' is not itself a biblical doctrine.

But do we want our children to embrace our biblical convictions with joy? Let our churches become environments fertile with revival potentialities. Let's shape our churches with the deliberate intention that their content and tone may encourage our children, and all others, in true experience of God. Let our convictions open up to their eyes a glorious vision of God and to their hearts the succulent pleasures of God. We cannot trigger a divine visitation on our churches, but it *is* our responsibility prayerfully to offer our Lord a church steeped in the gospel and tenderly responsive to his presence. His Spirit's blessing should not have to work against the logic and ethos we create.

As we navigate the currents of distortion and error all around, Francis Schaeffer proposes a wise course.[2] 'The final problem is not to prove men wrong,' Schaeffer writes, 'but to win them back to Christ.' And he counsels us that *winning* hearts requires of us an apologetic with three components. First, we must provide a clear explanation of what is wrong with the false view competing for the allegiance of people's hearts. Second, we must provide a clear explanation of what is right with the scriptural teaching at that point of controversy. And third, *we must demonstrate in real life that the biblical view satisfies human needs and desires in a way that the error does not*. People must see and sense the beauty of the truth. But reacting to distorted experience by backing away from biblical experience concedes too much and leaves yearning hearts with no alternative but to drink from the polluted fountain.

My plea comes down to this. *Let's not neglect the revival dimension in our churches*. It is biblical. It is right. It is of God. Let's stop being so timid. Let's trust God so much that we follow his Word without qualifying it to death. None of us has long to live. Why not do something boldly radical before you die? Follow God's Word fully. Don't censor it. Don't whittle it down to the narrow confines of your comfort zones. Trust that God is wise in all his Word and ways. *Pray* for more of him than you've ever had before. And then go beyond praying. *Expect* him to show himself near to you in new ways that will delight you and honour his own name. Venture your whole personal fulfilment on God, withholding nothing. He will be honoured, and you will be amply rewarded.

I delay no longer. Let's dig into the Bible to unfold in vivid detail, first, what God can do and, second, what we must do.

Part One

What God can do

Prologue

One might think that the role of God in revival would be obvious enough. 'In him we live and move and have our being' (Acts 17:28). And especially revival, however human in the moment-by-moment unfolding of history: is it not an unmistakable miracle of God? Yes, but we do manage to skew our perception of God's role in revival, and in more than one way.

Every time we drive past a church with a sign in front announcing, 'Revival meetings here next week', we are confronted with an understanding of revival that exaggerates the human dynamic. It may seem a small point, and I do not wish to be unfair. But how can we advertise a revival and expect to retain credibility? Presumably we do this because the very idea of revival has been diminished to an event on the church calendar. Evangelistic meetings – maybe that is all people mean when they announce a revival – are a legitimate church programme. But true revival is not a scheduled programme. It is a gift from the Throne wonderfully interrupting our little programmes. The Holy Spirit blows like the wind, unpredictably, mysteriously, uncontrollably, wherever he pleases (John

15

3:8). We cannot announce him in advance. We can only pray that he will blow our way.

Another distortion is to treat revival as a merely human artefact discovered amid the debris of history.[1] As a topic of scholarly interest, revivals fall within the history of evangelical Christianity. But if God's role is minimized in the scholar's historical analysis, if a revival is treated like a specimen in a petri dish to be turned over and over and looked at from various angles with too little sympathy and too much detachment, if biblical faith is not allowed to illuminate the whole, the net result is a dismissive reductionism. This way of thinking quenches the Spirit. It is less an insight into reality and more a function of intellectual fashion in our times.

I believe that God revives his people, because the Bible says he does. I respect revival as a real act of God on the human scene. Not everything called revival is revival; but authentic revival is a holy thing. Holy things can be thoughtfully studied but they must be thoughtfully studied *as* holy things. For me, therefore, it is a matter of principle to consider revival not merely as a species of evangelical experience but, far more, as an authentic act of God among us, much to be welcomed.[2]

So we can fall into two opposite errors. On the one hand, we can overinterpret an event as revival. We can attribute too much to God. We can celebrate an intense corporate experience as his work when in reality it is only, or mostly, a work of human religious psychology. The human personality, without one bit of the Holy Spirit, is capable of burning religious fervour. But we must not ascribe to God what he himself would not own. We must be chaste in our claims. We must think with careful discernment.[3] Scholars must not write hagiography. Pastors must not allow fanaticism.

On the other hand, we can underinterpret a spiritual event. We might make insufficient allowances for the presence of God, or exclude him altogether, when he is really at work. The presence of human error and eccentricity does not necessarily mean that God is not also blessing. Nor does the influence of strong human abilities or favourable historical trends render an event explainable in human terms only. We must allow for the profound mingling of the divine with the human, or we risk a kind of methodological naturalism.

It is not always easy to discern the hand of God in human

events, but we must thoughtfully and prayerfully avoid either over-interpreting or underinterpreting scenes of human experience that may qualify as revival. Both errors surely offend God. He has declared openly and repeatedly that he purposes to show himself among us.[4] Therefore we submit ourselves to God's own purpose when we look expectantly for his revealed glory. And we honour him when we require of ourselves that we not be deceived with counterfeits. He will not give his glory to another (Isa. 48:11).

So what can God do among us? What can we confidently pray for? What may we properly expect? What should we eagerly welcome? Only the holy Scriptures can answer these questions. And the Bible invites us to look for unmistakable visitations of God's glory. So let us allow God to be God to us. Let us give ourselves permission to see him at work. Not everything we call revival is really revival, and no real revival is perfect. But it remains true that God is able to revive his people. This is what the Bible says. Let me show you.

1
God comes down to us

It was a gorgeous September day in the north-east of Scotland, in 1984. I was standing atop the Hill of Fare, overlooking the valley where my family and I lived while I was doing my doctoral work at the University of Aberdeen. I had run the Hill, as I did every year on that day, my birthday, just to prove to the Lord I was not washed up yet! And now, as I rested at the summit, my eyes were exulting in the lovely view. Spread out before me was a patchwork of fields bordered with ancient stone walls, pastures dotted with sheep, stands of trees, a stone farmhouse here and there. The River Dee, fed from the mountains to the west, hurried silently toward the North Sea twenty miles to the east. An old castle ruin on the hillside off to my right stood guard over the serenity of the whole scene.

But at that moment I noticed how the puffy, cumulus clouds were casting shadows randomly on the valley floor. In one place, all was green and bright. In another place, it was shadowy, grey, subdued. And it came to me: the church is like this. In some quarters, the light of God is streaming down in unclouded brilliance. The church is flooded with life and truth and joy. In other places, a chill has set in. The colour has faded. God's people are living in the shadows.

19

The power of God is not evenly distributed throughout his church, geographically or historically. God himself has told us that his work can follow an uneven pattern: 'I sent rain on one town, but withheld it from another. One field had rain; another had none and dried up' (Amos 4:7). The church either blossoms or withers, as God sends or withholds the rains of his blessing.

And how is that fact significant? It is significant in that the church, and the church only, is the salt of the earth and light of the world. By God's own appointment, the church of the Lord Jesus Christ is *the* agent of divine redemption in human society. There is no other: not the Boy Scouts, not the Rotary Club, not any political party of any kind. That being so, what could be more important for the world than the condition of the church?

Isaiah 63:15 – 64:12 teaches us how to pray when we find ourselves living in the shadows. And this biblical prayer challenges us to scrap our routine expectations of God and seek him boldly for a fresh visitation from on high. He is able to come down to his people.

The people of God to whom Isaiah's prayer was originally given needed urgently to rediscover God in just this way. Judah had been conquered by the muscular, vigorous Babylonian empire early in the sixth century BC. The forces of evil stood triumphant over the broken body of God's people, savouring their victory with sadistic glee. To the Jewish survivors it seemed as if the whole moral order of the universe had been overthrown. The temple had been violated and its ministries halted. The holy city had been plundered and its people deported. And the stragglers left behind had to ask, 'Where is God now? Has he abandoned us?' The people of God were living in the shadows. And at that moment the prophecy of Isaiah calls them to pray that God would come down to them again with reviving mercies.

Where are you, Father?

Look down from heaven and see
   from your lofty throne, holy and glorious.
Where are your zeal and your might?
   Your tenderness and compassion are withheld from us.

But you are our Father,
   though Abraham does not know us
   or Israel acknowledge us;
you, O LORD, are our Father,
   our Redeemer from of old is your name.

(Isa. 63:15–16)

I remember hearing Francis Schaeffer pray in public many years ago. His opening words struck me: 'O God, we thank you that you exist.' It had never occurred to me to thank God for that; but how meaningful a prayer that was. Our only hope is that God is there. He may withdraw from us the enjoyment of his nearness but he is still there. Our present experience is not the full measure of his reality. God's glory is quite undiminished for its lying beyond the range of our vision. And as long as God is there, unchanged and unchanging, he can renew our experience of him here. The prophet encourages us to pray with that confidence in mind. So what may we ask for?

The cry 'Look down and see' calls for God to renew his attentive concern for us. In one sense, of course, God is constantly 'sustaining all things by his powerful word' (Heb. 1:3). If he looked away even for an instant, we would quickly disintegrate. Isaiah does not doubt that. But this verse invites us to ask God to renew the *visible demonstration* of his concern for us.

With God's attention redirected our way, as it were, we ask him the question 'Where? Where is your loving intensity ('zeal') toward us? Where is your manly strength ('might') on our behalf? Your agonizing concern ('tenderness') and your melting sympathies ('compassion') remain powerfully active within you. But you are withholding them from us.'

It is as if our King has retreated into his glorious palace on high, choosing to overlook the sufferings of his people. He closes his ears to their cries beyond his palace walls. He breaks off his once-familiar companionship. So we are faced with a painful incongruity. Up there, enthroned in heavenly glory, is God our Father. Down here, we, his very own children, languish in our wretchedness. How does *that* make sense?

But we should not read this prayer as whining criticism of God.

This cry arises from fresh stirrings of spiritual awakening, as the people of God begin to see how far they have drifted and how much they have lost ('Abraham does not know us or Israel acknowledge us'). If Abraham were to get into a time machine and push the fast-forward button, he would look at this generation of the people of God and wonder, 'Who are *you*?' They bear little resemblance to their godly forefather, much less their heavenly Father. But, certain that God must be true to himself, they cling to him as their family defender ('our *Redeemer* from of old is your name'). And how can God betray his own 'name'?

This way of praying expresses true faith struggling to find God afresh. We cannot pray in this way unless we believe that, no matter how barren our experience has become, our Father is still there for us.[1] In *The Screwtape Letters* C. S. Lewis has the senior devil explaining to the junior devil that this tenacious faith in God is the tempter's greatest defeat in our souls:

> Sooner or later He withdraws, if not in fact, at least from their conscious experience, all those supports and incentives ... It is during such trough periods, much more than during the peak periods, that it [the Christian] is growing into the sort of creature He wants it to be. Hence the prayers offered in the state of dryness are those which please Him best ... Do not be deceived, Wormwood. Our cause is never more in danger than when a human, no longer desiring, but still intending, to do our Enemy's will, looks round upon a universe from which every trace of Him seems to have vanished, and asks why he has been forsaken, and still obeys.[2]

Isaiah calls us to defy despair and pray for our renewed enjoyment of God's love. Our Father rules all things from his glorious throne in heaven, in full possession of his attributes and powers. Therefore our present experience does not determine our future. God our Father and Redeemer is the true measure of our future prospects. And we may seek him with that confidence.

But our attempts to seek the Lord can be neutralized by our own sinfulness, counteracting our higher aspirations. The prophet now subjects our spiritual malaise to a profoundly searching analysis.

Why do you harden us, Lord?

Why, O LORD, do you make us wander from your ways
and harden our hearts so we do not revere you?
Return for the sake of your servants,
the tribes that are your inheritance.

(Isa. 63:17)

The people of God ('your servants, the tribes that are your inheritance') perceive such extraordinarily paralysing power in their sinful
trends that a divine judgment must be at work. And if *God* is
against us, then who can be for us? Is this not a verse to make us
tremble? But there it is on the biblical page, and the Hebrew is
unambiguous. So what do we learn here about the ways of God?

When we wander from God, when our hearts harden so that we
binge on sin, it is not God's fault (Jas. 1:13–15). We have only ourselves to blame. But God may still use our sin for his own holy
purpose. If we provoke God by neglecting him and chasing after all
the wrong things, he is able to expose our wickedness to us. He is able
to lift restraint from our hearts. He is able to withdraw the support of
his Spirit. And when he does, we plunge into those lustful appetites,
which otherwise we would have been inhibited from indulging.

This verse explains why the best of human wisdom and therapy
can fail us. It proclaims the utter necessity of the mercy of God on
us, for our best efforts will crumble under the power of our sin. If
God withholds himself, sin takes over within our souls like a drug
gang gaining control of a neighbourhood.

Primarily, however, this verse explains the ultimate reason why
the church experiences dry times. God himself sends those spiritual
droughts to us. If we allow him to fade into the unnoticed backdrop of nominally Christian lives, we become hardened *under his
own discipline*. When the church is living in the shadows and God
seems far away, make no mistake: God is not inactive. He is still
very much at work, pursuing what Isaiah calls God's 'strange work'
of judgment (Isa. 28:21).

But it is we who drive him to it. Israel thought they could flirt
with the idols, and God would always be there to bail them out of
trouble. In a sense, that expectation is right. God's grace really is

cheap. It comes at no cost to ourselves and we cannot exhaust its resources. But it is also true that God will not allow his grace to be cheapened, trivialized, dishonoured. He intends his grace to be glorified (Eph. 1:6). And if we abuse his mercy as a pretext for sinning, God is not left helpless by his own gospel of grace. That same gospel declares that we reap what we sow (Gal. 6:7–8).

It is possible to coddle some secret sin, some pet indulgence kept hidden away in our back pocket for the occasional spree. We may think that, when we get tired of it or when it becomes a little too much for us, we can easily drop it and come back to God, no problem. Oh, really? How do we know God will *let* us come back? He may leave us in our mess for a while to teach us a lesson.[3] Our existence is more than the aggregate whole of our autonomous personal choices. Choice is one of our favourite words today. But we must never forget that God's choices underlie our own. We can fall before him and plead his mercies in Christ our Saviour but we will never outflank him or outsmart him.

Solemn as this warning is, it inspires an equally thrilling hope. If it is his to harden us, then it is also his to make us tender once more. Our sinful condition is not within our easy control but it is entirely within God's sovereign control. And that hope is the message of Isaiah 63:17. We can cry out to God from the prison we have created by our sins, and he will hear us even from there. After *we* have gone beyond the point of no return, *God* is able to 'return' for the sake of his servants, softening his sin-coarsened people.

> For a little while your people possessed your holy place,
> > but now our enemies have trampled down your sanctuary.
> We are yours from of old;
> > but you have not ruled over them,
> > they have not been called by your name.
>
> (Isa. 63:18–19)

Here the prophet calls a nominal generation to lament the depth to which they have fallen. We today might perceive the status quo of the church as acceptable, as long as outright disaster does not strike. But Isaiah would ask us why. Why do we accept the present condition of the church? Where is our sense of humiliation, of indignation, such as we see in these verses? The prophet refuses to rest content when the church is dominated by the world. Rather than following the trends of the world, the church should be setting the trends for the world. We must always be thankful for the wonderful things the Lord is doing in our day. But we must never stop asking God to make his people 'the praise of the earth' (62:7) until he does it. The church's unfulfilled potential and the world's undeserved prestige create a scandal contradicting our very identity as the people of the living God.

Deuteronomy 4:5–8 reminds us that we have two privileges which no other group on the face of the earth can claim. We have the wisdom of God in his Word and we have the nearness of God in answered prayer. And Moses says that the world should be looking at us with a sense of envy and awe. Deuteronomy 26:17–19 and 28:1 tell us that, if we humble ourselves under his Word, God will see to it that we are admired by the world. They will be drawn to us willingly, gladly. They will see that we have the answers to life's problems. They will see that God is with us. But if out of unbelief and insecurity we crave the world's approval more than God's favour, our lives, our churches, and our institutions will show it, as influence flows away from the church in favour of the world.

And what of us today? So many churches, so few solid conversions! As the prophet surveys the defeated condition of the people of God, their historic opportunity lost, his heart is bursting for a fresh visitation of God, for God can do for us what we cannot do for ourselves.

Oh, that you would come down!

Oh, that you would rend the heavens and come down,
    that the mountains would tremble before you!
As when fire sets twigs ablaze
    and causes water to boil,
come down to make your name known to your enemies
    and cause the nations to quake before you!
For when you did awesome things that we did not expect,
    you came down, and the mountains trembled before you.
                                                          (Isa. 64:1–3)

I love this imagery. The prophet envisions God taking the sky, which he has spread out like a curtain (40:22), taking that cosmic veil, which hides him from our view, grabbing it in his strong hands, ripping it apart from top to bottom, and stepping down into our world! It's a thought to make every believer tremble with joy.

Isaiah portrays the descent of God as something to be longed for. 'Oh, that you would rend the heavens and come down' is a vivid way of praying, 'Thy kingdom come, thy will be done on earth as it is in heaven.' God, who seems so far away up there, so removed from the cruel push-and-shove dominating our world, so careless about the fortunes of his own cause, suddenly rips through the sky to break in with his presence and power. Who would not long for it?

The paragraph has two bookends, as it were, surrounding it with one primary thought. 'Come down, that the mountains would tremble before you' appears at the beginning and again (with no change in the Hebrew) at the end. But the prophet is not thinking of a literal earthquake. The 'mountains' symbolize long-established, well-positioned, difficult-to-remove resistance to God. That is the world we live in. And that is what the church cannot change by her own efforts and programmes and good intentions. But the Lord's presence ('before you') changes everything. The evil that we cannot budge is, to God, like mere twigs before a fire or water set to boil. It has no power to resist.

God is able to come down in new, unanticipated ways here in this world, so that people actually change their minds about him. He is able to make his name known to his enemies. He is able to cause the nations to quake before him. He does it by his own power. He does it in his own surprising ways. In verse 3 Isaiah may have the Lord's descent on Mount Sinai in mind. But whatever the incident may have been, it accomplished 'awesome things that *we did not expect*'.

Our narrow expectations are not the measure of the entire work of God. When the Spirit came down at Pentecost, the people were 'utterly amazed' (Acts 2:7). In fact they were 'amazed and perplexed' (v. 12). God is full of surprises. This is why A. Skevington Wood, the historian of the First Great Awakening, proposes:

The next great spiritual awakening may be utterly unlike any that has gone before. We must beware, then, of an undue fixity in our concept of revival. The Holy Spirit is not limited to a stereotype. He enjoys and exhibits an unconditional liberty.[4]

'Awesome things that we did not expect' urges us to make allowances for the freedom of God. Obviously he will never contradict his own Word. It is not, therefore, Spirit-quenching to require of ourselves that we be searchingly biblical in our assessments. But God is not limited to our past experiences, our traditions, or what we think the church's next step should be. We must leave room for divine mystery, for surprises. God never acts out of character but he does exceed our expectations.

Isaiah is teaching us how to pray for the church in our generation. One senses the intensity of his plea. He draws us up with him into fervency with God. Calvin puts it this way: 'Here believers burst forth into earnest prayer, as usually happens when in sore adversity we do not find plain terms to be sufficiently forcible for our purpose.'[5] This kind of praying does not drone on in sleepy requests for what will probably happen anyway. This courageous prayer looks back to God's unexpected breakthroughs in the past ('you came down') for inspiration to pray for new breakthroughs today ('Oh, that you would come down!').

George Whitefield, the evangelist of the eighteenth century, was preaching once in Cheltenham, England. He relates in his Journals that suddenly, during the sermon, 'God, the Lord, came down amongst us.'[6] Something special happened through the ministry of the Word. God shook the mountains of resistance. He burned the brushwood of prejudice and false ideas. He warmed the indifference of cold and unbelieving hearts. He made his name known. And here in Isaiah's prophetic prayer God himself invites us to ask him for a renewed demonstration of his triumphant power.

Does this vision of God not put our brainstorms and programmes into a true perspective? At bottom, we do not need formulas for successful Christian living or techniques for successful church growth. Granted, there is a proper place for the wise use of the best means. But Isaiah's vision lifts us beyond praying for God's

blessing on our own ideas. He is proposing something more profound. He sets before us the glorious prospect of a surprising visitation from Almighty God himself.

How can we be saved?

> Since ancient times no one has heard,
>> no ear has perceived,
> no eye has seen any God besides you,
>> who acts on behalf of those who wait for him.
> You come to the help of those who gladly do right,
>> who remember your ways.
> But when we continued to sin against them,
>> you were angry.
> How then can we be saved?
>
> (Isa. 64:4–5)

The awesome vision of God coming down (vv. 1–3) is juxtaposed
with the depressing familiarity of our sinning, here in verses 4–5.
We may wonder whether our generation *can* be turned around
('How then can we be saved?'); not that there is any deficiency in
God, of course.

God is uniquely able to act here on the human scene. He has
proven it 'since ancient times'. All the speculating and philosophiz-
ing and searching of the world's religions have produced no alternatives. The other gods simply do not deliver the goods. But the
God of Abraham, Isaac, and Jacob, the God of Moses, the God of
David, the God of the prophets, the God and Father of our Lord
Jesus Christ, alone, has proven himself a God who *acts* on our behalf
(v. 4). But Isaiah argues that we must meet God on God's terms.[7]

So who are the ones to experience God's close support? Scripture
generally has much to tell us, but in this passage Isaiah identifies
three marks of those for whom God acts. First, they are 'those who
wait for him'. To *wait* for God means just that: to be patient, to
delay, to let God act in his own time and in his own way, rather
than rush forward according to one's own impulses. Isaiah uses the
same word in 8:17: 'I will *wait* for the Lord, who is hiding his face
from the house of Jacob. I will put my trust in him.'

The believer who waits for the Lord endures the delay in a spirit of confidence, as the parallel 'put my trust' implies. Waiting regards him with expectancy and yet with the humility that defers to his timing and methods. True faith is not leverage to force God's hand. True faith waits for God in a posture of confident submission.

Second, God comes to the help of 'those who gladly do right'. We offend God if we feel that he is cheating us out of life, as if obeying him were a fast rather than a feast. Obedience is a privilege not granted to everyone. After all, God 'comes to the help' of obedient people. The NASB translates more simply: 'Thou dost *meet* him who rejoices in doing righteousness.' God looks for, draws near to, and encounters the one whose heart embraces life as one vast panorama of opportunity for honouring God.

Third, God comes to the help of those 'who remember [his] ways'. But the prophet is not upholding merely an ethical ideal. The NASB's more literal rendering gets to the point: '[the one] who remembers *Thee* in Thy ways'. This mentality, so pleasing to God, appears brilliantly in the apostle Paul:

> I consider everything a loss compared to the surpassing great-ness of knowing Christ Jesus my Lord, for whose sake I have lost all things. I consider them rubbish, that I may gain Christ and be found in him, not having a righteousness of my own that comes from the law, but that which is through faith in Christ.
>
> (Phil. 3:8–9)

God does not require that we 'remember his ways', full stop. Any moralistic Pharisee is capable of mere observance, at least outwardly. God requires that we remember *him* in his ways, fixing our hearts on *him* and gladly walking in his ways because we treasure *him*.

So if we want the only active God to be active on our behalf, we must demonstrate a faith that waits patiently, an obedience that thrills at the privilege, and an observing of his ways for his own sake. But then that's the problem, isn't it? Who of us is like that?

Isaiah's generation infuriated God ('you were angry') with a per-sistent pattern of sin ('we continued to sin'). Despite blessings and in the face of warnings, they kept on sinning. So 'how then can we be saved?' How can mediocre believers ever hope to see God rend the heavens and come down? We would love to see the nations quaking before God (v. 2), but what if we ourselves are wasting away under the power of our sins (v. 6)?

Our sins sweep us away

> All of us have become like one who is unclean,
>   and all our righteous acts are like filthy rags;
> we all shrivel up like a leaf,
>   and like the wind our sins sweep us away.
>
> (Isa. 64:6)

Rather than the saving power of God coming down, Isaiah sees another power at work. With prophetic insight, he shows us four images of the crippling power of sin. This is a reality check. And his intention is to deconstruct the pretences of a nominal, sin-infested generation of the church. With false exteriors stripped away, we are then ready to be renewed. The prophet invites us to own up to our hypocrisies, layer by layer.

First, 'all of us have become like one who is unclean'. We are moral lepers, defiled and defiling, unfit for God's presence and spreading our disease to others.

Second, 'all our righteous acts are like filthy rags'. The metaphor is embarrassing. These 'filthy rags' are used menstrual garments. The point is that even our best performances ('righteous acts') flow from our sinful nature within. Their quality is tainted. If sin were blue, then everything about you and me – every thought, emotion, word, and deed, including our best moments – would show at least some tint of blue. Even our *righteousness* needs to be rinsed clean. One man's trenchant assessment is this: 'The devil is wildly optimistic if he thinks he can make human beings worse than they are.'[8]

Third, 'we all shrivel up like a [brittle October] leaf'. God created us to be vigorous and resilient. But we have sinned ourselves into such a state that we have no rejuvenating power within.

Fourth, 'like the wind our sins sweep us away'. Our foolish inclinations drive us in directions we never intended to go. And when we look for the moral stability to right ourselves, when we put our foot on the brake, nothing happens. Sure, we are nice people. But what is it really worth? We are nice, *evil* people. We are too often swept along by our baser impulses.

Let us not miss the significance of what Isaiah is doing here. The whole passage is a prayer for revival. But revival is not a mere power surge, or an emotional blowout. True revival front-loads questions of personal integrity. Verse 6 calls us to an unblinking honesty about ourselves, so that we forsake all self-admiration. It explains why our natural moral potential is ineffective in pre-serving our marriages and empowering our churches. We are sinful. And sin is not just bad; it is powerful. It neutralizes our good inten-tions. We do not even have it within ourselves to seek God convin-cingly.

> No one calls on your name
>   or strives to lay hold of you;
> for you have hidden your face from us
>   and made us waste away because of our sins.
>
> (v. 7)

When is revival necessary? When prayer has lost its power ('No one calls on your name') and other ways of coping seem more helpful, when sleepy Christians go through the motions without rousing themselves to lay hold of God, revival is necessary.

God isn't really far away. We have direct access to him through Jesus the Mediator (Heb. 10:19–22). But Isaiah sees the reason why his people are not taking fuller advantage of their privileges. The reason is this: 'You have hidden your face from us.' The means of grace lack saving power. And when God disciplines us in this way, we cannot blame him. We waste away 'because of our sins'.

Do you see the irony of verse 7, compared with verse 1? Far from ripping the sky open and coming down to show his face before the trembling world, Isaiah laments that God isn't even showing his face to his own people. The church's sinful indifference tells God to stay away. But, to the glory of God's grace, that is not the whole story. Isaiah now directs us back to his mercies, because our sins do not defeat his goodness.

Oh, look upon us!

Yet, O LORD, you are our Father.
We are the clay, you are the potter;
  we are all the work of your hand.
Do not be angry beyond measure, O LORD;
  do not remember our sins forever.
Oh, look upon us we pray,
  for we are all your people.

(Isa. 64:8–9)

God is a Father and he is also a Potter. He is a Father who loves his children and he is no less a Potter who freely shapes his lump of clay. We cannot be selective. If we resist Isaiah's bold affirmation of divine sovereignty, we cannot claim his assurance of divine love. God is not a menu, from which we choose our preferences. God is a person: a whole, complex person. We must accept him as he is or not at all. If we want his fatherly compassion, we must also accept his artistic freedom.

And isn't that the God we need? A helplessly pleading Father gives us no hope. But a Father who loves with an irresistibly transforming love is one who can revive his church. Having sinned our way into a low condition, our only part now is to cry out to our powerful Father with the urgency of faith, modelled in these verses.

Some will still object: if we are the clay and God is the Potter, why pray at all? If we lie within his sovereign control, like soft clay in the strong hands of a potter, then what incentive is there to pray? The powerful incentive that Isaiah provides is precisely that *we are the clay and God is the Potter*! We are not bound by an impersonal force or blind fate; neither are we finally left to the tender mercies of our own depravity. The church's future lies with God our Father. Our ever-changing world, in every aspect, is being shaped moment by moment by our Father's hand. The world that our children will live in forty years from today will have been shaped by that same loving hand. What a strong hope! Someone larger than ourselves, Someone larger than our enemies, a Grace greater than all our sins can at any moment choose to reshape us and our world with the ease of a potter running his hand down his spinning lump of clay.

He is our Father, and nothing restrains him. And here Isaiah invites us to invoke God's sovereign power for our reviving once again.

When the prophet writes, 'Do not be angry *beyond measure*,' he is not insinuating that God might overreact. Isaiah and Moses were theological soulmates, and Moses assures us concerning God that 'he is the Rock, his works are perfect, and all his ways are just. A faithful God who does no wrong, upright and just is he' (Deut. 32:4).

So what does Isaiah mean? He is pleading that God would give us less discipline than we really deserve. The Potter is sensitive not to crush us.

I do not clean a delicate vase the same way I scrub a greasy roasting pan; I would break it. In the same way, God knows best how to deal with us. And Isaiah's prayer is giving us permission to plead God's mercy when his awesome power is applied to our cleansing. We deserve a vigorous scrubbing. But God knows how to use a light touch. It may not feel light to us at times, but we can be sure it is less than what we deserve and only what our restoration requires.

God loves a fresh beginning. He is willing to show grace ('do not remember our sins forever') and manifest favour ('look upon us'). He is willing to regard us not as we are in ourselves but as we are in Christ. And we have good grounds for praying this way, for 'we are all [his] people'. It is he who chose us as his own. He will not back out now. He cannot void his own eternal purpose.

Therefore, when we find ourselves wondering how long we must live in the shadows and whether the night of discipline will ever pass, we may stand on this bedrock of encouragement: *it is not in God to be angry beyond measure. He knows when enough is enough.*

Will you hold yourself back?

> Your sacred cities have become a desert;
>> even Zion is a desert, Jerusalem a desolation.
> Our holy and glorious temple, where our fathers praised you,
>> has been burned with fire,
>> and all that we treasured lies in ruins.
>
> (Isa. 64:10–11)

Too late do we value our real treasures in life! The familiar and beloved ordinances of the church, the only means of grace existing on the face of the earth, those tokens of God's saving power – 'all that we treasured' – will suffer ruin if we bungle our priestly calling. But God is able to recover even the sacred things our folly has damaged.[9]

Precious though they are, the institutions of the church, analogous to 'your sacred cities', are not ultimate reality. At their best, they only symbolize God's 'lofty throne, holy and glorious' in heaven (63:15), which *is* ultimate reality. So after our sins, the world, and the devil have done their worst – and they will – God will still be there on high with all the resources he needs to re-create his church out of the ruins we leave behind.

He may restrain himself and keep silent for a time. But this prayer stands recorded in the public record of holy Scripture as a permanent declaration of his readiness to remake us. And if this is true, then our best days as the church militant still lie ahead of us, not behind us. That's why he put this prayer in his Word: to awaken in us the courage to venture bold new prayers for revival.

> After all this, O LORD, will you hold yourself back?
>   Will you keep silent and punish us beyond measure?
>
> (64:12)

The way Isaiah asks these questions shows him shaking his head in disbelief. It is inconceivable that God would completely abandon his people. He has too much invested in us. 'God will not permit his glory to be trampled under foot, though men provoke him by innumerable transgressions,' to quote Calvin.[10] And on infinitely greater authority: 'How can I let myself be defamed? I will not yield my glory to another' (48:11). Isaiah wants us to ground our deepest convictions in the bedrock of that strong confidence.

The prophetic prayer now comes full circle. The concern 'Your tenderness and compassion *are withheld*' (63:15) is echoed here with the question 'Will you *hold yourself back*?' with the same Hebrew verb. God has withheld his compassion from his people. But he can see the damage that has been done and he feels the loss. Verse 12 brings the prophetic prayer to a close with encouraging expectation of new favours from heaven. In the course of this prayer, we have been humbled, confronted, broken. But now, by providing the very plea for a reversal of his strict dealings, God shows us how ready he is to release his grace on us once again.

This one sample of revival praying is consistent with the tenor and direction of other biblical prayers. Jonathan Edwards observed:

> if we look through the whole Bible and observe all the examples of prayer that we find there recorded, we shall not find so many prayers for any other mercy as for the deliverance, restoration and prosperity of the church and the advancement of God's glory and kingdom of grace in the world.[11]

Revival praying, therefore, lies in the mainstream of God's kingdom purpose. This way of praying pleases God. As normative biblical theology, Isaiah's model prayer takes us down very deep into our sinful condition. It lifts us up very high to glimpse the majesty of God. This prayer is not calculated to encourage our natural levity and superficiality. It is calculated to draw from us a response of depth: depth of repentance before God and depth of confidence in God. This prayer is intended to search our hearts, shape our aspirations, enlarge our faith, and draw us nearer to God.

So what could it look like for God to come down to us today? Unfortunately, Bible-believing people cannot always agree on this. Some look for apostolic signs and wonders. Others are not convinced that we should entertain such expectations. The debate sometimes reminds me of the time when Jesus took Peter, James, and John to the Mount of Transfiguration, while the other disciples were down below. A man asked the disciples waiting at the foot of the mountain to heal his son, but they failed (Mark 9:18). I imagine it this way. Up steps one disciple: 'This is how you heal somebody. Abracadabra!' Nothing. Another disciple elbows his way forward: 'That isn't how you do it, stupid! Watch this. Shazam!' One after another, they all fail. *And then Jesus comes down.*

When God rends the heavens and comes down on his people, a divine power achieves what human effort at its best fails to do. God's people thirst for the ministry of the Word and receive it with tender meltings of soul.[12] The grip of the enslaving sin is broken.

Reconciliation between believers is sought and granted. Spiritual things, rather than material things, capture people's hearts. A defensive, timid church is transformed into a confident army. Believers joyfully suffer for their Lord. They treasure usefulness to God over career advancement. Communion with God is avidly enjoyed. Churches and Christian organizations reform their policies and procedures. People who had always been indifferent to the gospel now inquire anxiously. And this type of spiritual movement draws in not just the isolated straggler here and there but large numbers of people. A wave of divine grace washes over the church and spills out onto the world. That is what happens when God comes down. And that is how we should pray for the church today.

Increase Mather lived in a proud, darkened Boston in 1721. He cried out, 'Oh, degenerate New England! What art thou come to at this day? How are those sins become common in thee that once were not so much as heard of in this land?'[13]

But God rent the heavens and came down. When George Whitefield ministered there in 1740, just nineteen years later, he wrote, 'So many persons come to me under conviction and for advice, that I have scarcely time to eat bread. Wonderful things are doing here. The Word runs like lightning!'

And Benjamin Franklin had this to say about the effects of God's work that same year in Philadelphia:

It was wonderful to see the change in the manners of our inhabitants. From being thoughtless or indifferent about religion, it seem'd as if all the world were growing religious, so that one could not walk thro' the town in an evening without hearing the psalms sung in different families of every street.

We are grateful for God's reviving mercies in the past. But who can be content with past blessings? Is it not time to pray again for God to rend the heavens and come down? Is this passage in Isaiah not *calculated* to give us the courage to pray boldly for a new revival sent from God?

2

God reinvigorates us

For those of us who have been Christians for a while, it becomes easy to think that we have pretty much exhausted the possibilities of the Christian life. We can settle into a routine of activities at church and in our small groups and Bible studies, with little expectation of anything new. The familiar becomes the predictable, and everything from here on will be more of the same. We dip our teaspoon into the vast ocean of the living God. Holding that teaspoon in our hand, we say, 'This is God.' We pour it out into our lives, and we say, 'This is the Christian experience.'

God calls us to dive into the ocean. He calls us into ever new regions of his fullness, his immensity, his all-sufficiency. There is more for us in Christ than we have yet apprehended. Let us never think that we have him figured out or that we have seen all he can do. The Bible is not a guidebook to a theological museum. It is a road map showing us the way into neglected or even forgotten glories of the living God. George Smeaton, a nineteenth-century scholar of the Free Church of Scotland, warns us wisely:

And no more mischievous and misleading theory could be propounded, nor any one more dishonouring to the Holy Spirit, than the principle ... that because the Spirit was poured out at Pentecost, the Church has no need, and no warrant, to pray any more for the effusion [outpouring] of the Spirit of God. On the contrary, the more the Church asks the Spirit and waits for His communication, the more she receives.[1]

Our Lord is so vast, and our exposure to him is so small. Twice in quick succession, summarizing his own approach to the Christian life, the great apostle says, 'I press on' (Phil. 3:12–14). The Scriptures are pervaded by a Pauline spirit of 'straining toward what is ahead'. The Word of God fully intends to draw us out of our timidity, kindle in our hearts yearnings for newness, and set us on a pilgrimage of prayer into his magnificence, where we will be reinvigorated.

Prayer is boring when it's merely an attempt to maintain our present level of communion with God without slipping back. That's boring, because our present experience isn't all that satisfying to begin with. Why protect *that*? But prayer springs to life with meaning and urgency when we see it as an occasion for pleading with God to deepen and expand our experience of him through reinvigoration by the Holy Spirit.

Psalm 85 is another prayer for revival. It is a biblical prayer intended to stimulate our own prayers. We know that God likes Psalm 85, because he inspired it. So we can pray in this way with assurance that our requests are not at all extravagant but right on target.

But we need first to read the psalm as a whole:

You showed favour to your land, O LORD;
    you restored the fortunes of Jacob.
You forgave the iniquity of your people
    and covered all their sins.
You set aside all your wrath
    and turned from your fierce anger.

                                                      (vv. 1–3)

Restore us again, O God our Saviour,
    and put away your displeasure towards us.

Will you be angry with us forever?
    Will you prolong your anger through all generations?
Will you not revive us again,
    that your people may rejoice in you?
Show us your unfailing love, O Lord,
    and grant us your salvation.

(vv. 4–7)

I will listen to what God the Lord will say;
    he promises peace to his people, his saints –
    but let them not return to folly.
Surely his salvation is near those who fear him,
    that his glory may dwell in our land.

(vv. 8–9)

Love and faithfulness meet together;
    righteousness and peace kiss each other.
Faithfulness springs forth from the earth,
    and righteousness looks down from heaven.
The Lord will indeed give what is good,
    and our land will yield its harvest.
Righteousness goes before him
    and prepares the way for his steps.

(vv. 10–13)

The striking thing about Psalm 85 is this: even though it laments God's displeasure with his people (vv. 4–5), it nowhere calls them to repent of sin. It contains no confession of sin. Sin is not even mentioned, except as forgiven in the past (v. 2) and warned against in the future (v. 8, last line). In fact the people of God in view here are 'his saints' (v. 8) and 'those who fear him' (v. 9). So these people, yearning for revival, are godly people. And yet they sense their Lord's anger with them. How does this make sense?

God's anger in verse 5 ('Will you be angry with us forever?') is not a condemning anger, rejecting his people. It is a disciplining anger, refining his people. They are not living in such aggressive defiance of God that the psalmist calls for repentance. But God stands some distance away from his own people, because they have not been seeking him. They have been resting on the blessings of the past (vv. 1–3). They have drifted into spiritual complacency. And in fatherly discipline God is withholding the outpouring of new blessing until his children cry out to him in sharpened hunger.

It is like a church beginning to realize, 'We are not what we used to be. We are not what we ought to be or want to be. It has been too long since the immediacy of God's presence was a vital reality in our midst. It is time to seek the Lord.' That is the burden of Psalm 85: a good church with a strong past seeking the Lord for a fresh visitation in the present. Even good churches need revival.[2]

Think of a husband and wife walking together. Some time before, their marriage went through a rocky period. The wife ran off with another man. But the husband pursued her and won her heart again. Their reunion was sweet, like verses 1–3. So, as the psalm is being written, the husband and wife have been back together for some time. But by now things have changed. The glow of their rekindled romance has faded. They no longer walk hand in hand. They do not speak as tenderly as before. The wife's heart is cooling again. To her credit, she is still walking with her husband, not flirting with other men. But neither does she delight in her husband's company as she used to. She has lost her first love, and a chilly silence has set in. She is thinking of other things. But now, as Psalm 85 makes clear, she is coming to realize how far her heart has drifted, even though her steps have remained on course. She begins to notice that her husband is no longer initiating overtures of love as he used to. Feeling the loss, the wife stops, turns to him, looks up into her lover's eyes and says, 'Please take me in your arms again.'

Now, how does Psalm 85 express that spirit? In the first paragraph (vv. 1–3), the people gather strength for the great plea in verses 4–7 by recalling God's mercies in the past. A favourable past argues encouraging possibilities in the future.

Past mercies

You showed favour to your land, O LORD;
  you restored the fortunes of Jacob.

(Ps. 85:1)

The return of the Jews to the promised land after their long exile in Babylon in the sixth century BC may be the event assumed here. But whatever the original episode, the point is that God's smile had beamed down on his people. He restored them out of spiritual decline. So they have seen God's reviving work before.[3]

The verb translated 'showed favour' exudes the flush of personal warmth and delight.[4] God's policy toward his people turned from stern discipline to joyful affirmation. And he *demonstrated* his renewed favour with the unmistakable clarity of concrete action by lifting his hand of discipline and reversing their humiliation. He 'restored the fortunes of Jacob'. It was a landmark event, as divine restoration always is. The memory of it marked the people of God.

But how did this dramatic change in their corporate life come about? How can one explain such an unlikely but welcome turn of events? It was not merely human politics moving the pawns around on the board of history. It did not arise from the people of God deploying their own diplomacy or force. Verses 2 and 3 lift our eyes up to the Throne of heaven, where the decisions of life are really shaped.

> You forgave the iniquity of your people
>   and covered all their sins.
> You set aside all your wrath
>   and turned from your fierce anger.

We are inclined to regard our moral failings casually. We are inclined to congratulate ourselves with how well we complement God's contribution to the venture of life. We are so accustomed to our sin-infested condition that we feel 'normal' to ourselves. Only God can see us as we really are, and what we really are deserves his 'wrath' and 'anger'. But verses 2 and 3 argue the grace of God toward his people: not a theoretical grace, but a real-life grace that they have personally experienced. God will never violate his own integrity by winking at our sins. Our sins drove his Son to the cross. But the scope of God's glory is big enough to include both wrath and grace ('You *set aside* all your *wrath*').[5]

And God's grace was needed because of 'the iniquity of *your people*'. The fault was not the sins of the pagans out in the world. It

was the sins of God's own people that had antagonized him.
But God lifted that hindrance away ('you forgave'). God deleted
from his database ('you covered') his record of '*all* their sins'.
And with all their sins erased from his scorecard, his holy wrath
relaxed into a comfortable ease with his people. The tension was
over.

But it was all God's own doing. Do you see that God himself is
the subject of every verb in verses 1–3? As God's people review a
season of unusual favour in the past, not one word is said about
human initiative or causation. Why? Because it was all of grace. We
did not qualify for it. We did not deserve it. God himself, acting on
his own initiative, launched a new beginning for his sinful people.
And God has not changed.

Therefore, as verses 4–7 will show, we can go back to him again
and again with the confidence that our God is a God who gives his
sinful people new life. Our hope is not that our Father does not
really feel disciplinary 'wrath', for he does. Our hope is not that
God may come to realize that his concern is some kind of neurotic
overreaction to our little failings, for it is not. Our hope is that
God's mercy in Christ knows how to 'set aside' and 'turn from' his
wrath toward the sins of his people.[6] He is able to melt the frozen
tundra of our obstinacy into a fresh responsiveness. He did it
before. He is ready to do it again.

God's own actions, gratefully reviewed as precedent in verses
1–3, encourage our longings for revival, expressed in verses 4–7.
But the way this prayer unfolds is significant. It shows us that
revival is not our whimsical brainstorm, concocted out of wishful
thinking. Revival is God's own pattern of dealing with us. It renews
what God himself has already granted in the past. Therefore we
may be sure of this: true revival is not an aberration. True revival is
a firmly established biblical tradition. It deserves our acceptance as
accredited, orthodox experience with impeccable biblical credentials
and deep historical roots. It stands firm as a valid part of the ways
of God with his people, to be cherished in the past and sought after
for the present.

What then do the past mercies of verses 1–3 prompt us to ask
God for today? Verses 4–7 reflect the present distress, crying out to
God with deeply felt urgency.

Present distress

> Restore us again, O God our Saviour,
> and put away your displeasure towards us.
>
> (Ps. 85:4)

Verse 4 begins this section by appealing to 'our *Saviour*', and verse 7 concludes it with 'your *salvation*'. The plea framing this section is that God would renew his miracle of salvation. And significantly this prayer rises on behalf of the people of God, not the lost world. Unbelievers are not the only ones who need salvation. The burden of this paragraph is that God's own people would experience salvation in a fresh and vital way. And the confidence of the psalm is that we who have drawn from his deep reservoir of saving mercy in the past (vv. 1–3) will find him ever full for us again today (vv. 4–7).

The sad reality presupposed in these verses is that God's people have again lapsed into spiritual mediocrity. They have again provoked God's 'displeasure'. And that divine sense of annoyance ('displeasure' is a weak translation)[7] is the barrier to our recapturing the joy of salvation. Look at the way the two lines of verse 4 stand in parallel. 'Restore us again, O God' is joined with 'put away your displeasure towards us'. How is this parallelism significant? It means that we cannot manage our spiritual decline as a problem to be solved by our human devices; God alone must do this, because God is the only one who can put away his own displeasure. He is our Saviour. If he refuses to restore our generation, we have nowhere else to go. We lie in his power. He can make us; he can break us. But at the same time, the ultimacy of God also implies hopeful possibilities far beyond the range of what we might accomplish.

The word translated 'put away' could be more literally rendered 'break'.[8] It makes awkward English, but the force is clear: 'Break your irritation, Lord! Make a sharp break in your policy toward us!' The people of God are led to ask for a decisive change in the way God regards them and handles them. And their prayer, lying here on the page of holy Scripture, declares to us what God can do for our generation as well. He needs no favourable circumstances before he can act, for it all rests with him alone. 'How irritating we are to you, Lord. We see that now. But you can restore us to a vital experience of your salvation. Break off your understandable annoyance with us, and through Christ crucified let your renewing mercies flow!'

The urgency of their prayer is unmistakable:

> Will you be angry with us forever?
>   Will you prolong your anger through all generations?
>
> (v. 5)

The emphatic words here are *forever* and *through all generations*. To these people, it seems like ages since the immediacy of God's presence was felt in their midst. Full-strength joy is by now a distant memory. For too long they have been going through the motions of a religious role-play, and they cannot bear it any longer.

The contrast between the memories savoured in verses 1–3 and the struggle of the present in verses 4–7, and especially here in verse 5, argues that revival grows out of a godly tension, a hearty dissatisfaction with the status quo that prays boldly, 'Will you be angry with us forever?' This is not the voice of contentment with the present condition of the church. The prophetic heart pulsating here senses that the people of God are neither in complete darkness nor in the brilliant noonday of God's blessing. They are hovering somewhere between, in mediocrity and nominalism. But a wholesome tension has erupted at the realization that there is more for them in Christ than they are presently experiencing, and that their own past witnesses to it.

Do you sense the confidence driving this prayer? The people of God cannot believe that he will discipline them indefinitely. Their knowledge of God compels them to expect his anger to lift. Is that not the assurance of Psalm 30:5? 'For his anger lasts only a moment, but his favour lasts a lifetime; weeping may remain for a night, but rejoicing comes in the morning.'

God does not deprive us for fun, and he is always glad to get it over with. His deepest nature is biased toward mercy.[9] But he is sufficiently self-disciplined, if I may put it that way, to prolong a season of chastening if we need it. And sometimes we do.

What if God always answered our prayers and relieved our

distresses quickly? What if God were just a whim away? That kind of fathering produces spoiled brats. God knows when we need to struggle through. Time tests us, and that is good. It deepens us. God has no intention of encouraging superficiality in his children, for God himself is not a superficial person. He loves depth. And the long continuance of his discipline has the power to deliver us from our natural giddiness and set us apart as the very saints of God.

But there is even more goodness in God's anger. Our outbursts of temper tend to be erratic, moody, immoderate. They reveal our instability. We can even use an angry confrontation and its tense aftermath to control someone, keeping that person off balance and insecure. But God's anger is of another order both morally and psychologically. Morally, his anger is always a just, wise, measured assessment of what we need. Psychologically, his anger is entirely within his control. The question '*Will* you prolong your anger?' assumes that God will *decide* to prolong it or cancel it. He is in complete command of himself. After all, is not self-control the fruit of the Holy Spirit (Gal. 5:22–23)? So there is not even a tinge of emotional need in divine anger, tempting him to drag it out for *his own* sake. God is free to put his anger aside at any time and release an outpouring of mercy on us. This means that even when under his discipline, we can rejoice in hope. All God has to do is say the word, and everything changes.

Verse 6, the heart of the whole psalm, helps us envision what that change looks like in actual experience:

> Will you not revive us again,
>> that your people may rejoice in you?

The question in the first line is not 'Will you revive us again?' as if we had to wonder. The question expects a positive answer: 'Yes, I will revive you again.'[10] How could it be otherwise? Our God is the God of life.[11] His way is the way of life.[12] Out of his vast and vibrant all-sufficiency the living God will revive us again.

Verse 6 urges on us a strong confidence that God *will* command renewal for his people. We do not know his intentions toward our own generation, but he will never allow his church to die. The church must be revived, and revived again and again and again, as long as history endures. This confidence is as certain as is God's very being, for through Christ his Son we are in vital union with the living God.

The word translated 'revive' is used elsewhere in the Old Testament in a variety of ways: for restoring a city (1 Chron. 11:8); for recycling stones from an old ruin to build a new structure (Neh. 4:2 [in Hebrew 3:34]); and for sustaining the existence of the universe (Neh. 9:6). It is used for preserving a family line from extinction (Gen. 19:32), keeping people alive amid danger (Exod. 1:17); and restoring a man from near-fatal illness (Ps. 30:3). So this verb paints a picture of preservation, revitalization, recovery, renewal. And with people ('us') as the object of the verb, it suggests fresh *life* infused into them. God is able to reinvigorate his people.

But, perhaps surprisingly, 'revive' is not the most important word in verse 6a. The psalmist employs the verb 'revive' as the logical equivalent to restore back in verse 4, while he hurries on his way toward making another point here. The most heavily weighted word in verse 6a is *you*. This is where the emphasis falls.[13] Will *you* not revive us again? *You*, the God of the covenant, the God of the promises to the patriarchs, the God of the exodus and our settlement in the land, the God of the Messianic prophecies, the God who will bring everything to consummation in a new heaven and a new earth, our own God and Father – will *you* not revive us again? Is it even conceivable that *you* would allow *your* people to fall into complete decrepitude? No! The God who restored us before will surely revive us again. That aggressive little word 'you' steps boldly to the front of the verbal crowd to focus all our hopes where they properly belong.

God is the conspicuous figure in the landscape of Psalm 85. In addition to his being the 'you' here in verse 6, his promise is our hope (v. 8), his covenant defines our identity ('your people' in vv. 2 and 6, 'his people' and 'his saints' in v. 8), he is 'our Saviour' (v. 4), and his attributes stand forth in verses 10–13. Revival theology is grounded in the very person of God himself. Therefore revival is mainstream biblical theology, flowing from who our Saviour is, and it is the inheritance of all his people. We should not be timid about this. In fact if we do neglect the revival dimension in our ministries, how can we defend that neglect, given the nature of the living God to whom we are bound by his own gracious choice?

The great strength of that little 'you' repays careful reflection. We are reminded with the force of utter simplicity that it is God alone who reinvigorates his people. We cannot schedule our renewal. We cannot trigger it. We would be foolish to announce it. It is God who freely chooses to visit his people with fresh life by his Spirit. God does this *to* us. And what do *we* contribute? Our sin and lethargy and deadness. *He* is the Life-giver. And that makes true revival nothing less than a miracle.

Jonathan Edwards, the New England pastor who witnessed revival in the First Great Awakening, wrote a careful record of those events in his church.[14] His sense of amazement at how God worked prompted him to sprinkle his narrative with adjectives like 'extra-ordinary', 'remarkable', 'surprising', and 'wonderful'. He marvelled at what God accomplished:

> When God in so remarkable a manner took the work into his own hands, there was as much done in a day or two as at ordinary times, with all endeavours that men can use and with such a blessing as we commonly have, is done in a year.[15]

This is how we naturally speak when the *you* of Psalm 85:6 revives us again. God takes the work into his own hands, replacing the best that we can do with the best that he can do.

God's extraordinary reinvigorating of his people carries with it a liberating consequence. It allows us to be the ordinary people that in fact we are. The church no longer needs to falsify herself with trendy image-casting, which is hardly credible anyway.[16] To be compelling as the church, what we need is the outpoured life of our living God. We ourselves become delightfully secondary as God is magnified.

In another current flowing within the mighty river of the First Great Awakening, the parish of Cambuslang, near Glasgow, Scotland, was visited with unusual blessing. Upwards of thirty thousand people showed up for a remarkable communion service there in 1742. (And this was at a time when the total population of Glasgow itself was only around seventeen thousand.) But their season of blessing becomes all the more astonishing when we consider the human leadership that God was pleased to use. The parish minister at Cambuslang was the Reverend William M'Culloch, a steady, unspectacular, faithful man. What made the difference in that parish was not a sparkling human personality, supported by the apparatus of human promotion. What made the difference was the unusual touch of God on this ordinary man's ministry. And, although the magnetic George Whitefield did come up from England eventually to help M'Culloch in the exploding work, the revival was 'no foreign importation, but had issued directly from the faithful preaching and labours of a somewhat colourless parish minister'.[17] How could this happen? Psalm 85:6 explains. The subject of the verb revive is a mighty, divine *you*, whose power is made perfect in human weakness.

And why does God take the work of revival in hand so wonderfully? The second line of verse 6 reveals God's heart for his people: 'that your people may rejoice in you'. God delights to see his people rejoicing under his favour, rather than groaning under his discipline. He is willing to use the rod but he does not enjoy it. It was the Spirit of this God who moved the apostle Paul to summarize the object of all biblical ministry: 'Not that we lord it over your faith, but we work with you *for your joy*' (2 Cor. 1:24). So here in verse 6 the people of God are appealing to something deep and real in the heart of God. Our Father loves to see his children rejoicing. And their renewed happiness finds a very particular focus.

Verse 6 says that the revitalized people of God rejoice in *him*. They come back to the basics. They rediscover God. They become preoccupied with the being, works, and ways of God himself, revealed fully in Jesus Christ. They are captivated by a new fascination. The world's allure fades. The pleasures of sin are seen to be a scam. The people of God go back to *him* with actual experience that in his presence there is fullness of joy and at his right hand are pleasures forevermore (Ps. 16:11).

The appeal of this second line of verse 6 gathers increased momentum from its careful choice of words. The first line reads, 'Will you not revive *us* again?' So we might have expected the second line to say, 'that *we* may rejoice in you'. But instead we find, 'that *your people* may rejoice in you'. In addition to his great love for us, God has another strong incentive to renew us. We are *his people*. We bear his name here in the world, to bring greater glory to himself.[18] God has made a huge personal commitment not only to us but also to the display of his own glory before the wondering eyes of created beings. And if we exist here on the stage of history to fulfil this purpose, then God has a reason to keep working with us. He has a reason to lift us up out of our natural dullness into the intensity of joy. We are *his* people. And when the people of God are seen to be happy in him, he is highly honoured.

Joy is the very flavour of revival. We may have to go through deep humiliation to taste it, but rejoicing marks the church in revival. It must be so, for we were created primarily to glorify and enjoy God. So if he draws near to our souls with renewed life, we are wired in such a way that our natural response will be boundless joy. And this goes deeper than anything we can change about ourselves.

If we are spring-loaded to erupt in joy when God reinvigorates us, then verse 6b certifies strong rejoicing as a valid experience for the church, much to be sought after. The prayer is appealing to God on the assumption that the prospect of a rejoicing church is a meaningful argument to lay before him. This 'joy unspeakable and full of glory' (1 Pet. 1:8 AV) must be God's desire for his people. John Owen helps us sense the mystery and potency of spiritual joy:

> Of this joy there is no account to be given but that the Spirit works it when and how he will. He secretly infuses and distils it into the soul, prevailing against all fears and sorrows, filling the soul with gladness, exultations, and sometimes with unspeakable raptures of mind.[19]

This is a joy that the world never can give us, a joy the world can never take away, a joy the world is waiting to see. It is very real, it is deeply felt, and it is our inheritance as the people of the living God.

Verse 7 shows us that God is able to manifest himself to us with unmistakable clarity:

> Show us your unfailing love, O LORD,
>   and grant us your salvation.

The first line could also be translated, 'Cause us to *see* your unfailing love, O LORD.' The people do not doubt God's love, but they no longer sense it.[20] And they cannot endure the prospect of his love remaining a theoretical abstraction only. They yearn for the biblical doctrine to be made real to them. So they plead for divine attestation of his love in their actual experience. And they will 'see' his love as he 'grants them his salvation', releasing them from their present malaise.

The love of God, flooding our experience, acts with extraordinary power. When Jonathan Edwards gave the world an account of the revival in his church, he narrated the experience of his wife, Sarah. So what was it like when God showed Mrs Edwards his unfailing love and granted her salvation during this season of revival? To quote only a brief part of this beautiful passage, she enjoyed

> a very frequent dwelling for some considerable time together in views of the glory of the divine perfections and Christ's excellencies, so that the soul has been, as it were, perfectly overwhelmed and swallowed up with light and love, a sweet solace, and a rest and joy of soul altogether unspeakable. The person has more than once continued for five or six hours together, without interruption, in a clear and lively view or sense of the infinite beauty and amiableness of Christ's person and the heavenly sweetness of his transcendent love. So that (to use the person's own expressions) the soul remained in a kind of heavenly elysium and did, as it were, swim in the rays of Christ's love like a little mote swimming in the beams of the sun that come in at a window. The heart was swallowed up in a kind of glow of Christ's love coming down as a constant stream of sweet light, at the same time the soul all flowing out in love to him, so that there seemed to be a constant flowing and reflowing from heart to heart ... and this without being in any trance, or at all deprived of the exercise of the bodily senses.[21]

God does not grant such high-octane experiences to all his children, but we cannot deny that God is able to show us his unfailing love and grant us his salvation in far greater measure than many of us have known. When he does, to whatever degree he wisely chooses for each of us, we are released from the oppression of self and purified in the sweetness of his saving love. Who would not pray for this and pray for it with the urgency of verses 4–7? Is this not how the apostle Paul prayed for the Ephesian Christians: that they would stretch the wings of faith and soar in the atmosphere of the multidimensional love of God in Christ (Eph. 3:17b–19)?

A prophetic pause

How then will God answer the cries of his people? In verses 8 and 9 the psalmist himself speaks as a prophetic oracle announcing a decree handed down from God's throne. We may picture in our minds the psalmist leading the congregation in worship. As the people linger in the yearnings expressed in verses 4–7, he steps forward to address the worshippers:

> I will listen to what God the Lord will say;
>> he promises peace to his people, his saints –
>> but let them not return to folly.
>
> (Ps. 85:8)

The future of God's people hangs on this point. What will God say to us? What will he decree for our generation? It does not finally matter what the world says or what Christian leaders say, or scholars, or opinion polls. Ultimately our future pivots one way or the other, on the will of God. And whatever our own immediate prospects here on earth may seem to be, his word to his church is triumphant: 'He promises peace to his people.'

That word *peace*, heavily freighted with biblical connotations, conveys all the richness and fullness of life that we long for. We must not think of God as a cosmic miser, reluctantly parcelling out meagre blessings. Instead, we should think of ourselves as constantly assailing him with rude entreaties. He is astonishingly patient and kind. In the way he handles us, God abides by his own rule of open-handed generosity:

> And if someone wants to sue you and take your tunic, let him have your cloak as well. If someone forces you to go one mile,

go with him two miles. Give to the one who asks you, and do not turn away from the one who wants to borrow from you.

(Matt. 5:40–42)

God is like that. We ask (vv. 4–7), and he promises peace (v. 8). Every desire worthy of being granted is packed into that word *peace*, and it is all ours. His word to us in the gospel rings with an unambiguous 'Yes!' to our hearts' desires: 'For no matter how many promises God has made, they are "Yes" in Christ' (2 Cor. 1:20). God's peace flows from his open hand through Christ into our lives. Let no uncertainty about God linger in our minds. If we want to be happy with the happiness of the Ultimate Human Experience, we should ask God for it. God gives it, wrapped inside this priceless package called *peace*, promised to us by One who cannot lie, and secured for us by a crucified Saviour whose blood covers all our sins.

So verse 8 is calculated to awaken in all loyal hearts a sense of expectancy. As God approaches his people, what greeting falls from his lips? 'Peace!' (see Eph. 2:17). But that gives us no cause for complacency, either. Our part is to consecrate ourselves to him, and so prove ourselves indeed to be 'his people, his saints' who receive the benediction of peace. And the warning in the last line of verse 8, 'but let them not return to folly', calls us, once we have set our hand to the plough, to press on without turning back. If our prayer in verses 4–7 comes from the heart, we can never go back to nominalism and mediocrity. That was the folly that antagonized God in the first place (vv. 4–5).

We are capable of forfeiting God's blessing. We are capable of giving up on God, surrendering our principles, and slipping back to our former carelessness. We are capable of setting our minds on earthly things, not on things above. We are capable of a sensate, worldly existence. But what a costly miscalculation such a choice would prove to be! We never know but that, just around the corner, God's next decretive word for this generation may just be that special 'Peace!' that signals revival.

Like the speaker here in verse 8, let us be prophetic voices to our generation. The church is never in a static state. The scenes of life are constantly changing. We are always in danger of being drawn down by the gravitational pull of our own sinfulness.[22] Even our ideas for renewing the church, if they depart from the ways of God, generate unintended, unanticipated, and unwelcome consequences. The natural direction of human drift is such that 'every institution tends to produce its opposite'.[23] And one incentive for fighting that tendency and keeping close to the Lord is that he is always able to usher in for us a new era of recovery and advance. Our part is to press on with a rugged, unyielding confidence in his readiness to bless us at any time.

Verse 9 encourages us further as we set our faces toward God. It shows his salvation already knocking on our door:

> Surely his salvation is near those who fear him,
>   that his glory may dwell in our land.

God is never far away. He is so close that, at any time pleasing to himself, he can manifest his glory in our midst. No one can stop him and no one need help him. Nothing but his own sense of what is best stands between his glory and our churches.

When God's *glory* appears, his actual status as supreme over all the rest of reality is seen and his impressiveness is felt. The false appearances of this world are stripped away so that God stands forth in our sight as important, superior, awesome.[24] And his glorious greatness, manifest in our midst ('our land'), is what sets the church apart from other merely ordinary forms of human association. His glory is our distinction.

The word 'surely' cries out, 'Let me urge this truth on you with compelling certainty! However low the church may fall at a given moment in history, here is the rock we can always stand on. God's salvation is *near*. All he has to do is say the word, and revival materializes here among us. God may create, but he does not need, favourable circumstances. He needs only himself for revival to break in, fully assembled and operational, at any time.' And this assertion is not mere rhetoric.

His glory did dwell among us in its most brilliant manifestation thus far through the person of Jesus (John 1:14). Now the Holy Spirit glorifies Jesus by revealing him to our hearts (John 16:14). When the saving knowledge of his glory extends powerfully to many people at once, it is called revival.

As at his first advent, our Lord's visitations can be controversial. Verses 1–7 refer to God's people at several points. Then verses 8 and 9 sharpen our understanding of who are included within that circle. They are 'his saints' (v. 8) and 'those who fear him' (v. 9). These people welcome the advent of his glory. But others who identify outwardly with the institution of the Christian church may fear or even reject revival, because their hearts do not love the display of the glory of Jesus above all else. Their pulses do not quicken at the realization that 'his salvation is near those who fear him', and the prospect that 'his glory may dwell in our land' does not stir their hearts. They would prefer to return to predictable, safe nominalism.

As a result, every time our Lord manifests himself afresh, we see fulfilled again what Simeon prophesied long ago: 'This child is destined to cause the falling and rising of many in Israel, and to be a sign that will be spoken against' (Luke 2:34). If we were honest, would we not all have to admit that there is something in every one of our hearts that resists yielding all to the glory of Jesus?

Without even realizing it, we can slip into perceiving Christianity as useful for reinforcing our lifestyles rather than as challenging us to follow the way of the cross. We are capable of using even a Christian routine to seal ourselves off from engaging with our Lord himself. But that deeply personal 'flowing and reflowing from heart to heart' that Mrs Edwards experienced *is* authentic Christianity. And when its reality confronts us in revival, we face a choice. We may choose to humble ourselves, consider the event with fair-minded evaluation, and open our hearts to the Lord's blessing in it. Or we may choose to be offended, close off the possibility of understanding, and dismiss the whole as nothing more than emotionalism. To claim that 'the church always denounces every revival movement'[25] overstates the case; but there are enough evidences in its favour to make the statement, if not convincing, at least understandable. The resistance in our hearts is why verses 8 and 9 whisper to us all a caution. When revival comes, let us make certain we are not on the wrong side. It is 'those who fear him' who discover how near his salvation really lies. Let us not return to the folly of religious tedium claiming to be authentic Christianity.

But what does the glory look like when it dwells among us?

Verses 10–13 portray the experience of union and communion between God and his people in images so beautiful they are almost surreal.

Future glory

> Love and faithfulness meet together;
>> righteousness and peace kiss each other.
>
> (Ps. 85:10)

The psalmist's gorgeous portrait of covenant renewal could be interpreted more effectively with a musical symphony than with my wearisome prose. But even with a word processor one can at least say this: the covenant realities of love, faithfulness, righteousness, and peace had seemed abstract to God's people. Suddenly, in revival, they spring forth with fresh immediacy. These classic trademarks of God's gracious initiative toward sinful man move from words on the biblical page into our actual experience. The ideal comes within reach, if only in part. We savour a foretaste of heaven.

Is it not striking how these great principles are portrayed as if they were living beings? We see his love and faithfulness. They come together. They engage in glad recognition. His righteousness and peace also appear. They greet with a kiss. They touch in tender affection. Our season of discipline is over. The truths of the gospel now unite in meaningful and endearing reality. We experience God's 'unfailing love' and 'salvation' (vv. 7 and 9), his 'peace' (v. 8) and 'glory' (v. 9).

> Faithfulness springs forth from the earth,
>> and righteousness looks down from heaven.
>
> (v. 11)

Revival purifies the church, but not by sterilizing the church. Revival purifies us by making us fruitful in the Spirit. Luxuriant faithfulness to God 'springs forth' among us where before sin had grown rank. The infestations of sin naturally choke out a proper response to God. But he is able to draw up out of his people a new harvest, a new quality, a new ethos, favouring all that pleases him.

'Lord of harvest, grant that we / wholesome grain and pure may be.'
And his grace comes full circle as God in righteousness leans over,
so to speak, to look down on us from heaven with a smile of
approval.

> The LORD will indeed give what is good,
>> and our land will yield its harvest.
>
> (v. 12)

The word 'indeed' signals that we are now arriving at a climactic
affirmation. Each word carries weight. 'The LORD' – our covenant
God himself – out of his infinite store of goodness 'will give', with
the overflowing generosity of his gracious heart, 'what is good' –
everything that deserves to be hoped for as 'good'. The largesse of
God's grace pours out on us. We content ourselves with so little; we
need to stretch our desires out to match the bounty of God's
supply!

That word 'good' includes all that verses 1–3 remember, all that
verses 4–7 pray for, all that verses 8 and 9 wait for, and all that
verses 10 and 11 envision. The reinvigorating of the church is the
'good' that our Lord will indeed give to his people. So why should
we fear true revival? It is *good*. It takes us out beyond our predictable routines into unfamiliar territory, true. But verses 10 and
11 portray an interruption worthy of our thoughtful acceptance, a
vista worthy of our careful exploration. Revival is never perfect. We
always spoil it to some degree. We mean well but we cannot help it.
We are naturally off balance because of sin. But revival itself is not
the problem; it is the answer. Let us not be afraid of it; it is 'what is
good'.

And it *does* good: 'Our land will yield its harvest.' The NIV con-
ceals the fact that the word 'give' in the first line ('the LORD will
give') reappears here in the second line. We could translate: 'Our
land will *give* its harvest.' God gives out showers of blessing (12a),
and the church gives back to him a harvest of responsiveness (12b).
Reinvigorated by God, our worship and service are no longer
forced, stilted, reluctant, but natural, eager, and growing.

The psalm concludes with a dynamic vision of God's ongoing
movement among us:

Righteousness goes before him
   and prepares the way for his steps.

(v. 13)

God does not need us to open doors of opportunity before him. 'Righteousness', his ability to set things right, makes a way for him as he moves among his people. Wherever the Champion of righteousness appears, the wrongs of our lives have a remedy.[26] This means that our problems do not impede his movement; they invite his movement. He is sufficient in himself for his redemptive work to go on as long as he is pleased to linger in our midst. As the psalm arrives at its concluding glimpse of our great God, we see him moving forward in triumphant grace, and 'we are roused from basking to following'.[27]

Psalm 85, extending its field of vision from the past through the present and into the future, declares with confidence that our God is able to reinvigorate his people at all times and in all seasons. The fact that this psalm stands recorded in holy Scripture as ever relevant instructs us to perceive ourselves as ever in need of new life and to perceive God as ever able to meet us afresh. We see the history of God's people stretching out into a panorama of successive eras of strength and weakness, depending on God's reviving power.[28] A season of spiritual vitality, fuelling joyful and daring exploits for the gospel, is followed by fatigue, inertia, and a brittle, unimaginative status quo. A fresh wave of grace then washes over the church, lifting us again into vigorous life and mission. The wave recedes, then rises again, and so on. And Psalm 85 urges on us a certainty that God is committed to *keep on reviving* his people.

The psalm also argues, in an almost hidden way, the inevitability of change in a revived church. The Hebrew root *šûb*, meaning 'turn, return', appears five times in this brief psalm. It is translated 'restore' (v. 1), 'turn' (v. 3), 'restore' (v. 4), 'return' (v. 8), and it is hidden behind the English adverb 'again' in verse 6. The repeated use of this word alerts us to the reality of turning, of changing, in revival. Revival is pivotal in nature. God turns from his fierce anger (v. 3) and restores us to blessing (vv. 1, 4, 6). Our part is not to turn back to our natural folly. So revival is a change, a reversal, a turning toward what should be. Some people in our churches may not like it. They may feel threatened. They may criticize unfairly. They may argue, without realizing what they are saying, that the church should turn back to folly and live in it continually as a normative state of affairs. They may have sincere intentions, but their real need is to turn to their Lord, not to cling to that which is merely familiar. Revival is upheaval (if you don't like it), or it is restoration (if you do like it). But it *will* turn a church around.

Interestingly, Isaiah prophesied the church's final, eschatological deliverance in terms similar to Psalm 85.[29] It may be that the psalmist drew from Isaiah. But the similarity between the two biblical voices tells us something. If the psalmist found Isaiah's foretelling of the End useful for describing revival in the present, then there must not be an impenetrably solid barrier between the present and the future. That barrier must be semi-permeable. God is able to tilt the future back toward us a little, allowing those latter-day glories to slide part-way into our experience now. This may explain why Christians living in the atmosphere of revival have sometimes wondered whether they were living in the last days. In revival God does grant us a fuller measure of the powers of the age to come. The theological understanding of this will be given different nuances by sincere believers, but it is understandable why people in revival conditions raise such questions.

Verses 10–13 of Psalm 85 are stamped with a visibly eschatological impression. But they do not describe the End. They answer the cry, raised in verses 4–7, for revival in the present. And how is that significant? It confirms us in the conviction that true revival is no ordinary experience. We are grateful for all that God gives us, including his smaller bestowals, but revival is an *extraordinary* activating of covenant graces in our present experience. The future reaches back to touch the present. For this reason, we should be cautious about labelling just any event a 'revival'. Revival is extraordinary. It is as if God passes around hors d'oeuvres to the Marriage Supper of the Lamb.

We New Testament Christians have seen the future in Jesus Christ. God in Christ has unmistakably demonstrated his ultimate intentions for us. 'He promises peace to his people' translates into 'on earth peace, good will toward men' (Luke 2:14). That promise will carry us all the way into a new heaven and a new earth. And as we press on toward that goal, Psalm 85 encourages us to seek fore-tastes of the ultimate glory, until we are 'lost in wonder, love and praise'.

How then can we respond with indifference to the malaise within the evangelical church today? We have lowered our expecta-tions so far that the possibilities envisioned in Psalm 85 may seem unreal, even threatening. But God put this psalm in his Bible for the very purpose of encouraging us, challenging us, even prodding us, until we rise up with holy dissatisfaction and seek him for fresh vigour. There is more for us in Christ than we have yet appre-hended. So how can we justify our present stagnation? Our God is the living God. He has argued strenuously that we are rich with hope and destined for glory. We have no right to languish in com-placency. So may I ask you a question? If Psalm 85 does not make your mouth water spiritually, is Christ your Saviour at all?

3
God heals us

God so wants to encourage us with his reviving powers that he multiplies the images with which to press this confidence into our hearts. He knows how weak we are. He knows how easily discouraged we are. As we survey our lives, our homes, our churches, and our society, our faith can sag in defeatism. But God's grace is more than a match for our weakness. He refuses to quit. He keeps on reassuring us, meeting our objections, giving us strong reasons for the courageous openness of faith.

But God does not keep on declaring the same message in the same way. If he did, we might come up with (to us) an unanswerable objection, reinforcing our natural cynicism. So God builds his case in different, imaginative ways. He confronts us again and again with his goodness from different angles until we finally give up: 'Okay, Lord, you win. I believe. I believe you can renew your people. I believe you intend to. Nothing can stop you when you want to move in on us. I can never look at your church with the same eyes again. At any time you please, under any conditions, we can burst into flame by your Spirit. You are able to come down to us. You are able to reinvigorate us. And you are able to heal us.'

God reveals himself to us in Hosea chapter 14 as the Healer of his sin-sick church. Did you know that God is like a doctor? 'He heals the brokenhearted and binds up their wounds' (Ps. 147:3). Bending over his patients with wise and attentive care, God proves that he is the universe's ultimate specialist in treating the aggressive cancers of our sin. His expertise can be trusted. His prescriptions are effective. His bedside manner is reassuring. He declares in Jeremiah 30:12–13 and 17:

> Your wound is incurable,
> your injury beyond healing.
> There is no one to plead your cause,
> no remedy for your sore,
> no healing for you.
>
> But I will restore you to health
> and heal your wounds,
> declares the LORD.

Our own remedies for the church's ailments are worthless. But God has miracle cures that no one else can offer. Yet there is another side to this truth.

God is also able to wound us. In verse 14 of Jeremiah 30 the Lord explains to his hurting people, 'I have struck you as an enemy would.' And in Deuteronomy 32:39 God declares to us:

> See now that I myself am He!
> There is no god besides me.
> I put to death and I bring to life,
> I have wounded and I will heal,
> and no one can deliver out of my hand.

So God is like both an enemy who wounds and a medic who heals. And no one can stop him, either way, because he alone is God. If we offend him by clinging in self-confident independence to our own prescriptions for the church's healthy future, he will wound us. He will allow us to fail, and fail painfully, until we come to our senses, humble ourselves, and go back to his ways. Then our great Physician will touch us with effective remedies (Isa. 58:8; Jer. 33:1–9). So God is not arbitrary. He always has a reason for what he does. But he alone retains ultimate command of the church's health.

Hosea's vision of God as our Healer sets before us an invitation with an offer. In 14:1–3 the prophet invites us to return to the Lord, even explaining to us how. In verses 4–8 God himself speaks, offering to heal us of the malignancy of our sins and give us fresh spiritual health. Hosea helps us see that sin is more than bad. Sin, because it draws us away from the living God, is also enfeebling. A worldly church is a decrepit church, hobbling its way into the geriatric ward, even though it may perceive itself as vibrantly youthful. Such a church is like a cancer victim energetically pumping iron in a gym, admiring himself in the mirror, unaware that he is in fact dying from deep within.

Hosea helps us get in touch with reality by the sharply defined clarity of his categories. Sin is our disease, God is our doctor, and his treatment alone restores the church to health. Hosea begins with the doctor's prescription: an undiluted, full-strength dose of repentance.[1]

Return to the Lord your God

> Return, O Israel, to the LORD your God.
> Your sins have been your downfall!
>
> (Hos. 14:1)

If we want healing from God, thorough repentance is the way to receive it. I say *thorough* repentance because of the Hebrew lying behind the English words 'return to'. Hosea's wording connotes a kind of repentance that does more than just point a life in the Lord's general direction. The repentance implied by his idiom brings that life fully back to the Lord, withholding nothing from him.[2] It is not enough that we see our sins and feel bad about them. It is not enough even to stop sinning. True repentance comes all the way back to God, back to our original relationship with him, back to our first love, back to the basics of the gospel, back to the daily disciplines of holiness. We leave the world behind, including worldly Christianity, and go hard after God until we rediscover how to live in his nearness.

The very idea of 'returning' tells us to go back the way we came.

Retracing our wayward steps, we must undo what we have done, dismantle our idolatries, own up to our foolish judgment calls, recant our wrong ideas. Then we reassemble the life, personally and institutionally, that is pleasing to God, according to the Scriptures. We start to think more carefully about how we live. We get tough on ourselves and make some long-overdue, hard decisions. We prize God alone as our great delight and reward. This is real repentance. It is costly, inconvenient, and embarrassing. But it is the only way to healing. Anything less is humbug.

But isn't the nearness of God where we belong, anyway? 'Return to the LORD *your God.*' We are his covenanted people, chosen in Christ, redeemed at the cross, sealed with his Spirit. Despite what we deserve, his covenant with us still holds. He still identifies with us as our God. We have no true interest or advantage anywhere else. So we are not being required to grope after some strange, risky, unknown relationship. God is calling his own prodigals home. We are his people, set apart to him in the first place.

Our problem is not that God is inaccessible or unknowable. Our problem is with us. We have stumbled over our sins ('Your sins have been your downfall!'). Hosea has in mind here Israel's steep national decline during his lifetime. The country was on the skids. How could they put on the brakes? The people hoped that their weakening position might be secured through political alliances: 'When Ephraim saw his sickness, and Judah his sores, then Ephraim turned to Assyria, and sent to the great king for help. But he is not able to cure you, not able to heal your sores' (5:13).

The people of God did not understand that their nation was suffering social disintegration and international diminution for a moral reason, not a political reason: 'Your *sins* have been your downfall!' We can see our symptoms easily enough but we do not diagnose the disease wisely. And so we apply irrelevant, ineffective remedies. And we risk antagonizing God even further by treating him as if he were irrelevant. How dimly we grasp the true relevance of spiritual things for living real life in this tough world![3]

Moreover, Hosea's generation also felt that economic realities required them to mix in some Canaanite Baalism with their biblical faith. Portraying Israel as the Lord's unfaithful wife, the prophet read the nation's mind: 'She said, "I will go after my lovers [the

Baals], who give me my food and my water, my wool and my linen, my oil and my drink" ' (2:5).

The Israelites saw the good things in life as the pay-off for their dalliances with the rites of Baal worship. To this the Lord responded: 'She has not acknowledged that I was the one who gave her the grain, the new wine and the oil, who lavished on her the silver and the gold – which they used for Baal' (2:8).

But however the Israelites were rationalizing their compromises, they were not really being driven by material or economic necessity. The truth was far worse. Israel was madly in love, flirting with the Baals. Deep within the national mood there stirred an emotional craving for the exotic, sexy world of Baalism. And the familiar world of classical biblical faith seemed old and boring by comparison. This is worldliness. And the Lord tells us in Hosea 2:13 how he dealt with Hosea's generation of worldly semi-believers: ' "I will punish her for the days she burned incense to the Baals; she decked herself with rings and jewellery, and went after her lovers, but me she forgot," declares the LORD.'

These, then, were the two primary sins that proved to be the downfall of God's people in Hosea's time: futile hopes and vulgar desires. They hankered after the security of worldly alliances and the thrill of worldly pleasures. They did not really feel that their heavenly husband would either protect them or satisfy them. And so they were sniffing around where they had no business, caressing their darling sins, trying to get their needs met by others. The church in every generation is in danger of stumbling over the very same sins.[4]

What is it that brings the people of God low? What is it that obstructs our progress and frustrates our good intentions? What is it that sets us up to be caught out by unintended consequences? The answer is embarrassingly simple. We sin: 'Your sins have been your downfall!' And we sin today in essentially the same ways they did then. But Hosea is showing us the way out: 'Bend your will around and go back to the Lord. Go so far back that you begin to do something very radical, you begin actually, literally, to obey him. You begin to allow, by faith, that he might just be your all-sufficiency. It's your refusal to trust him enough to obey him; it's not your political weakness, not your finances, not anything else; it's your *sins* that have been your downfall. So go back to God. Relearn his ways. There is no healing for you any other way.'

How then do we return so fully, so thoroughly to God? What does he want from us when we approach him?

Take words with you

Take words with you
    and return to the LORD.
Say to him:
    'Forgive all our sins
and receive us graciously,
    that we may offer the fruit of our lips.'

(Hos. 14:2)

God wants to hear from us. He wants us to approach him with plain-speaking honesty: no evasion, no equivocation, no excuses. And he wants to hear from each one of us. I say 'each one of us' because of Hosea's Hebrew text. In verse 1 'return' was a singular imperative, and his pronouns ('*Your* sins . . . *your* downfall') were also singular. He was addressing the people of God all together as one corporate whole. But here in verse 2 Hosea changes to plural verbs when he says, 'Take . . . return . . . say.' He breaks the corporate whole down into its constituent members and speaks to us now as individuals. Could there be any other way? Repentance cannot remain a corporate act only and still be real. You and I must make it our own.

Is it not interesting that God wants us to bring to him, of all things, *words*? What else might we bring? We know that we cannot bring him our own merit, as if we deserved healing from God. Only Christ crucified can bring us back into God's good graces. But we might deceive ourselves into thinking that we can present him with religious acts and offerings, with pageantry and spectacle, with programmes and organizations and events, as the church's trumpets blare and drums beat in triumphalistic enthusiasm. We might think that is what God wants from us. It will not work: 'When they go with their flocks and herds to seek the LORD, they will not find him; he has withdrawn himself from them' (5:6). And God spoke through Isaiah, Hosea's contemporary: 'When you come to appear before me, who has asked this of you, this trampling of my courts?' (Isa. 1:12). No insolent barging into God's holy presence! It leads only to desecration. No patronizing rubbish tricked out in pious performance! It leads only to polished blasphemy. We do not intend it that way, of course. We mean well. But sometimes we do not think, we do not see it through God's eyes.

So what *does* God want from us? He wants not display but words: words of brokenness, words of renunciation, words of fresh resolve, words of praise. He wants a thoughtful, meaningful encounter with each one of us. We have unfinished business with God, and it has to be prayed through. If we cannot think of anything to say to God, then we may not yet feel with sufficient intensity our need for him. Maybe we need to suffer some more. But if we do sense our need and are uncertain that our effort will do any good, Hosea is coaching us in what to say and encouraging us that God really will listen.

As we approach God in individual repentance, what are we going to say to him? First, we confess our sins, holding nothing back. 'Forgive *all* our sins' – or, to paraphrase the force of these words, 'Carry off all our sins, every single one of them. We don't want them around any more. We are sorry we ever flirted with them. They have done us nothing but harm. Remove all our sins far from us.'

God is more willing to forgive us than we are willing to seek his forgiveness. And God is better able to release us from our sins than we are to get free of them.

Is it not significant that, in returning to God for healing, we must first face into our sins? We must place ourselves under the judgment of the Word of God. Outward success can seduce us into a spirit of self-admiration: 'Ephraim boasts, "I am very rich; I have become wealthy. With all my wealth they will not find in me any iniquity or sin"' (Hos. 12:8). In other words, 'I'm so successful, no one will notice or care about my hidden failings.' Such boastfulness drives God's healing presence away. So it makes no sense to ask the Lord for greater blessing on our unexamined status quo. We need to be released from what we now are. That is where we begin.

Secondly, we ask God to show us new favour: 'Receive us

graciously.' Severe honesty in confessing our sins is not a waste of time. It opens the way to renewed communion with God. We are graciously reinstated to the enjoyment of his goodness. Richard Sibbes helps us see the largeness of this divine grace:

> God's mercy to his children is complete and full. For he takes away ill, and does good. Men may pardon, but they also think that they have done wondrous bountifully when they have pardoned. But God goes further. He takes away ill, and does good; takes good out of his fountain, and does good to us.[5]

In other words, God does not merely remove our defect. He restores us to something better. He not only takes away our problem ('Forgive all our sins'), but he also does us good ('receive us graciously'). God's moral calculus is factored very much to our advantage. It is not for us to tell God exactly *how* he should bless us: the wording here is not specific but general ('receive us graciously'). It is God who decides how to answer that prayer. And he is wise enough to know just what to do in each of our lives. Our part is to welcome his renewed favour, however it comes to us, with a sense of undeserved privilege.

Thirdly, we pledge our renewed devotion to our Lord: 'that we may offer the fruit of our lips'. Thorough repentance is a new way of living, a moment-by-moment responsiveness to God's goodness. It's a sensitive, personal engaging with God, rendering back to him thanks for what we receive from him. This is so because true spirituality is circular in design. God sends blessing to us, and we offer the blessing back to him in praise. All good begins with God and returns to God. Our lives are not to be graves, where blessings go to die, but altars, where blessings are returned to God in thanksgiving.

Verse 2 charts for us a positive new course by showing us what to turn *toward*. But God does not intend that we merely add pious ornamentation to the surface of otherwise unchanged lives. So verse 3 now adds depth and texture to our rededication by showing us what to turn away *from*:

> Assyria cannot save us;
>   we will not mount war-horses.

We will never again say 'Our God'[6]
  to what our own hands have made,
  for in you the fatherless find compassion.

When we lay hold of the 'solid joys and lasting treasures' of our
God, we also let go of the stylish mythologies of the world that disappoint us. Hosea articulates for us a twofold vow, followed by an
affirmation of confidence mingled with relief.

Our vow renounces all vain hopes through self-help. We resolve
to live in complete dependence on our Lord alone. How? First, we
swear off all alliances with the Assyrias and Egypts[7] of our day
('Assyria cannot save us; we will not mount war-horses'). Hosea's
Israel had turned to these powers for national security: 'Ephraim is
like a dove, easily deceived and senseless – now calling to Egypt,
now turning to Assyria' (7:11). 'Ephraim feeds on the wind; he
pursues the east wind all day and multiplies lies and violence. He
makes a treaty with Assyria and sends olive oil to Egypt' (12:1).

Now, what is wrong with this picture? Simply put, the people of
God feel nervous if all they have is God. So they are fawning before
the bullies of worldly power; that is what is wrong. Today we
profess that we have taken refuge in the King of kings and Lord of
lords. At the same time we sometimes stoop to curry favour with
politicians and earthly powers, as if the safety of the church de-
pended on human protection and political favour. Do we demonstrate confidence that the Lord himself, and the Lord alone, is our
power, our security, our boast? Human politics is an honourable
calling, of course, but we dishonour our Lord if we feel naked when
surrounded with his care only.

Some Christians wrap the cross in their national flag. Granted,
citizenship in a human nation is a meaningful dimension of this
life, even though the nations are only specks of dust to God (Isa.
40:15). But Jesus Christ did not come to this earth so that we could
subordinate his eternal kingdom to any human cause. Nations rise
and fall. And rather than panic with those who have no hope firmer
than election-day victories, we who name Christ as Lord should
present to the world living validation of his all-sufficiency, come
what may. Shadrach, Meshach, and Abednego declared this faith
with heroic clarity:

O Nebuchadnezzar, we do not need to defend ourselves before you in this matter. If we are thrown into the blazing furnace, the God we serve is able to save us from it, and he will rescue us from your hand, O king. But even if he does not, we want you to know, O king, that we will not serve your gods or worship the image of gold you have set up.

(Dan. 3:16–18)

Courageous emotional detachment from human approval is the natural outcome of strong spiritual attachment to God. By contrast, the people of God in Hosea's day gambled their future on placating worldly powers. They not only discredited their witness to the world; they also antagonized God. But the repentant people of God find their hearts saying, 'What really matters is not what they decide about us in the Assyrian throne room but what God decides about us in the heavenly Throne room. That is where our future is really determined. So we will put our hope in *him*, come what may' (cf. Ezra 8:21–23).

The second way we reaffirm our faith in God alone is to swear off the gods we have devised ('We will never again say "Our God" to what our own hands have made'). In Hosea's day, idolatry was laughably obvious: 'And now they sin more and more, and make for themselves molten images, idols skilfully made of their silver, all of them the work of craftsmen. Sacrifice to these, they say. Men kiss calves!' (Hos. 13:2 RSV). The idolatry of the modern world is more subtle than that, but it is still possible to invest unrealistic power in the works of our own hands and expect very little from God himself. The dreariness of a prayer meeting, contrasted with our gushing enthusiasm over the latest church technique, reveals where our confidence really lies.

I hasten to admit that it is not always easy to discern when the proper use of means degrades into idolatry. We have to think it through. But the church scene today is crowded with temptations to venture little on God. And because God has no intention of supporting human ideas, methods, and standards, his power withdraws. We are then left with our own programmes still to fuel, but little of the divine Presence. So we look even more desperately to the works of our own hands, although we may continue to describe ministry outcomes in the pious terms of 'our God', the old term of covenant endearment.

A repentant church has abandoned itself to God alone. It risks everything on the promises of God. It is on its face before God. It understands that our ancient confession of faith, that he is 'our God', makes a difference in our practical execution of ministry and church development. A repentant church understands that methods are never value-free but always reveal where our trust really lies. Therefore methods are placed under the judgment of the Word of God. And repentant people rediscover the experiential reality of 'our God', so that they never again want to go back to their own plastic substitutes.

The sweet brokenness we sense in this verse shines forth most clearly in the last line: 'for in you the fatherless find compassion'. Is that not what we are: needy, hungry, penniless orphans, stumbling around in life desperate to find love? But 'As a father has compassion on his children, so the LORD has compassion on those who fear him' (Ps. 103:13). A repentant church rests in the truth of this and delights in the living reality of it. They feel that they have 'come home': in from the cold, hostile, foreign atmosphere of worldly alliances and self-worship, back to where they belong. We are far better off with our heavenly Father than with the illegitimate children of our own idols.

The very length of the vow here in Hosea 14:3 tells us something: true repentance aims at vital dependence on the Lord in all areas of life. This repentance is convincing. But not all repentance is so persuasive. Back in 6:1–3, the people of God had said:

Come, let us return to the LORD.
   He has torn us to pieces
   but he will heal us;
he has injured us
   but he will bind up our wounds.
After two days he will revive us;
   on the third day he will restore us,
   that we may live in his presence.
Let us acknowledge the LORD;
   let us press on to acknowledge him.

As surely as the sun rises,
    he will appear;
he will come to us like the winter rains,
    like the spring rains that water the earth.

Let us not be fooled by this pretty language. This is not true repentance. Trust without surrender is no trust at all. We see no renunciation here, only glib assurances: 'Two or, at the most, three days and God will make everything fine again. Hey, no problem.' But the very next verse shows us what God thinks of 'repentance' without reformation: 'What can I do with you, Ephraim? What can I do with you, Judah? Your love is like the morning mist, like the early dew that disappears' (v. 4). Warm feelings that quickly evaporate, producing no real life-change, are like a morning mist or dew: thin, insubstantial, fading. But true repentance is more than a momentary emotion. It is a sorrow for sin so deep that we re-centre our lives on God, whatever the personal cost.

And it *is* worth it. God wants us to know that if we will draw near to him with real repentance, he will draw near to us with a generous outpouring of healing power.

I will heal

I will heal their waywardness
    and love them freely,
    for my anger has turned away from them.

(Hos. 14:4)

If we sinners had to fear that going back to God he would only slap us around and scream at us and humiliate us, we would never approach him. We would safely keep our distance. But that is why verse 4 is here: it assures us that God's *kindness* leads us to repentance (Rom. 2:4). God *receives* broken sinners (Ps. 51:17). He has a soft spot in his heart for them. He pours out his favour on the penitent. So we have nothing to lose and everything to gain. Who would refuse his offer of healing? What sin could be worth the wounds it inflicts?

Verse 4 brings us to the gravitational centre of this entire passage.

We have spoken to God, bowing low before him (vv. 2–3). Now God speaks to us. We have declared our intention to take the courageous steps of true repentance. Now God declares what he will do for us: 'I will heal their waywardness.'

Actually, 'waywardness' is a weak translation. The NASB reads, 'I will heal their *apostasy*.' This is breathtaking, because apostasy is a serious sin: a life-threatening malignancy, so to speak. And the covenant people of Hosea's day were lying at death's door. With herdlike conformity, his generation had veered off into a persistent pattern of unreasoning but fashionable alternatives to obedient confidence in God. Their hearts were so hard they viewed the ways of God with an 'Anything but that!' mentality. Running every which way but toward God, 'My people are determined to turn from me' (11:7).

But here Hosea shows us that God's commitment to us is even more profound than our apostasy from him. Our crises do not overthrow his mercies. God can take us back at our *worst* and heal us. Isaiah agonized over the same distressing condition in the people of God:

> Why should you be beaten any more?
>   Why do you persist in rebellion?
> Your whole head is injured,
>   your whole heart afflicted.
> From the sole of your foot to the top of your head
>   there is no soundness –
> only wounds and welts
>   and open sores,
> not cleansed or bandaged
>   or soothed with oil.
>
> (Isa. 1:5–6)

Sin is a soul-destroying disease, draining us of spiritual vitality and appetite and joy.[8] Original sin is like a congenital birth defect, and acquired sins are like self-inflicted wounds. But God is able to perform radical surgery on his deformed and injured patients, with miraculous cures. In ourselves we are beset with 'the demented proclivity *for* rebellion and *against* return to Yahweh'.[9] But his healing touch is able to restore us to the spiritual life that can only be described with the lavish poetic imagery of verses 5–7, as we shall see. Under God's care, but nowhere else, our prognosis for a full recovery is encouraging.

Seeing how astonishingly God can recover his apostate people has forced me to change my mind about something or, at least, to admit a possibility I would not otherwise have entertained. I now realize that Hosea 14:4 should give us pause before we completely write off our more wayward denominations today. Hosea's generation was just as bad. So how do we know? Maybe some mainline denomination will lead the parade into God's glorious kingdom. Maybe he will do something like that just to highlight his grace all the more wonderfully. And if so, then there might be room there for you and me as well.

God's therapy for his sick people is love, not condemnation. We must come clean about our sins (vv. 1–3). We must move over and take God's side against our own sins. But when we do, God's answer is not more reproach but help ('I will love them'), and that at no charge ('freely'). He has within himself all the motivation and resources he needs to work with us, to transform us, to see us through. He does not wait until we are healthy. He only waits until we are repentant. His Son declared, 'It is not the healthy who need a doctor, but the sick. I have not come to call the righteous, but sinners to repentance' (Luke 5:31–32).

If we will only put away false appearances and admit how weak and sick we really are, how pathetic compared with verses 5–7, so that we check ourselves into God's hospital and place ourselves under his care, he promises to heal us by loving us freely. The eternal Word of God is calling to us today as much as he did to Israel so long ago. He wants to draw us to himself with an offer of his free, spontaneous, abundant love, so that our generation of the church comes alive with new life and real growth – despite the fact that we have so often spurned his love. Why do we punish ourselves one moment longer? Why do we not *run* back to him?

Our sins do incite his disciplining anger. That is a solemn truth. But his anger is not his final word to us ('my anger has *turned away* from them'). God's ultimate intentions for us are merciful, because he is merciful. If we were to dig through all the attributes of the person of God, if I may put it that way, we would hit bedrock at his mercy.[10] We could dig no deeper. So, while we are by nature inclined to turn away from him in apostasy, he is by nature inclined to turn toward us in mercy. It is simply his way. That is why he himself is all our hope. So what can the power of God's love actually accomplish for his penitent people?

I will be like the dew

I will be like the dew to Israel;
    he will blossom like a lily.
Like a cedar of Lebanon
    he will send down his roots;
    his young shoots will grow.
His splendour will be like an olive tree,
    his fragrance like a cedar of Lebanon.
Men will dwell again in his shade.
    He will flourish like the grain.
He will blossom like a vine,
    and his fame will be like the wine from Lebanon.
(Hos. 14:5–7)

After the plainly stated incentives offered in verse 4 – and 'clarity is vital to the anxious and conscience-stricken'[11] – now the poetry takes wings and flies. Hosea's imaginative language is describing what a renewed, healthy church looks like in real life – the church in the book of Acts, for example. The prophet heaps metaphor on metaphor to enforce one overall point: how the church, restored to health, flourishes with a miraculous quality of life. God's love inspires the wholesome growth of godliness, not the rank growth of licence. Freshness ('dew'), depth ('he will send down his roots'), beauty ('splendour ... fragrance'), influence ('men will dwell again in his shade'), abundant life ('he will flourish ... blossom'), and prestige ('fame') mark the character and ministry of the healthy church. The church explodes with life! No longer is an insecure church nervously craving the approval of the world, unwittingly stifling its own vitality. Now the world comes to the church, seeking shelter under its ministries and ordinances.

Ironic, is it not? We bless the world when we aim to please not the world but our Lord. Why? Because it is *his* life in us that makes us attractive. And he infuses his life into us when we set our hearts on him alone. After all, isn't the world looking for an alternative? Why should they show any interest, beyond passing amusement, in a church that is just a religious version of the values and beliefs they already live by? The salt of the earth is effective because it is *different*.

Do you see here the good terms God offers us? He puts into our hearts a new desire that he would 'forgive all our sins and receive us graciously' (v. 2). We take these simple words to God in prayer. And what does he grant in response? He transforms the church into a Garden of Eden (vv. 5–7). How largely, how imaginatively, God answers our prosaic little prayers, as the dew of God falls on us so that we blossom like a lily!

Finally, in verse 8, God stretches out his hands to us in appeal, as it were. Having stated his case, he does not leave it there. God appeals to us one more time to see how sharply incompatible our idols are with his own glorious reality. He offers himself to us and confronts us with a decision.

Your fruitfulness comes from me

O Ephraim, what more have I to do with idols?
    I will answer you and care for you.[12]
I am like a green pine tree;
    your fruitfulness comes from me.

(Hos. 14:8)

The vision of divine healing in verses 4–8 should have one powerful effect on us. By now we see God's love and power as unspeakably superior to the alternatives clamouring for our allegiance. 'What more have I to do with idols?' is a way of saying, 'The issue has now become clear. I am your God, your Father, your Healer. I alone am your all-sufficiency. Your idols bring nothing but corruption and death. How can any confusion now linger in your minds? How can any hesitation linger in your wills? The time to be decisive has now come. So choose!'

Hosea's image of God as a luxuriant evergreen implies that the *normal* experience of the church is a life of rich fruitfulness. The living God does not produce a dead, dry church. Abundance may be expected of a people in vital union with such a God. And when it comes, we must not fear it. We must not push it away in suspicion. We must not perceive it as aberrant. God's grace is by its very nature extravagant. How could it be otherwise, given our deep sinfulness and desperate illness? A meagre supply of grace is not even conceivable, if the all-holy God is to heal sinful people like us. Our part is to open our hearts in genuine repentance, welcoming the flow of grace until it rises to fill us all. But this will not happen automatically. We must turn from our idols and cast ourselves on the living God.

Baal can be manipulated, but not God. So God forces the issue of our personal engagement with himself. The words 'I' or 'me' appear conspicuously in each line of this verse. Why? Because God is not a genie to be stroked; neither is he a mere doctrinal abstraction to be recited. God is a person. And here he is calling us to fix ourselves on him, on him personally, him alone.

Where else can we go? Do the political parties love us? Do the credit card companies care for us? Do the education authorities show us wisdom? How we have miscalculated and been taken advantage of! But there is a God in heaven, our prayer-hearing God ('I will answer you'), our devotedly conscientious God ('I will care for you'), who will be there for us when it counts, as no one else can ever be. The only logical choice (if our minds have been cleared of the idols' hoopla), the only helpful course (if we consult our own best and truest interests), is to go back to our God and never let go again. Everything we most hope for in life comes from him alone, our ever-luxuriant God.

To wait on the Lord, to live the life of prayer, to abide in Christ, to walk in the Spirit, the *modus operandi* of the open Bible with the open heart, is a way of doing the business of life that does not come naturally to us. If in real life it is true that 'your fruitfulness comes from me', then we must allow for mystery. Our methods are not ultimate. God accomplishes his work by his own means, at his own pace, for his own ends, and we cannot manage him. God does not need you or me to be his nanny. Our part is humbly to cling to

God as God, and let God be God. We must neither seek our fullness from other sources nor resist the real thing when God grants it,
for 'your fruitfulness comes from *me*'.

The venoms of our sins are running in our veins. But God, who
made the soul with all its hidden capacities, also knows the soul.
'He is an excellent anatomist,' as Richard Sibbes put it:

> Seeing that our God is a healing God, as we can admire the
> wisdom, skill and excellency of our physician, so let us much
> more make use of him upon all occasions ... He is a healing
> God, who will heal all rebellions and the most grievous sick-
> nesses ... God is never at a loss. His skill cannot be set down.
> He is good at all diseases, to pardon all kinds of sins. There-
> fore let us go to him for cure, seeing there is neither sin, nor
> grief, nor terror of conscience arising from sin, which can be
> so great but God can cure both the sin and the terror ... And
> as he is a healing physician, so he puts his patients to no
> charge. For as he says, 'I will heal their backslidings,' so he
> says, 'I will love them freely.'[13]

Will the weak and sick church of today trust the Great Physician
enough to submit to his healing care? Let it be our aim, our
message, and our own practice for his gospel to be our clinic every
day, *for life is in Christ, and nowhere else.*

4

God pours out his Spirit upon us

As I write, the El Niño weather phenomenon is triggering uncommon rainstorms over the deserts of the American south-west. The usually barren sands are blossoming with the colour and beauty of wild flowers. And so we may thank an eccentricity in the Pacific Ocean's behaviour for an illustration of the Holy Spirit's effect on fallen mankind. A vast landscape of spiritual drought – that is what we are in our natural barrenness. A vast landscape of spiritual drought miraculously transformed into vibrant life and fiery colour – that is what we become in a supernatural, Spirit-drenched condition.

Our generation of the evangelical church is less than Spirit-drenched. We need a fresh outpouring of the Holy Spirit upon us today. The world does not perceive us as a potent spiritual force to be reckoned with but – at most – a block of votes, a demographic collectivity, a market niche to be manipulated. But it has not always been so.

A. W. Tozer, a twentieth-century prophetic voice, reminds us that the church of the apostolic age 'was not an organization merely, not a movement, but a walking incarnation of spiritual energy. And she accomplished within a few brief years such prodigies of moral conquest as to leave us wholly without explanation – apart from God.'[1] But today? Some of our churches go through a whole year without seeing even one person solidly converted to Christ. And the converts we already have are, in some cases, less than jaw-dropping by the witness of their lives. Tozer argues that we need spiritual energy of sufficient voltage to produce great saints again. The breed of mild, harmless Christians grown in our generation is but a poor sample of what the grace of God can do when it operates in power in the human heart. The emotionless act of 'accepting the Lord' practised among us bears little resemblance to the whirlwind conversions of the past. We need the power that transforms, that fills the soul with a sweet intoxication, that will make a former persecutor be 'beside himself' with the love of Christ. We have today theological saints who can (and must) be proved to be saints by an appeal to the Greek original. We need saints whose lives proclaim their sainthood and who need not run to the concordance for authentication.[2]

It is not just that our church members, and even our ministers, are falling into scandalous sins with painfully embarrassing frequency. It is not just that the great doctrines of our faith, which are meant to inflame our hearts, have little hold on us, so that they suffer neglect and even erosion. Our problem is that, with some encouraging exceptions, our Christianity today seems so utterly insipid.

If we were honest, many of us would have to admit that we are bored and boring. So let's face it: the world is not going to be won by Christians like us. We have no compelling power; mediocrity never does. And no matter how brilliant our devices for church development may be, no matter how effectively we may conceal our weakness under a façade of outward success, one thing is certain: we will continue as we are 'till the Spirit is poured upon us from on high, and the desert becomes a fertile field' (Isa. 32:15).

God is able to pour out his Spirit upon his church again like a refreshing rain shower relieving a drought. Moreover, God has promised to do so. And still more, as we shall see, God is keeping his promise. The storm rages. Is it refreshing you?

Unlike Isaiah 63 and 64, Psalm 85, and Hosea 14, which are

ready-made for direct application to any generation of the church, Joel 2:28–32 is firmly grounded in the unfolding sequence of human events that we call history. The passage begins with 'And afterward', it uses future tense verbs ('I will pour out'), and its time orientation is marked with the eschatological code language 'in those days'. This is a prophetic prediction of what will occur, not a general affirmation of what does occur. So we will explore Joel's revival message by asking two questions: first, what did Joel foresee? As he peered into his prophetic crystal ball, so to speak, what future prospects unfolded before him? Second, has Joel's prediction been fulfilled yet? If so, when? How? Are we a part of it today?

What did Joel foresee?

God raised up the prophet Joel during a time of intense national hardship. A massive swarm of locusts had attacked the promised land like an invading army, devouring the people's food supply. To compound their troubles, they had to endure a drought as well. The nation was devastated. So what was God's word to his people at such a time? It was, in fact, more complex and more profound than we might initially expect.

Joel's inspired vision perceived in the adversities suffered by his generation a foreshadowing of the ultimate megadisaster: the day of the Lord. To the prophetic eye, the troubles of history have a hidden meaning, which CNN or the BBC cannot see or report. The events of this present age stand forth as dress rehearsals for the Final Act. In each spasm of tragedy afflicting human history the prophets could feel a tremor signalling the eventual shaking of the foundations at the world's end.

Sensitive to both the immediate emergency and its ultimate significance, therefore, Joel addresses his people at two levels. He foresees that their present troubles will be reversed with an outpouring of divine mercy (vv. 18–27), expelling the 'army' of locusts from the land and restoring the rains in abundance. But Joel also envisions a later season of infinitely greater blessing, occurring at the threshold of the awesome day of the Lord (vv. 28–32). At this later time, God will not pour out a literal shower of rain to relieve parched throats. He will pour out his Spirit, drenching his people with spiritual blessing and filling their mouths with truth. And we live in that rainy season today.

I will pour out my spirit

And afterward,
I will pour out my Spirit on all flesh.[3]
Your sons and daughters will prophesy,
your old men will dream dreams,
your young men will see visions.
Even on servants,[4] both men and women,
I will pour out my Spirit in those days.

(Joel 2:28–29)

God loves to shower blessing on his people, lavish blessing, spread far and wide. Joel envisions the floodgates of grace opening up as God democratizes the gift of his Spirit. Young and old, men and women, and boys and girls, the lowly and the great, all alike without distinction, the people of God stand tall with spiritual privilege. Our Father is rich, and he is a big spender!

Three things invite our attention in these verses. First, God says that he will 'pour out' his Spirit. (To reinforce his point, he repeats it in the last line.) The imagery implies the unrestrained generosity of the Spirit's effusion. It is as if the Holy Spirit were a liquid – not literally, of course, but figuratively. The bestowal of the Holy Spirit cannot be described in literal terms. I mean, does he literally descend or fall or come down? None of these. But in a figurative and *yet real sense*, the Spirit is to be granted in such extravagant measure that the giving can only be imagined as the outpouring of a heavy rain on parched land. Isaiah 44:3 encourages this expectation with the same imagery: 'For I will pour water on the thirsty land, and streams on the dry ground; I will pour out my Spirit on your offspring, and my blessing on your descendants.'

The bountiful measure of the Spirit's outpouring is also evident in its effects. God's people prophesy with striking demonstrations of a new giftedness, 'dreaming dreams' and 'seeing visions'. The evidences of the Spirit's increased presence explode in incidence as God's people finally open their eyes and find their voices. This is significant. It shows us that the Spirit registers his power not through raw experiential voltage without theological content but through the knowledge of God abounding in the church. God's truth is grasped and declared; faith is personalized; orthodoxy is universal; God becomes very real. Jeremiah sees this level of privilege as the ultimate blessing God gives his people: ' "No longer will a man teach his neighbour, or a man his brother, saying, 'Know the LORD,' because they will all know me, from the least of them to the greatest," declares the LORD' (Jer. 31:34).

So what is the proof that the Spirit is being poured out on us? The voice of the church rings with prophetic clarity. The people of God are no longer passive, intimidated, unresponsive, uncertain. They are no longer preoccupied with self, convenience, comfort. They are no longer complaining, whining, griping. Instead, they become outspoken in God's praises and gospel truth, 'declaring the wonders of God' (Acts 2:11). The Spirit-drenched people of God 'speak to one another with psalms, hymns and spiritual songs. [They] sing and make music in [their] heart to the Lord, always giving thanks to God the Father for everything, in the name of our Lord Jesus Christ' (Eph. 5:19–20). And the unbeliever, observing a church eloquent with prophetic power, 'will be convinced by all that he is a sinner and will be judged by all, and the secrets of his heart will be laid bare. So he will fall down and worship God, exclaiming, "God is really among you!" ' (1 Cor. 14:24–25).

The second thing to catch our attention in Joel 2:28–29 is that God says, 'I will pour out *my Spirit.*' He has no greater gift to give. To receive in lavish measure the Spirit's illumination, his encouragement, his felt presence, his purifying power, and more, is to lay hold of the best this life can offer and everything we long for in our own deepest intentions.

I remember a film I saw during my college years. In one scene a man was throwing handfuls of money into the crowds of people passing through Trafalgar Square in London. They were quite willing to degrade themselves to get their hands on the money. The whole episode was a cynical exposure of our distorted values. And yet here in the heart of God is something very different. He pours out upon us the riches of his Spirit. Far from demeaning us, he lifts us up as we receive the outpouring, and then we have the dignity of serving as his voice to our generation. We could receive no greater gift. Jesus said:

> Which of you fathers, if your son asks for a fish, will give him a snake instead? Or if he asks for an egg, will give him a scorpion? If you then, though you are evil, know how to give good gifts to your children, how much more will your Father in heaven give the Holy Spirit to those who ask him!
>
> (Luke 11:11–13)

Fish and eggs are good gifts to our hungry children. So are 'grain, new wine and oil' (Joel 2:19) to God's children. But isn't it striking how Jesus assumes that the Holy Spirit is the ultimate gift to be desired and received? He does not even argue the point. It is too obvious. He just takes it for granted. If we don't share his assumption, it is because our hearts do not prize his values.

Our hearts may hanker after a new job or a younger body or more money. So when we read those words of our Lord in Luke 11, we may be frankly disappointed. 'How much more will your Father in heaven give *the Holy Spirit*.' 'The Holy Spirit?' we may say to ourselves. 'Shucks. I wanted a new car. Now where can I find a biblical promise for that?' But we can see both in the logic of Jesus' words and in the contextual flow of Joel 2 that the Spirit is a greater gift to God's hungry and thirsty people. The keener our yearnings for the Spirit, the more we will rejoice as we turn our faces upward into the falling rain shower, open our mouths, and drink him in. Let us never think, 'Great. Just great. This rain is going to ruin my new suit,' as we put up our umbrellas. If we despise God's gift, he may well take away from us the blessing of his Spirit (Ps. 51:11).

Third, we see that God will pour out his Spirit 'upon all flesh'. Two things stand out here. One is that we are only *flesh*. Not much to brag about, is it? I mean, what do our lives really amount to? Youthful schooling and good times, adulthood's labours and burdens, followed by the advancing decrepitude of old age, and then death. We live in weakness; we die in weakness. We spend about a third of our lives asleep in bed, recouping our strength, and then we die! Why? We are just flesh – weak, vulnerable, dying. Yet our unutterably wearisome existence becomes the scene where nothing less than the very Spirit of God is poured out to impart the fullness of true life.

The other thing to dwell on here is that the Spirit will descend upon *all* flesh: both sexes, all ages, all stations in life. Moses had longed for this: 'I wish that all the LORD's people were prophets and that the LORD would put his Spirit on them!' (Num. 11:29). When the Spirit came upon King Saul so that he started to prophesy, the people were surprised (1 Sam. 10:9–11). In the Old Testament age, such endowment was restricted to a few leaders.[5]

But now God promises a new era of spirituality for all. No longer does the Spirit fall only upon the privileged few. We are now the privileged many. The Spirit grants all God's people illuminated understanding, greater than in the old covenant community (2 Cor. 3:12–18 RSV). He empowers the church's witness as never before, from Jerusalem in the first century to the ends of the earth today (Acts 1:8). The New Testament church under God's blessing has a fuller prophetic vision and a more compelling prophetic voice than Old Testament Israel ever had. And this is the inheritance of the *whole* church, 'for you and your children and for all who are far off – for all whom the Lord our God will call' (Acts 2:39).[6] When the Spirit falls upon us, far from establishing a new religious elitism, he destroys all the barriers created by human pride.

But this reviving shower from heaven will not usher in an age of undisturbed bliss. Not yet, anyway. Until the day of the Lord comes, the outpouring of the Spirit will be matched with an out-pouring of distress.

I will show wonders

> I will show wonders in the heavens
>   and on the earth,
>   blood and fire and billows of smoke.
> The sun will be turned to darkness
>   and the moon to blood
>   before the coming of the great and dreadful day of the LORD.
>
>   (Joel 2:30–31)

This world is not our home. But, as C. S. Lewis described it, the world is still 'a merry inn along the way'. God made it to be so. In Acts 14:17 Paul explains that God shows us kindness 'by giving [us] rain from heaven and crops in their seasons; he provides [us] with plenty of food and fills [our] hearts with joy'. In describing our experience so delightfully, Paul is not denying human tragedy. People starve, drown in flood-swollen rivers, and are swept away by mountain avalanches. This world is not heaven, but it is still good. That is the reason the calendar in my room is able to feature a beautiful scene of the Pass of Glencoe this month, Cavell Gardens in Inverness next month, Loch Leven the following month, and so on. The goodness of this life testifies to the goodness of our Creator God (1 Tim. 4:1–5). But Joel shows us that the human race does not have forever to respond to God's gracious witness.

A time is coming when the familiar routines of earthly life and the pleasant surroundings we often enjoy will break down in dramatic upheaval. The day of the Lord will trigger awesome convulsions in the apparently settled state of nature. So we should not be lulled to sleep. The annual round of the seasons we enjoy now, with their variation and interest, does not mean that God is pleased with the sinful human race. It means that God is holding back, giving the world a little more time to repent (2 Pet. 3:9–10). But all the while, the flood of divine judgment on high steadily gathers and grows. At the appointed time, it will be released with terrible fury, as the apostle John describes in Revelation 6:12–17:

I watched as [the Lamb] opened the sixth seal. There was a great earthquake. The sun turned black like sackcloth made of goat hair, the whole moon turned blood red, and the stars in the sky fell to earth, as late figs drop from a fig tree when shaken by a strong wind. The sky receded like a scroll, rolling up, and every mountain and island was removed from its place. Then the kings of the earth, the princes, the generals, the rich, the mighty, and every slave and every free man hid in caves and among the rocks of the mountains. They called to the mountains and the rocks, 'Fall on us and hide us from the face of him who sits on the throne and from the wrath of the Lamb! For the great day of their wrath has come, and who can stand?'

I remember one time as a boy in California, sitting at the desk in my room, when suddenly the whole room began to tremble. I had never felt an earthquake before. It caught me off guard, of course. Because the earth beneath my feet had always been so stable, I had never thought about it. It was the unnoticed foundation for the things that did draw my attention. But at that moment everything shuddered, alerting me that nothing in this world is ultimately stable. That earth tremor was a prophetic voice – just a whisper, thankfully – foretelling this final shaking of all things prophesied in Scripture.

So the scenario Joel portrays for us has two primary features. God in grace will pour out his Holy Spirit upon all of his people, and God will also disrupt the normal course of life with frightening demonstrations of his wrath. It will be the best of times and the worst of times. Jesus also told us so:

> There will be signs in the sun, moon and stars. On the earth, nations will be in anguish and perplexity at the roaring and tossing of the sea. Men will faint from terror, apprehensive of what is coming on the world, for the heavenly bodies will be shaken. At that time they will see the Son of Man coming in a cloud with power and great glory. When these things begin to take place, stand up and lift up your heads, because your redemption is drawing near.
>
> (Luke 21:25–28)

The very catastrophes that terrify the world should be occasions of joyful anticipation for God's people, for we are 'longing for a better country – a heavenly one' (Heb. 11:16). 'Let goods and kindred go, this mortal life also.' Our true home is out in the future, where righteousness dwells (2 Pet. 3:13). And the judgment of this present evil age will take us there.

So God is forewarning us of a season of unimaginable dread. The sky will darken, not because of a swarm of locusts, as in Joel's day, but because of something infinitely more ominous. The very creation itself will shudder with dismay as 'the great and dreadful day of the LORD' draws near. Whether the sun will literally be darkened and the moon literally become blood red, or whether this language simply intimates massive disruptions of normality, can be argued either way.[7] But one thing is unmistakably clear. The day of the Lord is an occasion to prepare for!

Call on the name of the Lord!

> And everyone who calls
>> on the name of the LORD will be saved;
> for on Mount Zion and in Jerusalem
>> there will be deliverance,
>> as the LORD has said,
> among the survivors
>> whom the LORD calls.

(Joel 2:32)

However dreadful the final act in history's drama, it can also be a day of salvation for anyone at all (Rom. 10:12–13). The prophetic voices of verses 28 and 29, empowered by the Holy Spirit, will declare the gospel to the world. And everyone who responds by merely calling on the name of the Lord will be saved. There will be deliverance among the people of God ('on Mount Zion and in Jerusalem'), but nowhere else. Dialling 999 will do no good. Storing tinned food in the basement will do no good. Calling on the name of the Lord – humbly invoking his mercy through Jesus Christ[8] – will be the only way to survive.

The connection between the outpouring of the Spirit and the great and dreadful day of the Lord, with its attendant upheaval, is significant. It means that a great effusion of the Spirit does not promise smooth sailing, but it does ensure survival. And the real threat, pressuring us to seek a way of survival, is not what we sometimes think. We wring our hands over the rising tide of sin in our society, over crime and crumbling neighbourhoods. And may our Father lead us not into temptation but deliver us from evil! But our concerns may be misplaced, or at least incomplete. We can be so intimidated by our degenerating society around us that we might be distracted from an infinitely greater threat looming overhead: the judgment of *God*, breaking into this world with catastrophic finality. Only the Spirit poured out can bring us through, as Joel implies. And only the Spirit poured out can rouse our sleepy world into a great awakening to its danger, so that its people too call on the Lord.

If revival and cataclysm are interrelated in the purposes of God, as our passage suggests, then an outpouring of the Spirit might not 'save our country'. I wish it would and I hope it does. But an outpouring of the Holy Spirit may just perform the service of preparing the way for our nation's final collapse. It may have the net effect of witnessing to the tragic avoidability of the judgment, for by simply calling on the Lord so many could have saved themselves.

But all who do call on him are not left to trust in their own good intentions. Our evil hearts may betray us at the moment of crisis. So, even as we must call on the Lord, he himself graciously calls us ('the survivors *whom the* LORD *calls*'). God is ultimately the one who preserves his own. Joel's final word about the survivors is that the Lord draws them to himself.

In C. S. Lewis's *The Silver Chair* Jill encounters Aslan the Lion – by chance, as far as she is concerned. But then he speaks of having called her to himself. She explains her perplexity:

> 'I was wondering – I mean – could there be some mistake? Because nobody called me and Scrubb, you know. It was we who asked to come here. Scrubb said we were to call to – to Somebody – it was a name I wouldn't know – and perhaps the Somebody would let us in. And we did, and then we found the door open.'
>
> 'You would not have called to me unless I had been calling to you,' said the Lion.[9]

God's persistent pursuit of us is our only absolute certainty now and forever. The God on whom our faith calls for deliverance is also the one who enables us to keep faith with him by his own faithfulness to us. We can't make a move without God. Therefore we do not trust in our own faith. We entrust ourselves to our Lord, who imparts and sustains our faith and who will see us through.

To sum up: Joel foresees a time when the deceiving appearances of this present evil age will collapse under the weight of reality. Everything will finally be seen in its true colours: God in his grace and wrath, the people of God in their prophetic power, the universe in its delicate vulnerability. The stage will have been set for that final act, 'the great and dreadful day of the LORD'.

Has Joel's prophecy been fulfilled?

We come now to our second question in this chapter. We know what Joel foresaw. But has his vision been fulfilled? And if it has, does the fulfilment include us today? I have already alluded to the answer in some ways but I shall make it clearer now.

Shortly before he ascended to his Father in heaven, Jesus told his disciples that they would soon be baptized with the Holy Spirit (Acts 1:5). He promised them that they would be empowered by the Holy Spirit to be his witnesses to the ends of the earth (v. 8). Then, on the day of Pentecost, the Spirit came. He rushed down suddenly like a violent wind (2:2). He appeared like tongues of fire upon the followers of Jesus (v. 3). The Spirit filled them so that they declared God's praises in foreign languages they had never studied (vv. 4, 11), enabling the visitors crowding Jerusalem for the Pentecost celebration to hear the gospel in their own native languages.[10]

Some of the onlookers dismissed the disciples' behaviour as drunkenness. Revival always attracts ridicule. Some people are offended by it, because it implies that they may not be as advanced as their carefully groomed spiritual image suggests. So they despise revival. They write it off as 'enthusiasm' or merely psychological. And sometimes they have a point, because no revival is pure. But these mockers in Jerusalem were wrong. So Peter explained what was really happening. And much to his credit, he was wise enough to deflect their prejudice with a little self-deprecating humour: 'These men are not drunk, as you suppose. It's only nine in the morning!' (v. 15). But then his tone changed to solemn earnestness:

No, this is what was spoken by the prophet Joel:

'In the last days, God says,
    I will pour out from[11] my Spirit on all flesh.[12]
Your sons and daughters will prophesy,

your young men will see visions,
   your old men will dream dreams.
Even on my servants, both men and women,
   I will pour out from[13] my Spirit in those days,
   and they will prophesy.
I will show wonders in the heaven above
   and signs on the earth below,
   blood and fire and billows of smoke.
The sun will be turned to darkness
   and the moon to blood
   before the coming of the great and glorious day of the Lord.
And everyone who calls
   on the name of the Lord will be saved.'

(Acts 2:16–21)

Peter identified what was happening there in Jerusalem as the kind of event Joel had predicted. The Spirit had come, imparting to God's servants a miraculous prophetic fluency. And the point for the onlookers was obvious: it is time to call on the Lord for salvation! The terrible disruptions prophesied by Joel could usher in the day of the Lord at any time. The door of mercy stands open, but not forever. The Lord Jesus will act decisively in awesome triumph over his enemies. Therefore Peter called the people to come to terms with the exalted Lord, receive the Holy Spirit, and save themselves from the coming doom (Acts 2:32–40).

But this event at Pentecost was not the only outpouring of the Holy Spirit. It was just the beginning. The rest of the book of Acts records the Holy Spirit's continued work in the early church. The Spirit filled Peter and the whole church to speak out prophetically (4:8, 31). The Spirit confirmed the public testimony of the church (5:32). The Spirit gave Stephen power to perform miraculous signs and to argue cogently for the gospel (6:5, 8, 10), filling him with grace when under intense pressure (7:55). The Spirit came upon converts in despised Samaria, drawing them into the circle of grace (8:14–17). The Spirit told Philip to approach the Ethiopian eunuch (8:29) and later took him away (8:39). The Spirit encouraged the growing church (9:31). The Spirit alerted Peter to the three men looking for him on Cornelius's behalf, men whom the Spirit himself had sent (10:19–20; 11:12). The Spirit was poured out even on lowly Gentiles (10:44–47) just as he had come down upon Jews at Pentecost (11:15; 15:8). Barnabas was full of the Holy Spirit and encouragement (11:24). By the Spirit, Agabus predicted a famine (11:28). The Spirit ordained Barnabas and Saul for their ministry (13:2) and sent them on their way (13:4). Filled with the Holy Spirit, Paul had the courage to confront Elymas the magician (13:9). The new converts of Paul and Barnabas were filled with joy and the Holy Spirit (13:52). The Spirit guided the proceedings at the Jerusalem Council (15:28). Paul and his companions were forbidden by the Spirit to go into Asia and Bithynia (16:6–7). The Spirit came upon disciples of John the Baptist in Ephesus, just as he had come down at Pentecost (19:1–6). The Spirit compelled Paul to go to Jerusalem, warning him that he would suffer for it (20:22–23). The Spirit appointed men as overseers in the Ephesian church (20:28). The Spirit prompted believers in Tyre to caution Paul about going on to Jerusalem (21:4). By the Spirit, Agabus prophesied Paul's imprisonment (21:11). And through it all, the gospel surged forward with overruling power and the church spread by leaps and bounds across the ancient world.[14]

Now *that* is an outpouring of the Holy Spirit! His presence pervaded the early church as their constant companion and secret power. *And our Lord Jesus continues to pour out his Spirit upon his church.* Pentecost did not exhaust the fulfilment of Joel 2. It only inaugurated the age of the Spirit, which Peter calls 'the last days' (Acts 2:17; cf. Heb. 1:1–2). For this reason, Peter may have found suggestive the Septuagint's wording 'I will pour out *from* my Spirit.'[15] In other words, 'I will grant, out of my inexhaustible resources of grace, effusion after effusion of the Holy Spirit throughout the course of these last days' – a point that Joel would doubtless have gladly affirmed. The entire Christian era, beginning at Pentecost, is one extended fulfilment of Joel 2:28–32, leading to ultimate fulfilment in 'the great and dreadful day of the Lord'.

So even as Pentecost marked the beginning of a great movement of the Holy Spirit in the book of Acts, the book of Acts is itself only the beginning of Christian history. After all, Peter said that the promise of the Spirit is 'for you *and your children*' in subsequent generations (Acts 2:39). Until our Lord returns, we will serve by the

Spirit's power as his prophetic presence in this age. And we may expect a rough ride on our way toward the day of the Lord, as history's upheavals (such as the destruction of Jerusalem in AD 70) roar one warning after another that the day of the Lord is coming. The Christian's ultimate aim, therefore, is not a normal life but an anointed life. We will have time enough in heaven for ease and security.

Moreover, as our biblical text allows and as church history shows, Jesus is not pouring his Spirit upon the church steadily, evenly, or predictably. At some times and in some places, the church languishes even as Judah did in Joel's day. The 'locusts' of worldly influence can eat at our souls and the 'drought' of spiritual deprivation can leave us dry. But then the risen Lord pours out upon his church a fresh measure of his Spirit, and we are revived. So we can think of a season of revival as rather like a storm system moving across a parched area of the church, bringing 'times of refreshing' (Acts 3:19).

In the introduction to Jonathan Edwards's 'Faithful Narrative of the Surprising Work of God', Isaac Watts and John Guyse describe that surprising work like this:

> There is a spot of ground, as we are here informed, wherein there are twelve or fourteen towns and villages, chiefly situate in New Hampshire, near the banks of the river of Connecticut, within the compass of thirty miles, wherein it pleased God, two years ago, to display his free and sovereign mercy in the conversion of a great multitude of souls in a short space of time, turning them from a formal, cold, and careless profession of Christianity to the lively exercise of every Christian grace and the powerful practice of our holy religion. The great God has seemed to act over again the miracle of Gideon's fleece, which was plentifully watered with the dew of heaven, while the rest of the earth round about it was dry and had no such remarkable blessing.[16]

The Lord poured out his Spirit with sovereign freedom. This is encouraging. We cannot trigger the Spirit's downpour but we should always abound in hope, for we live in the age of the Spirit.

The Lord Jesus may at any time and under any circumstances grant us a fresh bestowment of his Spirit. And we can be certain that nothing will defeat God's purpose whenever he chooses to renew a season of unusual spiritual richness. How can any opposition down here on earth restrain the outpouring of the Spirit from on high? It is God's free decision, effortless accomplishment, and sovereign purpose. 'I will no longer hide my face from them, for I will pour out my Spirit on the house of Israel, declares the Sovereign LORD' (Ezek. 39:29). At any time, in any measure, upon any church, the Sovereign Lord is able to send the showers of his Spirit, for his greater glory, our richer joy, and the salvation of the nations.

God has promised us this blessing. 'I *will* pour out my Spirit on all flesh' (Joel 2:28). 'The *promise* is for you and your children and for all who are far off – for all whom the Lord our God will call' (Acts 2:39). Now let us seek his promise. Let us seek it earnestly, laying hold of him in prayer and not letting go. Let us seek it wisely, not sitting around waiting for 'a special motion of the Spirit'[17] before we act, but confidently obeying our Lord's commands to go and speak at any price and against all opposition and ridicule, even as we continue to pray. He will empower us, according to his will, as we are moving forward in faithful obedience.

I remember arriving at work one morning in 1986. Someone said, 'The space shuttle just blew up.' One of the men had a television in his office, so we crowded in there to watch the news. Again and again we saw the video of the shuttle climbing into space so gracefully and powerfully, slowly rotating as it surged upward. And then, in an instant, it disintegrated in a cloud of white smoke and flying debris. I cannot think of a better image of this present world when the day of the Lord finally comes. History will be proceeding in its usual course, 'all systems go', when God will suddenly appear. He will not ask anyone's permission. He will not apologize for himself. He will not hesitate. God will bring this present evil age to a decisive end forever with a cataclysmic shaking of all things.

Therefore we must not trivialize revival as if it were a tool for the promotion of 'our church' or 'my ministry'. We must see revival as divine empowerment for us to lift our prophetic voices, that the nations may call on the name of the Lord before that great and dreadful day. God is in earnest with us. Let us be so with him.

Drawing on his outpoured Spirit, let us speak his Word to our generation. The door of mercy stands open now, but we have not got forever. My mother helps us sense the urgency of the hour with her hymn 'Macedonia':

> The vision of a dying world is vast before our eyes;
> We feel the heartbeat of its need, we hear its feeble cries.
> Lord Jesus Christ, revive thy church in this, her crucial hour!
> Lord Jesus Christ, awake thy church with Spirit-given power!
>
> The savage hugs his god of stone and fears descent of night;
> The city dweller cringes lone amid the garish light.
> Lord Jesus Christ, arouse thy church to see their mute distress!
> Lord Jesus Christ, equip thy church with love and tenderness!
>
> Today, as understanding's bounds are stretched on every hand,
> O clothe thy Word in bright, new sounds, and speed it o'er the
>   land.
> Lord Jesus Christ, empower us to preach by every means!
> Lord Jesus Christ, embolden us in near and distant scenes!
>
> The warning bell of judgment tolls, above us looms the cross.
> Around are ever-dying souls – how great, how great the loss!
> O Lord, constrain and move thy church the glad news to impart!
> And Lord, as thou dost stir thy church, begin within my heart.[18]

When we reflect on where we stand in God's plan for history, what dignity it lends to our existence! God has ordained that you and I live not in some obscure Sumerian village four thousand years ago but here in 'the last days', in that season of history when the Spirit is more generously poured out, when the day of the Lord may at any time appear with a wrath unmitigated, full and vast, terrifyingly final. As we proceed toward the End, the wheat and the weeds are growing together (Matt. 13:24–30). And we are a part of all this! Let us live with urgency. Let us exploit the opportunity of life. Let us not drift. Let us live intentionally. We have not got forever to make up our minds and we must not trifle our lives away.

Charles Simeon held his friend Henry Martyn in the deepest affection. Simeon ministered in Cambridge while Martyn went to India as a missionary. A portrait of Martyn, sent to Simeon in 1812, had something of the influence on Simeon that his friend's own presence would have had:

> The portrait was hung in Simeon's dining-room, over the fire-place. He used often to look at it in his friends' presence and to say, as he did so, with peculiar loving emphasis, 'There, see that blessed man! What an expression of countenance! No one looks at me as he does; he never takes his eyes off me, and seems always to be saying, "Be serious – be in earnest – don't trifle – don't trifle."' Then, smiling at the picture, and gently bowing, he would add, 'And I won't trifle. I won't trifle.'[19]

Your life and mine have greatness – if not in accomplishment, at least in potential. And God has granted that we live during that era of the world's history heaviest with gospel potential. Let us not trifle, as worldlings do. They are living for the weekend; we are living for the End. Let us seek the Lord's anointing on our lives. Let us seek it now.

5

God raises us up

Jeremy Bentham, the champion of Utilitarianism, died in 1832. He willed his estate to the University College Hospital in London, on one bizarre condition. He required that his dead body be dissected and then his skeleton reassembled, preserved, and clothed so that he could 'attend' all subsequent board meetings of the hospital. To this day, dressed in his nineteenth-century attire, Jeremy Bentham is wheeled into the hospital's board meetings and the chairman pronounces, 'Jeremy Bentham, present but not voting.'[1]

This is a picture of too many people in our churches today. They are 'present but not voting'. They hear the Word. They receive the Lord's Supper. But they are not voting, not responding. They have little sense of the glory of God and the thrill of living flat-out for Christ. They expect little from God and venture little for God. God's promises and assurances in Scripture seem unreal. A. W. Tozer's assessment is trenchant, as always:

> To the absence of the Spirit may be traced that vague sense of unreality which almost everywhere invests religion in our times. In the average church service the most real thing is the shadowy unreality of everything. The worshiper sits in a state of suspended thought; a kind of dreamy numbness creeps

upon him; he hears words but they do not register; he cannot relate them to anything on his own life-level. He is conscious of having entered a kind of half-world; his mind surrenders itself to a more or less pleasant mood which passes with the benediction, leaving no trace behind. It does not affect anything in his everyday life. He is aware of no power, no Presence, no spiritual reality. There is simply nothing in his experience corresponding to the things which he heard from the pulpit or sang in the hymns.[2]

What really matters to too many Christians is all in this world – its politics, economics, entertainments, and lifestyles, and even its troubles. 'There is a pleasure in being to a certain degree agitated by events,' to quote Boswell.[3] When, in the mind of the Christian, the reality of God is eclipsed by the passing parade of worldly distractions, one's faith becomes worthless for much more than the personal comfort of an evangelical Muzak, however sincerely intended it may be.

It has all happened before. Israel and Judah sank into a worldly malaise as well. God warned them through his prophets to change course. He gave them strong incentives. He gave them ample opportunity. But they would not listen. So eventually God disciplined them. The salt had lost its savour and was no longer good for anything except to be thrown out and trampled underfoot (Matt. 5:13). The generation of the prophet Ezekiel was 'trampled underfoot' when the Babylonian army conquered Judah and deported the people to exile far away. But their affliction, though richly deserved, could not by itself restore. In fact it created a new problem.

As God's people languished in exile in Babylon, their unbelief, which before had taken the form of moral complacency, gave way to new unbelief in the form of spiritual despondency. His prophetic threats of discipline had seemed empty to the people as they binged on moral and doctrinal recklessness. Now, when Ezekiel comes to them with divine promises of restoration (chap. 36), his new message of hope seems equally unreal. God promises his people that he will reinvigorate them spiritually and morally, returning them to the land and lavishing them with blessing in it. But how do his people assess their future prospects? 'Our bones are dried up and our hope is gone; we are cut off' (37:11), they moan in discouragement. Back when they were running wild, they could not take God's warnings seriously. Now as they are suffering, they cannot bring themselves to take God's assurances seriously. How foolish we are and slow of heart to believe *all* that the prophets have spoken (Luke 24:25)!

Sometimes we really do need to feel the sting of God's discipline (Heb. 12:3–11). But we need more than discipline, because discipline alone does not create faith. To rise up from the low condition that prompted God's discipline in the first place, we also need his reviving touch. We need grace that is greater than all our sin. We need a new spirit within to expel our addiction to worldliness (Ezek. 36:25–27).[4] So here in Ezekiel 37 God declares his intention to resurrect his deadened people. He is able to transform our casualties into a living army. Or, as the hymn 'Fairest Lord Jesus' puts it, 'He makes the woeful heart to sing.' And Ezekiel 37 is calculated to make woeful hearts to *sing* again.

But can this passage be applied to the Christian church today? Ezekiel predicts a 'resurrection' of Israel from Babylonian captivity and their return to the promised land in a spiritually revived condition, all of which occurred long ago.[5] Ezekiel's prediction was fulfilled. But did that fulfilment exhaust the value of our passage? Does Ezekiel's text now lie dormant on the biblical page as merely a historical artefact? I do not think so. The passage is more than an ancient prediction of an event by now long past. It declares the eternal ways of God, for what he promises to do here emerges out of his unchanging character. Ezekiel's great burden is not just a particular moment in the history of Israel but the nature and purpose of *God* for his people. There is nothing in the passage that requires us to limit its significance to a specific historical situation, past or present. It finds its immediate significance in the return of the Jewish exiles in the sixth century BC. It predicts their return against the backdrop of the New Covenant theology of chapter 36 and promises the implementation of that covenant with the daring metaphor of resurrection. But the New Covenant is the inheritance of all the true people of God in every age. In all places and at all times we will need to be raised up out of our personal and institutional graves. Ezekiel 37 labours to assure us of God's power-ful all-sufficiency for us. As long as our God remains the living God, and until we are with him in heaven, our dead hearts and dead churches will need him just as much as the Jewish exiles did twenty-five hundred years ago. And this passage announces that he is there to fill us with New Covenant life.

Before we were saved, we were 'dead in trespasses and sins'. But then God 'made us alive together with Christ' (Eph. 2:1–10). That is brilliantly true. But it is possible even for those who are 'alive together with Christ' to become cold and sluggish, deadened in their experience of Christ. This tragic condition may lie concealed beneath a busy church programme and peppy choruses, but God sees. The risen Lord said to his church at Sardis, 'You have a repu-tation of being alive, but you are dead' (Rev. 3:1). We are all too familiar with this in our own lives and in our churches as well. And Ezekiel's vision applies to the church today whenever our experience of God fades to a mere memory, whenever we lie defeated before the triumphant world, whenever our faith is exhausted and our expectations flattened in despair, so that we say of ourselves, 'Our bones are dried up and our hope is gone; we are cut off.' But our barrenness does not stop God. When we have nothing left to offer, he is able to impart to us fresh life out of his limitless all-sufficiency.

We know that Ezekiel 37 is meant for God's own people because the Lord calls them 'my people' in verses 12 and 13. And verse 11 explains that the vision applies to 'the whole house of Israel', the people of the covenant. But what the people of God need is to be *revived* in their spiritual experience. When God asks Ezekiel, 'Can these bones live?' (v. 3), Ezekiel does not say, 'Of course these "bones" can live again. They both can and will, for we are your people.' Instead, Ezekiel answers, 'O Sovereign LORD, you alone know.' His answer makes sense only if God is asking him not about their status as God's people but about the prospects for *revival* in that generation of God's people. Their identity is not subject to question. It is the ultimate reason why they receive this prophetic assurance in the first place. But God's own people have died as a vibrant force for his glory. They are no longer a compelling witness to and manifestation of his reality and worth in the eyes of a God-neglecting world. So when Ezekiel is asked about the revival of his generation, the question knocks him off-balance. He seems unsure or even paralysed in shock. The people of God seem beyond recovery.

The prophet looks out on the exiled Jews in Babylon as if they were a valley strewn with dry bones, a sort of spiritual Death Valley, perhaps reminiscent of scenes of slaughter during the final days of Judah's collapse. It may be the darkest moment thus far in the history of God's people. If this 'army' of bones ever fights again, it will be a miracle. But God loves to perform miracles.

The passage divides into two sections. In verses 1–10, we are shown Ezekiel's vision. The prophet does not see literal bones, literal tendons, and so on. This is a visionary experience, not a concrete experience (see 8:3; 11:24–25). It is happening inside Ezekiel's head, not out in real life. And then in verses 11–14 we are told the interpretation of the vision, where we see what Ezekiel is literally to do with his actual people in Babylonian exile. Although the visionary experience does not take place in space and time, it does give Ezekiel new eyes with which to see the real people of his generation. It gives him a new insight, a new hope, a new message to proclaim.

The vision: a valley of dry bones

> The hand of the LORD was upon me, and he brought me out by the Spirit of the LORD and set me in the middle of a valley; it was full of bones. He led me back and forth among them, and I saw a great many bones on the floor of the valley, bones that were very dry. He asked me, 'Son of man, can these bones live?'
>
> I said, 'O Sovereign LORD, you alone know.'
>
> (Ezek. 37:1–3)

God does not wait for his people to kick-start their own renewal. He takes the initiative himself. He opens up a new vision of hope for them by laying his hand on Ezekiel.

The Spirit seizes the prophet, bringing him into a valley full of human bones. The scene is enough to give him the creeps. It looks as if a defeated army of a bygone day has been left to rot right where they fell. Imagine the scene: Skulls and rib cages and pelvises and femurs strewn around in disarray, some partially buried in the sand, baking in the shimmering heat of the Mesopotamian sun; the whole scene utterly still, quiet, deathly. But Ezekiel is not allowed to behold the ghastly sight and then turn away in disgust. God takes him on a guided tour of death, death, death everywhere around, death visibly triumphant among the people of God.

What lays hold of Ezekiel with overwhelming force is the vast number of bones ('a great many bones') and their brittle, bleached condition ('very dry'). They have been lying there under the sun for a long time, the marrow thoroughly baked out of them. They will soon turn altogether into dust. There is nowhere the slightest sign of life whatever. At this moment of unblinking realism, God asks the question that drives the entire passage: 'Son of man, *can these bones live?*'

In other words, is there any realistic hope of new life in this scene of defeat and death? Can you devise some method for re-invigorating these bones? Do you have consultants and experts to help you 'deal with the problem'? Or have these bones gone beyond any human prospect of restoration to life? Is the covenant community not doomed to remain forever in its pathetic helplessness?

The very many and very dry bones of this vision, which Ezekiel can only gape at in disbelief, declare to us a solemn warning. Sin breeds death. And the death at work in us all has a big appetite; it is never satisfied. The vast number and the arid condition of these bones bear silent testimony to the ravenous hunger of death, the predator of our souls. Ironically, the Jews in Babylon were thriving outwardly. They were raising families, doing business, making money. But this vision reveals the true state of their souls. God's discipline has brought them into this condition, and only God's grace can take them out of it again.

But God presses the question 'Son of man, *can these bones live?*' We could paraphrase the force of it like this: 'You've taken a good look all around here, Ezekiel. Does this scene of death look to you like the birthplace of new life? What do you think, mortal man?' Ezekiel is forced to ponder a new question and face a staggering possibility. His stammering answer is both affirming and revealing: 'O Sovereign LORD, you alone know.' His words affirm a truth about God, and they reveal a weakness in Ezekiel.

'O Sovereign LORD' affirms God as Israel's Master, who keeps his covenant with his people. The biblical names of God are packed with meaning. Here, the divine name Yahweh ('LORD') resonates with assurance that he is 'near at hand and mighty to control'.[6] The prefixed title Sovereign emphasizes his status as Master over all. In the face of a hopeless situation, with nothing else to say, Ezekiel takes his stand here.

Our sovereign Lord, by his very existence and nature, creates new possibilities. I remember sitting over lunch with Dr Carl Henry, the great evangelical theologian, several years ago. We were discussing evangelicalism's future. I was lamenting our prospects, but his reply to me was encouraging: 'Our God is a God of surprises.' It must be so, with One who is the 'Sovereign LORD'. Who can overpower him, outwit him, outmanoeuvre him? He anticipates, surrounds, and accounts for everything, simply everything. Even if he blundered – absurd supposition! – but even if he did blunder, 'the foolishness of God is wiser than man's wisdom' (1 Cor. 1:25). In other words, God's worst idea is still infinitely cleverer than man's best idea. And 'the weakness of God is stronger than man's strength'. Therefore, *what is hopelessly impossible for us is no longer absolute in its finality.* We may not *know* how God would rescue a dead church, but we must confess that the 'Sovereign LORD' *can* rescue any church: 'See now that I myself am He! There is no god besides me. I put to death and I bring to life, I have wounded and I will heal, and no one can deliver out of my hand' (Deut. 32:39).

But Ezekiel's answer also reveals a weakness in him. It falls short of unambiguous certainty. 'You alone know' is another way of saying, 'What I see in this valley is so discouraging, its remedy so inconceivable, I can't bring myself to an unqualified reply. If there is any hope, it must lie with you alone. But I can't even imagine it. So I believe, but help my unbelief.' Ezekiel's head knew too much good theology to deny God's power. But Ezekiel's heart could not quite muster a resolute 'Yes, of course, these bones can live!' So he refers the question back to God. If these bones do in fact come back to life again, it will be due not to the faith of the prophet but to the sovereign act of Israel's covenant-keeping God, 'near at hand and mighty to control'.

But what *are* these 'bones'? What is the point? Verse 11 interprets this aspect of the vision:

> Then he said to me: 'Son of man, these bones are the whole house of Israel. They say, "Our bones are dried up and our hope is gone; we are cut off."'

Israel in exile is dead. As a force for God, the nation is spent. And this is not only God's assessment of them; it is how they see themselves. They have completely lost heart. They look out into their future and see stretching out before them one long death sentence. In Jackson Browne's song 'The Pretender', he says that he sees the ships, bearing his dreams, sail out of sight. In other words, 'There goes life. There goes happiness. There goes hope, sailing away over the horizon. My life is now over.' Similarly, the exiled Jews in Babylon see nothing for themselves but more exile, more abandonment, more humiliation. They have no spirit left, because they see no future before them.

That their bones are 'dried up' is a figurative expression for 'Our hope is gone; we are cut off.' In effect, 'We are beyond recovery.' Now, if this were unalterably true, it would have been bad news not just for the Jewish exiles but for the whole world as well. If the 'kingdom of priests and holy nation' of Exodus 19:6 were history, then with its death the hope of the world would have expired, for it was through this nation that salvation was to come to the world (John 4:22). So the demoralized people of God are really saying that his great project of world redemption has failed. The only true light of the world is extinguished. In the great conflict of the ages, the darkness has triumphed. But the defeat of God's people is not the defeat of God. And to project one's own failure onto God is just plain irrational, for God is never at a loss.

When I was going through a season of crushing discouragement myself some years ago, I corresponded with Mr William Still, a minister in the Church of Scotland and a father in the Lord. He was kind and sensitive throughout our exchange of letters. But at one point he did write to me, 'Of course, your feelings are quite irrational.' That helped. I had not seen it so clearly. In that instant of surprised recognition at the unexpected appearance of truth, I had to throw my head back and laugh. In the same way, the feelings of the Jewish exiles were irrational. If we are tethered to the eternal purpose of God, how can we be utterly cut off? God cannot fail when he intends to succeed. And he does intend to succeed. In fact even our feelings of desolation can ultimately bear fruit in his dealings with us.

God understands how weak we are. He understands that what we need in a despairing condition is not more discipline but hope. We need to see beyond ourselves and our failure, up out of this world, all the way up into the grandeur of the living God. And that hope in God – hope for a revival totally improbable from a human point of view but decreed by the Father, bought for us by his crucified Son, and implemented by his Spirit – that hope in our all-sufficient God is the prophetic burden of this passage.

You will come to life

> Then he said to me, 'Prophesy to these bones and say to them, "Dry bones, hear the word of the LORD! This is what the Sovereign LORD says to these bones: I will make breath enter you, and you will come to life. I will attach tendons to you and make flesh come upon you and cover you with skin; I will put breath in you, and you will come to life. Then you will know that I am the LORD." '
>
> (Ezek. 37:4–6)

Sometimes God requires us to do things that do not make sense in our own eyes. In Ezekiel's case, he has to preach to a valley of dry bones. 'This was as if one should water a dry, rotten stick, and say, "Grow." '[7] But then, is all preaching not equally absurd? We do not even have within ourselves the wherewithal to hear and respond to the Word of God properly. 'Though seeing, they do not see; though hearing, they do not hear or understand' (Matt. 13:13). Any vital response to the proclamation of God's Word is a miracle of grace.

The striking thing about verses 4 and 5 is that, although the prophet must preach, it is not really his preaching that gives life. '*I* will make breath enter you, and you will come to life,' God says. His *means* of sparking new life is the promise declared through the mouth of the prophet, but the *cause* of that new life is God's own gracious action. He alone is the God of life. He reinforces his point by repeating it in verse 6: 'I will put breath in you, and you will come to life.'

Preachers are 'God's fellow workers' (2 Cor. 6:1). Their efforts are not causative in power, but they may be instrumental in function (1 Cor. 3:5–9). As our passage unfolds, Ezekiel acts only in obedience to divine orders, and he notes that fact carefully (vv. 7, 10). Why? To confess that the power is God's alone. Ezekiel is *not* the proverbial flea on the back of the elephant. (Once upon a time, a flea was riding on the back of an elephant as it crossed a rickety old bridge. The narrow bridge swayed and shuddered with each movement of the great creature, sending other animals scurrying out of harm's way. After the elephant had crossed, the flea looked back and said, 'Well, I guess we really shook 'em up that time!')

God does use preachers, but they do not shake anything up. It is God himself who raises his deadened church to life. Therefore our self-exaltation is preposterous. The great principle driving all history applies with special force to God's reviving mercies: 'Then you will know that I am the Lord' (v. 6).

The weakness of human preaching was illustrated forcefully in a class at Trinity Evangelical Divinity School near Chicago, where I used to teach. The professor took the students into a local cemetery. He told one of them to preach to the gravestones. He insisted. The student was dumbfounded, of course. But the lesson was clear: human preaching alone may expect true, spiritual results as much as preaching in a cemetery raises the dead. Only God can return life to the dead.

So verse 5 promises the impossible – revived life for the dead-ened people of God – while verse 6 describes the process leading to that glorious outcome. The two-stage process described here in verse 6 (first the body, then the breath) alludes to Genesis 2:7, where God makes Adam: 'The Lord God formed the man from the dust of the ground and breathed into his nostrils the breath of life, and the man became a living being.'

First stage: God forms Adam's material body. Second stage: God breathes into him the immaterial breath of life. Net result: the man becomes a living being. And how is the structure of this verse significant? *It includes the second stage.* The material is not enough for Adam to become a living being. He also needs the immaterial breath of God within him. Only then does Adam come alive. The exiled Jews must reflect on this. We must reflect on it. Most people do not understand it.

Most people do not understand that we do not live from the ground up but from heaven down. Attractive shopping malls and well-stocked refrigerators do not define the essence of human existence. What makes for life is intangible, supramundane, spiritual. God alone can give it. As we come to realize this, it magnifies the value of God in our eyes, giving us strong incentives to seek him as our *only true life*.

That is the purpose driving all of God's dealings with us – that we should come to acknowledge and experience him as our personal all-sufficiency: 'Then you will know that I am the LORD' (v. 6). He aims to persuade us that he really is 'the God who makes the dead live and calls into being things that are not' (Rom. 4:17 REB). And if this is our God, then the church may look for revival at any time. It is in God's very nature. The living God is able to impart life to any and all at any time at all.

In *The Lion, the Witch and the Wardrobe*, by C. S. Lewis, Aslan the Lion, a figure of Christ, enters a castle. It is the home of the Witch. Aslan and his two human friends find it filled with statues of animals and people turned to stone. Aslan brings them back to life, beginning with a lion:

'Oh, Susan! Look! Look at the lion.'

I expect you've seen someone put a lighted match to a bit of newspaper which is propped up in a grate against an unlit fire. And for a second nothing seems to have happened; and then you notice a tiny streak of flame creeping along the edge of the newspaper. It was like that now. For a second after Aslan had breathed upon him the stone lion looked just the same. Then a tiny streak of gold began to run along his white marble back – then it spread – then the colour seemed to lick all over him as the flame licks all over a bit of paper – then, while his hind-quarters were still obviously stone the lion shook his mane and all the heavy, stony folds rippled into living hair. Then he opened a great red mouth, warm and living, and gave a prodigious yawn. And now his hind legs had come to life. He lifted one of them and scratched himself. Then, having caught sight of Aslan, he went bounding after him and frisking round him whimpering with delight and jumping up to lick his face.

Of course the children's eyes turned to follow the lion; but the sight they saw was so wonderful that they soon forgot about *him*. Everywhere the statues were coming to life. The courtyard looked no longer like a museum; it looked more like a zoo. Creatures were running after Aslan and dancing round him till he was almost hidden in the crowd. Instead of all that deadly white the courtyard was now a blaze of colours; glossy chestnut sides of centaurs, indigo horns of unicorns, dazzling plumage of birds, reddy-brown of foxes, dogs, and satyrs, yellow stockings and crimson hoods of dwarfs; and the birch-girls in silver, and the beech-girls in fresh, transparent green, and the larch-girls in green so bright that it was almost yellow. And instead of the deadly silence the whole place rang with the sound of happy roarings, brayings, yelpings, barkings, squealings, cooings, neighings, stampings, shouts, hurrahs, songs and laughter.[8]

In the same way, the Sovereign Lord declares to his people covered with 'all that deadly white' and living in that 'deadly silence', 'I will make breath enter you, and you will come to life'. And we may think of a church enjoying his reviving mercies as that courtyard of happy creatures, filling the place with 'shouts, hurrahs, songs and laughter'.

But there was no breath in them

> So I prophesied as I was commanded. And as I was prophesying, there was a noise, a rattling sound, and the bones came together, bone to bone. I looked, and tendons and flesh appeared on them and skin covered them, but there was no breath in them.
>
> (Ezek. 37:7–8)

Ezekiel passes the test of his faith. Disregarding the odds against success (humanly calculated), he prophesies as he was commanded. And as the very words fall from his lips, the bones start moving around, organizing themselves into recognizably human skeletons. Ezekiel watches in astonishment as human tissue appears over the bones, so that they become actual bodies. There they lie. The Word has a visible effect, a token of greater blessing to come. *But the bodies are still dead.*

Some churches, like these bodies, are incomplete in their restoration. They are well organized. Their structures may even claim a pedigree rooted in the Reformation. But where is the *life*? Or we may think of some individuals: they profess the faith, submit to the ordinances, and fulfil the expectations. Outwardly they fit the profile of 'a good Christian'. But where is the *life*?

Preaching to the dry bones of a dead church is God's way of moving them into revival. The importance God places on preaching toward revival is reinforced not only by the obviously strategic role of Ezekiel's prophesying in the unfolding drama here but also by the fact that the very word 'prophesy' appears seven times in our passage (vv. 4, 7, 9, 10, and 12). The bones are to 'hear the word of the LORD' (v. 4). The phrase 'This is what the Sovereign LORD says' occurs three times (vv. 5, 9, 12).[9] The passage simmers with confidence in the Word of God as a dynamic force for revival (see Rom. 1:16; 1 Cor. 2:4; 1 Thess. 1:5).

There is certainly no reviving power in what the people themselves are saying: 'Our bones are dried up and our hope is gone; we are cut off' (v. 11). They must stop listening to themselves, to their own despair and defeatism and self-pity, and start hearing the word of the Lord: 'You will come to life. Then you will know that I am the LORD' (v. 6). This is why our ears are on the outside of our heads rather than on the inside. Even at our best, our good ideas cannot impart life. They can only reconfigure the outward appearance of our naturally geriatric inner selves. Our words have no divine efficacy, however stylish and popular they may be. But God gives life.

The Scriptures rejoice in the divine instrumentality of the Word. Think of the Psalter. Psalm 1 'high-fives' (the congratulatory word 'blessed' is a biblical 'high-five') the man who rejects worldliness (v. 1) but gladly delights in the law of the Lord (v. 2). He flourishes like 'a tree planted by streams of water' (v. 3). Is that not suggestive? Some people think the Bible is a dry book. No; it is *soaking wet* with 'streams of water' flowing from the Spirit through the Word into the soul. And Psalm 19:7 affirms, 'The law of the LORD is perfect, reviving the soul.' And Psalm 119 – some ancient saint's devotional journal, arranged alphabetically – looks for reinvigoration through the Word. The psalmist is emotionally exhausted: 'My soul cleaves to the dust; revive me *according to thy word*!' (v. 25 RSV). He is suffering: 'This is my comfort in my affliction, that *thy promise* gives me life' (v. 50 RSV). He needs protection: 'Plead my cause and redeem me; give me life *according to thy promise*!' (v. 154 RSV). How clearly he sees the potentialities of the Word of God! How confidently he exploits them!

God is bearing witness to us through Ezekiel's prophesying, and through other Scriptures, that authentic renewal is a ministry of his Word. Not only does the Word preserve us from imitation revival, but it is itself God's primary means of sparking genuine revival. Why? Not because the Bible is a magical book, but because God engages us primarily through our minds and transforms us through new understandings. 'Such is the nature of man, that no object can come at the heart but through the door of the understanding.'[10]

Contemplating the dry bones of our churches today, many can see that we need revival. That is beyond question. For some churches, a move toward mediocrity would be an improvement. But we must be wise in the strategies we deploy to seek revival blessing:

> It is not just spiritual experience which will rectify our situation, but a complete re-orientation to biblical truth and a return to right thinking and doctrine ... Heightened experience certainly leaves its mark, some of which may be good wherever it meets orthodoxy, but a *reformational revival* is a life-giving river which has continuing positive effects.[11]

The word 'just' in the first sentence there is important; the revival that will rectify our situation *is* spiritual experience. But chasing theologically indefensible experiences promoted as 'revival' will ultimately betray us.

Contemporary evangelicalism tolerates an elusive but coercive antidoctrine atmosphere. It is everywhere but nowhere at the same time – just a vague mood in which one senses that requiring theological justification for our practices, especially when they appear to be working effectively, is rude or even Spirit-quenching. Most Christians would never come out and say that the Bible is a dead book, but too few rejoice in it as the living Word of God. Biblical teaching is dismissed as 'mere doctrine'. 'Doctrine divides,' we are told. 'Not doctrine, but power' – that sort of thinking. But what is biblical doctrine? That is simply a formal term for the Bible's vision of *God*, the glorious face of God in Christ unveiled before us by the Spirit with transforming power (Exod. 33:18 with 34:5–7; 2 Cor. 3:12 – 4:6). *If we want true revival, we will stop disparaging the Word and start exploiting it.*

But then, is there not a problem with that? If *all* we needed were the Word of God *only*, how could we explain all the faithful, soundly orthodox, Bible-preaching, dead churches out there? Without the Word, we will certainly drift. But still, something more is required.

Prophesy to the breath

> Then he said to me, 'Prophesy to the breath; prophesy, son of man, and say to it, "This is what the Sovereign LORD says: Come from the four winds, O breath, and breathe into these slain, that they may live." So I prophesied as he commanded me, and breath entered them; they came to life and stood up on their feet – a vast army.
>
> (Ezek. 37:9–10)

God has used Ezekiel's preaching to reassemble the bones into bodies. But now, nothing less than a massive stirring of the winds from the four corners of the earth will revive this vast congregation of corpses to fresh life. So God calls for a great blowing of the winds to breathe life into 'these slain', the victims of the Babylonian invasion and deportation, in 'a major offensive against the forces of death'.[12]

Ezekiel's role here is equivalent to prayer – but not just any prayer. This is prophetic praying, because it agrees with God's clearly revealed will. Ezekiel calls for the breath (the Holy Spirit, according to v. 14) to breathe on the dead congregation. Only then will they be quickened. One can imagine a gentle stirring of air growing steadily into a gale as the winds converge to whoosh down on and into all these bodies. And those who had been 'the slain' are transformed into 'a vast army'.

It is a sheer act of God. True, Ezekiel obeys God's command. But this outcome can be explained only in terms of divine action. The prophet does not create the new life; he only witnesses it and reports it to us. Similarly, our confidence is not in ourselves but in God who raises the dead (2 Cor. 1:9).

If this is true, and it is, then we should see the living church as an ongoing miracle and we should see revival as an occasional megamiracle. Especially in revival, the 'vast army' is seen to be in vital union with the Lord of life, bursting the limitations of merely human ideas, methods, promotion, and enthusiasm. Revival is not a Finneyite 'right use of the appropriate means'.[13] The ordinary rules of human cause and effect are suspended, and God is seen to be all in all.

But the New International Version hides something here. In verse 2, Ezekiel tells us that he saw 'a great many bones' and that they were 'very dry'. The Revised Standard Version translates more literally, 'very many' and 'very dry'. The RSV shows us that the same Hebrew adverb (translated 'very') is used to amplify the force of both the adjectives, 'many' and 'dry'. Here in verse 10 that same adverb is used again, twice, to modify the 'great army'. That is to say, the animated bodies have leapt to their feet as (literally) a 'very, very great army'. Ezekiel's careful wording tells us something. It tells us that the two verys of verse 2 are now fully reversed here in verse 10. *Utter desolation has become irrepressible energy, by the power of God.* We are overwhelmed by the extent and depth of our deadness, but God is not. He is able by his Spirit to transform a profoundly dead church into 'a vast army', standing on their feet in readiness to obey his orders and serve his cause.

The Word had reconstituted the dry bones into, if you will, 'fresh' corpses. But the Spirit also was needed to energize them as a living army. A. B. Simpson helps us see the necessity of the Spirit along with the Word:

The Word of God alone can bring about only an outward reformation like the baptism of John, which changed the lives of men
and the forms and habits of their conversation; but it cannot put
breath in them. And so the first effect is the abandonment of sin,
the reformation of life, the assuming of the forms of righteousness, but there is no breath in them. The great agent in the
real and vital transfiguration is the Spirit of the Living God, 'the
breath of life from the four winds of heaven'.[14]

A church may so react against those who highlight the Spirit but
neglect the Word that it overreacts by employing the Word only.
This is theologically invalid and tactically foolish. What we find in
our passage is new life bursting forth as the Word and the Spirit
powerfully collaborate. This is the divine strategy, and it works.
Whole human forms *now* stand forth with new life.

With the apostle Paul, we must resolve to exercise fully trinitarian
ministries: not Father, Son, and Holy Scripture but 'the testimony
about God', 'Jesus Christ and him crucified', and 'the Spirit's power'
(1 Cor. 2:1–4). Both Old and New Testaments bear witness to this
kind of ministry as God's own strategy, filled with power for life.

When God attends the preaching of his Word with the powerful
breathings of his Spirit, a decrepit church stands up on its feet like a
mighty army. God's Word can kill: 'Now as I was prophesying,
Pelatiah son of Benaiah died' (Ezek. 11:13). But the Word also
enlivens, when accompanied by the Spirit. Weak preaching does not
expose failure in the Word. The Word is powerful. Weak preaching
only exposes the carnal, superficial understanding of the preacher
and his hearers. The Word is not the problem; with the Spirit, it is
the answer.

God has promised that he will never completely remove from us
his Spirit and his Word:

> 'As for me, this is my covenant with them,' says the LORD.
> 'My Spirit, who is on you, and my words that I have put in
> your mouth will not depart from your mouth, or from the
> mouths of your children, or from the mouths of their descen-
> dants from this time on and forever,' says the LORD.
>
> (Isa. 59:21)

We as the people of God may find ourselves scattered in many and various cultures from now until the End. But we will never encounter a situation so alien to God's provision that we must use other measures for doing his work. By his own wise ordering of things, two resources will always be there for us to draw on – the Spirit and the Word.

The interpretation: I will put my Spirit in you

> Then he said to me: 'Son of man, these bones are the whole house of Israel. They say, "Our bones are dried up and our hope is gone; we are cut off." Therefore prophesy and say to them: "This is what the Sovereign LORD says: O my people, I am going to open your graves and bring you up from them; I will bring you back to the land of Israel. Then you, my people, will know that I am the LORD, when I open your graves and bring you up from them. I will put my Spirit in you and you will live, and I will settle you in your own land. Then you will know that I the Lord have spoken, and I have done it, declares the LORD."'
>
> (Ezek. 37:11–14)

The Lord finally explains to Ezekiel what this whole business has been about. Thus far, Ezekiel has been blindly obeying God. Reading the biblical account today, our eyes can glance down the page to see the whole story at once; but for Ezekiel, the experience is unfolding step by step. And only now does God tell him how the vision connects with reality. Defeated, humiliated, intimidated, exiled Israel is as dead as dry bones, as they themselves acknowledge. God is well aware of their despondency:

> Son of man, say to the house of Israel, 'This is what you are saying, "Our offences and sins weigh us down, and we are wasting away because of them. How then can we live?"'
>
> (Ezek. 33:10)

Why do you say, O Jacob,
  and complain, O Israel,

'My way is hidden from the LORD;
 my cause is disregarded by my God'?

(Isa. 40:27)

But Zion said, 'The LORD has forsaken me,
 the Lord has forgotten me.'

(Isa. 49:14)

Perhaps the Jews themselves came up with this idea of 'dry bones'. Maybe, when God quotes them as saying, 'Our bones are dried up,' such talk was actually heard in their homes over meals or in the streets where they met for business and conversation. We can sympathize. They were far from the promised land, their place of special blessing. They had watched in horror as gleeful pagan conquerors looted the temple in Jerusalem – the holy temple, the one pinprick of heavenly light in the overwhelming darkness of this evil world. They had been forced to march hundreds of miles over the Fertile Crescent to be resettled as exiles in a foreign land.

Picture it with me. As they enter the world-class city of Babylon through the magnificent Ishtar Gate and onto the great Processional Way, they walk on a surface of limestone slabs, each one three-and-a-half feet square, the bevelled edge of every slab inscribed with a motto in honour of the god Marduk.[15] As they trudge into the city with downcast faces, their every step is confronted with 'To the honour of Marduk', 'To the honour of Marduk', 'To the honour of Marduk'. Their God, Yahweh, seems outclassed as they are swallowed up in an outwardly superior culture, which confidently denies their faith. The exiles are drowning in a sea of paganism, and the old verities of Jerusalem's creed feel quaintly out of date, remote, and inadequate.

But God uses their very disillusionment as the occasion to reaffirm their future. In direct response to their complaint 'Our bones are dried up' God frames a thrilling vision of their national resurrection. Let me paraphrase the message of verses 12–14: 'O my people' – and we can feel the tenderness of those words – 'I am going to open up this graveyard called Babylon, raise you up and bring you home, back to your place of blessing. I want you to know that ultimate reality is not the throne room of King Nebuchadnezzar. Ultimate reality is not death. Ultimate reality is not your own cynicism. I am ultimate reality. "I, even I, am he."[16] And at my merest command life and goodness and renewal will spring forth for you with power. You have lost heart, but I am still your God. Therefore, your future is glorious.'

And the final objective realized through it all? That 'you, my people, will know that I am the LORD'. At a cerebral level, the exiles have known this since they were little children in Sabbath school. But their sins tarnished and diminished in their hearts the felt glory of that truth. This will change. Through God's reviving mercies, that doctrinal commonplace will become a fresh discovery filled with depth, joy, nuance, and colour through vivid personal experience. How? 'I will put my Spirit in you and you will live.'

In one sense, of course, the exiles are already living. Their hearts are beating. But when God says, 'You will live,' he means, 'You have endured a depressing existence, far from me, in your Babylonian "graves". But I am bringing to you a new life, a spiritual life, a heavenly life, a life of nuclear-powered joy. I am going to breathe my Holy Spirit into you, just as I breathed the breath of life into Adam so long ago. And you will truly *live*.'

Along with 'prophesy', another key term in the passage is the Hebrew word *rûᵃḥ*. It appears ten times in the text, translated variously as 'Spirit' (vv. 1 and 14), 'breath' (vv. 5, 6, 8, 9, 10), and 'winds' (v. 9). And these uses of *rûᵃḥ* are framed within two references to the Holy Spirit of God, the first in verse 1 and the second here in 14, like bookends at either end of the passage. So what is the point? The point is that, contrary to conventional wisdom and human instinct – Babylonian, Jewish, and our own – true life is found only in *intangibles*, rendered vivid by the Spirit of God.

It seems so obvious I am embarrassed to say it, but it needs to be said again and again: the church is to be set apart by *spirituality*. Revival triggers a firm rejection of the foolish devices of carnality firing up the engine of the church, and a joyous rediscovery of the awesome power of simple, biblical spirituality.[17] The revival of a dead church occurs through spiritual awakening granted by God, not through our programmes and devices. A church invigorated with other animating forces may be *active*, but it is not *alive*.

The One whom we name as our Lord is 'a life-giving spirit'

(1 Cor. 15:45). He comes to us through his Holy Spirit. And the Spirit works with his Word, as Ezekiel's prophesying demonstrates. Jesus said, 'It is the spirit that gives life, the flesh is of no avail; the words that I have spoken to you are spirit and life' (John 6:63 RSV). Spirit, Word, life: this is God's method for the revival of his church, for every aspect of his church. Affirming this does not answer all our practical questions, but it does require that we look most confidently to those strategies deployed by God himself. We cannot improve on his genius. We dare not replace it.

The church's resurrection to vitality is a miracle of the Holy Spirit, the Lord and Giver of life. What breath is to the human body, the Spirit is to the church (vv. 9–10, 14). Without the breathings of the Spirit, the church, however orthodox, is like those dead bodies lying on the valley floor in verse 8. Therefore, limiting ourselves to appropriate structures (1 Cor. 14:40), and testing the spirits with proper discernment (1 John 4:1), we must allow for fresh breezes of the Holy Spirit to blow on our churches today. If we believe the theology of Ezekiel 37, how can we accept churches of well-assembled and even numerous, but lifeless, troops? The life-giving ministry of his Spirit is God's good will for us. Let us seek his gracious visitations. Let us have the courage to welcome them gratefully when they appear.[18] Spurgeon prayed:

> We must preach, but it is thine to apply. Lord, apply it. Come forth, great Spirit. Come from the four winds, O breath, and breathe upon these slain, that they may live. In the name of Jesus of Nazareth, O Spirit of God, come forth! By the voice that once bade the winds cease from roaring, and the waves be still, come, thou Spirit of the living God![19]

6

God restores us

As a college student I read Viktor Frankl's fascinating book, *Man's Search for Meaning*. Frankl, an Austrian psychiatrist, had been imprisoned in a Nazi concentration camp during World War II. In his book he explains what made the difference between the survivors and the statistics in that hellish place. It was not a matter of physical health and strength. What made the difference between the living and the dead was hope, something to live for beyond the barbed wire, something to look forward to, something to go home to:

> The prisoner who had lost faith in the future – his future – was doomed. With his loss of belief in the future, he also lost his spiritual hold; he let himself decline and became subject to mental and physical decay. Usually this happened quite suddenly, in the form of a crisis, the symptoms of which were familiar to the experienced camp inmate ... Usually it began with the prisoner refusing one morning to get dressed and wash or to go out on the parade grounds. No entreaties, no blows, no threats had any effect. He just lay there, hardly moving. If this crisis was brought about by an illness, he refused to be taken to the sick-bay or to do anything to help

himself. He simply gave up. There he remained, lying in his own excreta, and nothing bothered him any more.[1]

I wonder how many people in our world today have lost faith in their future. They have given up. And nothing bothers them any more.

Unless we have something to look forward to beyond the barbed wire, we will not survive. Hope for a better future is what makes the difference. We look out on the shopping malls, hamburger stalls and used-car forecourts of this world. If that is all there is to reality, we shall give up. We shall never find in our everyday existence enough incentives to keep our heads held high for long, especially when life gets tough, as inevitably it does. Many people today see reality as wholly confined to the here and now, and they live accordingly. There is no fear of God before their eyes, nor is there any hope in God within their hearts. And that is why our world is in such a mess. Without hope lifting the human heart to higher expectations and loftier aspirations, people inevitably fall back into the lifestyle that Malcolm Muggeridge called 'licking the earth' – ego, carnality, materialism.

If you are a Christian, you already know that the world has no ultimate answers. But God does have something to say to us, lifting our eyes beyond the barbed wire of our own captivity to worldliness. One of God's great ministries to his people is encouragement – rich, undeserved, liberating encouragement. He is 'the Father of compassion and the God of all comfort' (2 Cor. 1:3). He draws near to us with promises of restoration. And he arms us with strong incentives to keep on struggling until his restoration appears.

Psalm 126 proclaims this message. It reveals God's desire to encourage us with hope and fortify us for sustained effort. It is a psalm to enlarge our vision and stiffen our resolve. It is short, and we need to read it first:

When[2] the LORD restores the fortunes of Zion[3]
> (we are like those[4] who dream),
then[5] our mouths will be filled with laughter,
> our tongues with songs of joy.
Then it will be said among the nations,
> 'The LORD has done great things for them.'

The LORD has done great things for us,
  and we are glad.[6]

(vv. 1–3)

Restore our fortunes, O LORD,
  like streams in the Negev.
Those who sow in tears
  reap[7] with songs of joy.
He who goes out weeping,
  carrying seed to sow,
will return with songs of joy,
  carrying sheaves with him.

(vv. 4–6)

Psalm 126 invites us to believe again. It claims that God is able to restore his captive people. He is able to do great things for us. He is able to replace our tears with laughter. He promises that our hard sowing will be compensated with abundant reaping.

Psalm 126 is woven together into a beautifully coherent whole. The key words are 'restore' (vv. 1, 4), 'laughter', 'joy', and 'glad' (vv. 2, 3, 5, 6), 'tears' and 'weeping' (vv. 5, 6), and 'sow' and 'reap' (vv. 5, 6). Verses 2 and 3 also affirm that 'the LORD has done great things'. And the net purpose of the whole psalm is to encourage God's weary reformers, drawing them into the joys of the coming harvest and sustaining their efforts right now with vivid hope. Psalm 126 affirms the value of our dogged effort, and it lifts our eyes to glimpse the joys of rich divine reward.

If we dwell thoughtfully in the atmosphere of Psalm 126 for long, we cannot remain disheartened. We will find in it a tonic for our tired arms, legs, and souls, for that is why God put this psalm in his Bible. Verses 1–3 could be called 'What it will be like then' (the church released into new joys), and verses 4–6 'What it is like now' (the church pressing on toward that happy day).

Our mouths will be filled with laughter

When the LORD restores the fortunes of Zion
  (we are like those who dream),

then our mouths will be filled with laughter,
 our tongues with songs of joy.
Then it will be said among the nations,
 'The LORD has done great things for them.'
The LORD has done great things for us,
 and we are glad.

(Ps. 126:1–3)

Our sinning not only hurts us; it also inflicts collateral damage on the work of God. We can discredit his cause. When David committed adultery and murder, the prophet Nathan confronted him with the wider consequences of his sin: 'By this deed you have given occasion to the enemies of the LORD to blaspheme' (2 Sam. 12:14 NASB). David handed to the world on a silver platter excuses for dismissing the God of the sixth and seventh commandments as a joke. How the royal courts of the surrounding nations must have relished the juicy gossip: 'Oh, that David over there in Jerusalem! What a "man of God" he is!' The tittering giggles – that particular kind of laughter we reserve for the amusement we find in things we know are wrong – must have been heard far and wide. God's name was dragged down into the slime of David's blasphemous self-indulgence. But God in his mercy restored David, and the work of God went on. Psalm 51 shows us the depth of David's repentance, and Psalm 32 bears witness to the joy of his restoration.

But what David did personally in his day, the whole people of God did corporately in the following centuries. By their worldliness, they became unusable for winning the world. They did not give the nations occasion to praise God but to blaspheme God. Hos. compared the Israel of his generation to a 'faulty bow' (Hos. 7:16), a warped bow that cannot shoot an arrow straight any more. So what is it good for? The people of God had become useless in his hands. So eventually God sent them off into Babylonian captivity to learn some hard lessons.

That is where Psalm 126 comes from. There, behind the barbed wire of Babylonian exile, the covenant people returned to their senses. A remnant reconsecrated their lives to God and laid hold of his promises. And our inspired psalmist lifts up his voice with a word of hope and encouragement for them, and for us, from the

Throne. God is able to restore us. God is able to undo the damage we have done to his cause, so that even the world looks on in wonder. God is able to retrieve us from captivity with fresh displays of his power. For all who are under grace, the best is yet to be.

The key to understanding the first paragraph (vv. 1–3) appears in the second line of verse 1, marked off by parentheses:

> When the LORD restores the fortunes of Zion
>   (we are like those who dream),
> then our mouths will be filled with laughter...

'Those who dream' are prophets or seers, who receive a vision from God of what he intends to do. In the Old Testament, a dream could reveal the purpose of God. For example, young Joseph was granted a prophetic dream of his eventual ascendancy over his family (Gen. 37:5–10). And the improbable came true by a divinely orchestrated chain of events. The prophetic significance of dreaming can also be seen in Deuteronomy 13:1, which refers to 'a prophet or one who foretells by dreams'.[8] And so here in our psalm, 'we are like those who dream' whispers in parentheses that the people are not yet restored. They are anticipating a wonderful visitation from God. They are foretelling it, as if they were prophets. In effect, they are saying, 'When the Lord restores us (we can see it by faith even now), our mouths will be filled with laughter.' The Jews may still be in captivity but they have a hope out beyond the barbed wire. What they foresee by faith thrills them even now.

These verses declare the power of hope. Looking out into their future, the exiles can already taste that moment when God will restore his people to their inheritance. Their spirit of hope transforms how they see themselves in the present. They are not just a bedraggled band of Jewish exiles. They are not victims of history with the pagan foot placed firmly on their necks. Even now, they are 'Zion'.[9] Their sufferings do not define them; God defines them. They do not perceive themselves with a victim mentality. They are more than conquerors. The people of God stand tall in their true dignity.

And what do they see awaiting them? They see God reversing the real-life circumstances they are presently stuck with. They see God returning to them, restoring them. And when he does, the whole flavour of their experience will change. Their prophetic vision cheers their hearts right now, but then their mouths will be filled with laughter and their tongues with songs of joy. Their happiness will know no bounds.

Let us grasp what this reversal actually entails. Picture in your mind the holy city of Jerusalem in 586 BC, surrounded by the attacking Babylonian hordes furiously at work with their battering rams, defending archers on the city walls shooting down at them, and so on. It's judgment day. The moment has finally come for Jerusalem to bear the consequences of her long-standing, open contempt for her covenant God. The people are trapped within the walls of the city. They have no way to replenish their food supplies. They have no army out in the countryside to come and rescue them. The invaders hammer, hammer, hammer their way into the city, blood flows in the streets of Jerusalem, and the dazed survivors are led off into exile while their beloved city behind them burns to the ground.

And where was God in all this? He stood by and let it happen, and for good reason. His people deserved everything they suffered and more. But the question that now demands an answer is this: what does the future hold for people like that, under discipline like that? Can God's people, his 'faulty bow' (Hos. 7:16), be straightened out and made useful again?

To his eternal glory, God does not deal with his covenant people strictly on the basis of what they deserve. He figures into his moral equation the merit of his crucified Son and he gives us good things we do not deserve. And that means one thing for us who bear his name. Discipline may be necessary but it is never final. We may ruin our lives; we may bungle the stewardship of God's cause in our generation. But God is the greatest junk dealer in the universe. He deals in secondhand merchandise. In his wisdom and mercy, he takes the damaged goods of our lives and he restores us. No one else can do this. No one else cares enough to try. All our hope lies in God. And this vision of God our Restorer fills the people of God with hope, even as they remain for now under discipline. God will restore our fortunes. But there is still more.

The dreamed-of divine visitation will have one conspicuous

outcome for God's people. Their reversal of circumstances will be so complete, so stunning, so astonishing that they will explode with an uncommon *joy*. No longer will the church be laughed at. The church will do the laughing, with the laughter of God-honouring joy.

How the people describe it is interesting. They do not say, 'We will laugh; we will be joyful.' No, modest language just will not do. What they say is, 'Our mouths will be filled with laughter, and our tongues with songs of joy.' They heap terms on terms to convey something of the fullness and the intensity of joy they know is on its way to them from God. Calvin puts it this way: '[The prophet] describes no ordinary rejoicing, but such as so fills their minds as to constrain them to break forth into extravagance of gesture and of voice.'[10]

One of the marks of a restoring work of God among his people is this explosion of fresh joy. Our prissified, stiff, stilted worship is swept away as a mighty wave of joy, industrial-strength *joy*, washes over God's newly liberated church. Our mouths are filled with laughter and our tongues with songs of joy.

So does true revival spark laughter? Yes, obviously. Verse 2 says, 'Our mouths will be filled with *laughter*.' James reminds us that authentic Christianity calls us to embrace repentant sorrow (Jas. 4:8–10), but Psalm 126 shows that it also brings us the most potent joy. And the strong language of our psalm requires that we allow for joyful expression when God restores his people. In Psalm 126 it is this very joy that the people are looking forward to: 'When the LORD restores the fortunes of Zion ... *then* our mouths will be filled with laughter.' They treasure their restoration as an occasion for delight. That is the point.

God's mercies toward his people demand a joyful response. One thinks of the first verse of Psalm 100 in the Scottish Psalter:

> All people that on earth do dwell,
> Sing to the Lord with *cheerful* voice,
> Him serve with *mirth*, his praise forth tell,
> Come ye before him and *rejoice*.

A church restored to the enjoyment of its inheritance in Christ sings to God with cheerful voice, serves him with mirth, and comes before him rejoicing. Today we call it enthusiasm.[11] And we can say still more.

Jonathan Edwards reminds us that it is wrong not to exult when the Lord draws near to his people:

> There are many things in the word of God showing that when God remarkably appears in any great work for his church and against his enemies, it is a most dangerous thing, and highly provoking to God, to be slow and backward to acknowledge and honour God in the work.[12]

Edwards goes on to argue that we must not be neutral but should 'most cheerfully yield to the call [of God], and heedfully and diligently obey it'.[13] He cites the triumphal entry of Jesus, when the whole crowd of his disciples 'began joyfully to praise God in loud voices' (Luke 19:37). But the Pharisees insisted that Jesus should reproach his exuberant followers. Jesus replied, 'I tell you, if they keep quiet, the stones will cry out' (v. 40). Edwards then draws out the lesson for us:

> If Christ's professing disciples should be unaffected on such an occasion, and should not appear openly to acknowledge and rejoice in the glory of God therein appearing, it would manifest such fearful hardness of heart that the very stones would condemn them.[14]

Outbursts of revival joy still scandalize, partly because joy can disrupt church decorum. And for some people, religion consists in decorum. Underlying this may be a streak of self-admiration, absolutizing one's own staid personality type, as if one's own self were the criterion by which all experience of God should be assessed. It is one thing to see a church glorifying and enjoying God with overflowing feeling and to say, 'Well, that's not quite my own way, but good for them!' It is another thing to be offended and say, 'Their exuberance is *wrong.*'

But it is also true that wildly chaotic 'worship' does offend God. It is alien to his very nature. All things should be done decently and in order (1 Cor. 14:40), because God loves order. And in the name of revival some people go off the deep end. As Edwards argues, if the devil can no longer keep us quiet, he tries to drive us to excess.[15]

In fact Edwards warns us against a certain kind of laughter. His argument is subtle. Improper behaviour may originate in an authentic experience of God. Genuine experience can be filtered through such a distorted theological understanding that the net result becomes defective. He explains:

> Christians therefore should diligently observe their own hearts as to this matter, and should pray to God that he would give them experiences in which one thing may bear a proportion to another, that God may be honoured and their souls edified thereby; and ministers should have an eye to this, in their private dealings with the souls of their people. It is chiefly from such a defect in experiences that some things have arisen which have been pretty common among true Christians of late, though supposed by many to have risen from a good cause; as particularly, *talking of divine and heavenly things and expressing divine joys with laughter or light behaviour.* I believe in many instances such things have arisen from a good cause … High discoveries and gracious joyful affections have been the occasion of them; but the proper cause has been sin, even that odious defect in their experience, whereby there has been lacking a sense of the awesome and holy majesty of God as present with them and their nothingness and vileness before him, proportionable to the sense they have had of God's grace and the love of Christ.[16]

In other words, you and I may have a true experience of God, in which our own lack of theological proportion allows the behavioural outflow of the experience to be marred. We sinners are so tricky that we can mix our own evil in with a good gift of God. So we must ask the Lord to protect us from ourselves and moderate us with as strong a sense of his 'awesome and holy majesty', humbling us, as we have of his grace and love, thrilling us.

We must guard our hearts. Every one of us is trouble waiting to erupt. If we are heedless of our own bizarre tendencies, we may become eccentric, in the proper sense of that word. 'Ec-centric' is 'off-centre', like a wheel with the hub off-centre, so that it turns roughly. And when unbalanced theology unleashes our own foolish impulses, the wholesome laughter and joy of Psalm 126 can degenerate into tragic buffoonery.

The reason Jonathan Edwards addresses this question is that the Great Awakening was drawing fire from critics. They derided it as fanaticism. And, sadly, excited Christians were doing some strange things, as Edwards acknowledges. Mistakes are inevitably made in revival, for our fallenness has knocked us off-balance in every way. Even in our best moments, we fall short. But joy is not in principle alien to our faith, nor is it intrinsically inappropriate to worship. It is intrinsically appropriate. The wording of Psalm 126 argues forcefully for this conviction. Therefore we must always keep ourselves under the judgment of the Word of God, for we face two opposite dangers. We may grieve the Spirit by reckless frivolity or we may quench the Spirit by claustrophobic reserve. Are there not *two* kinds of excess?

God loves order. He also loves joy. And authentic spiritual joy can *thrive* under the light touch of sensitively maintained order. It is simply a matter of wise, non-oppressive pastoral oversight. Let each church work out its own salvation.

I was on the phone recently to another pastor who is a dear friend. He had just returned from visiting a church where the Lord is powerfully at work in his restoring mercies, and the joy is overflowing. My friend was refreshed and challenged. His heart longed to see the same responsiveness in his own church. He confessed to me that he had been treating 'church' more as a forum for a lecture than as an occasion for joy. And he commented in self-reproach, 'If I had lived back in the days of the Great Awakening, *I would have been on the wrong side.*' Who wants to be on the wrong side? Let us not give the stones all the fun (Luke 19:40)! When our Lord restores the fortunes of Zion, let us sing to him with a cheerful voice and serve him with a proper mirth.

Among the nations

A striking feature of the psalmist's vision of coming revival is the awestruck response of the nations:

Then it will be said among the nations,
    'The L<small>ORD</small> has done great things for them.'

(Ps. 126:2)

When the Lord punished his rebellious people, he did it out in the open. The nations saw everything. The prophet Jeremiah warned his generation ahead of time:

People from many nations will pass by this city and will ask one another, 'Why has the L<small>ORD</small> done such a thing to this great city?' And the answer will be: 'Because they have forsaken the covenant of the L<small>ORD</small> their God and have worshipped and served other gods.'

(Jer. 22:8–9)

Today the question goes something like this: 'Why is this great, historic denomination losing members, funds, and influence?' And the correct answer may be, 'Because they have forsaken the covenant of the L<small>ORD</small> their God and have worshipped and served other gods.' The world has eyes. They can see when a church or denomination or college or seminary has lost touch with its true identity, has become rootless, is no longer inhabited by the living God, has sunk into an utterly inconsequential existence, and is captive to alien ideologies. The world is not stupid.

But the world can also see the church's restoration. Revival is not something that God does off in a corner. It is a public work. It can be widely reported and marvelled at. A true divine visitation is unmistakable. It is visible, concrete, palpable. The world may not like revival but they cannot ignore it. Psalm 126 anticipates such a striking reversal of the church's fortunes that the world is compelled to acknowledge it. It is obvious that no one less than 'the Lord' is at work, doing 'great things' for his people. He owns them publicly. He stands forth among them. He identifies with them.

God has no intention of limiting the visibility of his movements to the church's eyes only. He is not a tribal god, a territorial god, a privatized god, content with a parochial sphere of influence. He claims the adoring recognition of all the nations by making his work visible before their very eyes. Many biblical authors anticipate the universal acknowledgment of God's work; for example:

> This is what the Sovereign LORD says: On the day I cleanse you from all your sins, I will resettle your towns, and the ruins will be rebuilt. The desolate land will be cultivated instead of lying desolate in the sight of all who pass through it. They will say, 'This land that was laid waste has become like the garden of Eden; the cities that were lying in ruins, desolate and destroyed, are now fortified and inhabited.' *Then the nations around you that remain will know* that I the LORD have rebuilt what was destroyed and have replanted what was desolate. I the LORD have spoken, and I will do it.
>
> (Ezek. 36:33–36)

> The LORD has made his salvation known
>   and *revealed his righteousness to the nations.*
> He has remembered his love
>   and his faithfulness to the house of Israel;
> *all the ends of the earth have seen*
>   the salvation of our God.
>
> (Ps. 98:2–3)

> The LORD will lay bare his holy arm
>   *in the sight of all the nations,*
> and *all the ends of the earth will see*
>   the salvation of our God.
>
> (Isa. 52:10)

The restoring work of God is too extraordinary to overlook. He intends it to be publicly acknowledged, for his greater glory.

The return of the Jews from Babylon to the promised land in 537 BC fulfilled the expectation of verse 2, but only in part. The fulfilment of Psalm 126, and of other passages like it, increases in the course of time, as God repeatedly undertakes on his people's behalf. The first advent of our Lord and the explosion of belief in his name around the world during the apostolic era accelerated the forward movement of this prophetic vision toward its ultimate realization (Acts 15:12–18). And the work continues through church renewal and world missions today, eventually to be consummated at our Lord's glorious second advent.[17] Through it all, God is redeeming us from the ruin of the fall; he is bringing his enemies under his feet; he is gaining a universal kingdom and a pure bride for his Son. The Scripture bears witness to his great driving aim, and we have the privilege of participating in its actual unfolding in space and time. So whenever God grants us a remarkable visitation, restoring our fortunes with joy, compelling the attention of the world, he is simply re-actualizing the words of Psalm 126 in our own experience. Again and again, the revival of the church bears witness to the prophetic hope:

> But you, O LORD, sit enthroned forever;
>   your renown endures through all generations.
> You will arise and have compassion on Zion,
>   for it is time to show favour to her;
>   the appointed time has come.
> For her stones are dear to your servants;
>   her very dust moves them to pity.
> The nations will fear the name of the LORD,
>   all the kings of the earth will revere your glory.
> For the LORD will rebuild Zion
>   and appear in his glory.
> He will respond to the prayer of the destitute;
>   he will not despise their plea.
>
> (Ps. 102:12–17)

Is it not encouraging, even astonishing, to realize that our existence together as the church, even with all our failings, is no impediment to God, but just the reverse? Our existence is an historical vehicle, created and shaped by the great God of heaven, to make his work known here on earth. And therefore he is well able at any time to reshape our experience into the beautiful prophetic patterns revealed in his Word.

If the report of God's great work is circulating out there among the nations, then the church herself must confess the same.

We are glad

> The LORD has done great things for us,
>   and we are glad.

> (Ps. 126:3)

What the world remarks on with wonder – or in some cases with grudging admiration, bitter regret, or plain bewilderment – the church rejoices in as her own inheritance. The restoring work of God is to *our* advantage uniquely ('for us'). The nations look in from the outside, but we stand within the circle of grace, where we boast in God (Rom. 5:2, 11).

But if Psalm 126 was written while God's people were still in Babylonian exile, looking forward to their restoration as a future event, why does verse 3 treat it as an accomplished fact? Why does verse 3 say, 'The LORD *has done* great things for us, and we *are* glad'?

Think of it like this. A homeless tramp lives in a cardboard box somewhere in the ghetto. He picks his meals out of rubbish bins. He pushes his shopping trolley through the alleys, collecting soft-drink cans to sell to the recycling company. It is not much of a life. But then one day he receives a telegram, informing him that his long-lost uncle has died, leaving him a million pounds. The cheque is on its way. As the man holds that telegram in his hands, standing there in his ragged clothing, hope leaps up in his heart and a smile spreads across his face. In an outward sense, of course, nothing has changed yet. But in a more profound sense, everything has already changed. He looks around at his old surroundings: 'I can live with this for another couple of days. No big deal. The cheque is on its way. My uncle has done great things for me. And I am glad.'

Verse 3 witnesses to a great reality in the ways of God: the glad-dening power of hope. A great future transforms a dreary present. Everything changes already. In fact the greater the future, the greater the power to bolster present morale. Verses 1 and 2 look forward to God's great restoring work (summarized in 'The Lord has done great things for us'), while verse 3 marks the beginning of great celebration in advance ('and we are glad'). Let us not refuse to be glad in God until his work is fully completed; let us begin now. And let our gladness rise in proportion to the greatness of our restoration. God is committed to restoring his people from captivity to great joy. And as long as God is God, this hope remains solid and real.

The infallible certainty of our hope in God fires the prayer of verse 4, even as it also sustains the efforts of verses 5 and 6.

Restore our fortunes!

> Restore our fortunes, O LORD,
>   like streams in the Negev.
> Those who sow in tears
>   reap with songs of joy.
> He who goes out weeping,
>   carrying seed to sow,
> will return with songs of joy,
>   carrying sheaves with him.
>
> (Ps. 126:4–6)

The people of God cannot contain themselves. In verse 4 they pray for their prophetic dream to become their personal reality. They yearn for God's reviving touch intensely. They confess that they have become dry but they lay hold of God with strong confidence that he can refresh them. And he can, richly and suddenly, 'like streams in the Negev'.

The desolate Negev region, lying south of Judah, is 'an adverse environment to human activity or extensive settlement. It provides only the barest of existence for bedouin...'[18] Dr Willem VanGemeren reports his personal observation of 'streams in the Negev':

> The wadis in the steppe south of Hebron, around Beersheba, were generally dry; but on the rare occasions when during the winter months it rained even as little as one inch, the water ran down its 'streams' with great rapidity and often with destructive force. I have seen roads and bridges destroyed by the force of these torrential streams. The 'streams in the Negev' were not ordinary phenomena, as much as they represent proverbially the sudden unleash of God's blessing.[19]

Your 'Negev' and mine – that place of drought, of parched lives, of dry worship, arid marriages, and barren evangelism – can become a scene of 'the sudden unleash of God's blessing'. God is able to grant an extraordinary *downpour* of blessing.

Savour this thought with me for a moment. What do we contribute to this remarkable work of God? Nothing but our own captivity and dryness. All the initiative, all the power, all the fullness come from God alone. And his outpoured blessing can come *suddenly*, in full measure, like streams in the Negev transforming barrenness into abundance in minutes. This is the divine mystery of humanly uncaused, unforeseen, overwhelming revival.

But the 'streams in the Negev' are not the only metaphor for revival used here. Another image appears in verses 5 and 6, where we see the complementary truth of our own hard work and rugged disciplines and sighs and tears.[20] Revival is a season of refreshing from the presence of the Lord. It is sheer miracle. But it is also true that we are not to sit idly by, doing nothing while we wait for God to bless. We are to get busy sowing the seeds of revival, plentifully and constantly, praying that God will honour the proper use of his own means.

Verse 5 sounds like a proverbial saying: 'Those who sow in tears reap with songs of joy.' What is the point? The pay-off is worth the pain! We sow our 'seed' – whatever we have to give to the work of God – by seeking the Lord in prayer, serving his will with faithful effort, steadily believing God's promises without becoming cynical; declaring his reviving power to his worldly church, consecrating our money to his glory; waiting patiently for the divine visitation. Our efforts are attended with tears of yearning, tears of frustration, tears of sorrow. We work hard without always seeing the eventual outcome. We scatter our efforts out in God's field, unable to predict when he will grant the harvest or whether it will be a hundredfold, sixty, or thirty. But still, we have a strong incentive to go on and go on and go on without quitting. What is that incentive?

Our incentive is precisely what verse 5 declares. Tearful sowers *do* reap with songs of joy. It is simply a law of God, analogous to a law of nature.[21] So let us never give up. 'Weeping must not hinder sowing,' as Matthew Henry rightly urges us.[22] What is more, the weeping *helps* the sowing. Does not the little scenario in verse 5

imply that our tears water the seed as it is being sown? Are our tears
not *essential* to the joyful reaping? In other words, we sow not only
in tears but also *with* tears. Setbacks and disappointments, losses
and crosses, obstacles and delays, thorns in the flesh, opposition and
betrayals – if they do not deflect us from our persistent sowing, they
actually advance our cause, for our tears are the seeds of new life.
Matthew Henry continues:

> As the ground is by the rain prepared for the seed, and the
> sower sometimes chooses to sow in the wet, so we must
> improve times of affliction, as disposing us to repentance, and
> prayer, and humiliation. Nay, there are tears which are them-
> selves the seed that we must sow, tears of sorrow for sin, our
> own and others', tears of sympathy with the afflicted church,
> and tears of tenderness in prayer and under the Word.[23]

In the ways of God, it is those who mourn that shall be comforted (Matt. 5:4). It is those who love God for whom all things
work together for good (Rom. 8:28–30). It is those who stand firm,
without being moved, always giving themselves fully to the work of
the Lord, who work with the only labour that is not ultimately in
vain (1 Cor. 15:58). Let us not hold back the tears. Let us not
shrink from the life that causes them (Acts 20:17–38).

Verse 6 applies the proverbial truth of verse 5 to each one of us
personally (plural 'Those' becomes singular 'He'). Verse 6 also
strengthens the proverb of verse 5 into a promise (timeless 'reap'
becomes predictive 'will return'):

> He who goes out weeping,
>   carrying seed to sow,
> will return with songs of joy,
>   carrying sheaves with him.
>
>   (Ps. 126:6)

Our faithfulness to God, however ordinary and even feeble, *will*
bear fruit, and at two levels. First, the absolute confidence of this
verse is that, in God's grand scheme of things, no faithful effort is
wasted. We do not see the full significance of our little labours, but

we can trust that God preserves their worth by fitting them into *his* omnipotent work sweeping through history. We are a part of something vast and ancient and glorious, extending far beyond the range of our own awareness. Let us not lose heart, even as we weep.

Secondly, the unqualified confidence of verse 6 seems to lengthen our vision through the remaining course of history, up out of time, all the way up into ultimacy; into heaven, which will be the grandest, sweetest revival of all. It is there, in the irreversible victory and unfading glory and unalloyed laughter of heaven, that the real value of our present exertions will be eternally revealed and forever enjoyed.

Therefore we who labour in God's field may banish from our minds any fear of futility. The struggles of a life spent for the glory of God through the restoration of his church and the amazement of the nations cannot, *simply cannot*, be wasted effort. God's Word declares that our labour in the Lord is not in vain. But a life of self-protecting ease, a stress-free life of stinting, miserly investment – *that* life is a waste! Yes, sowing for the Lord is laborious. But we are going to give ourselves to *something*; why not give ourselves to the only effort offering a payoff both certain and infinite? Let us throw ourselves into the work of restoring God's church without regret or reservation! No false heroics; no self-pity; no longing glances back over our shoulder; no moaning about worldly opportunities sacrificed: weeping sowers are the *only* joyful reapers.

Not long ago I visited the Vietnam Memorial in Washington, DC, with my friend Dr Al Mawhinney, Dean of Reformed Theological Seminary in Orlando. It was a solemn experience for us, walking slowly past the thousands of names etched into that black wall. Those men were our contemporaries. In fact Al found the name of a high-school friend there on the wall. Apart from providence, there is no reason why our names should not be up there too. But, as it happened, neither of us fought in Vietnam.

As I reflected on it personally, it struck me with great force that I will never be included in the brotherhood of suffering to which all Vietnam veterans belong. I wandered that day over to a vendor's stand not far from the memorial, where a man was selling military insignia from our various armed forces and even from the battles of the Vietnam War. But I cannot wear any of those insignia. I never will. I did not fight those battles. I will never walk into a dinner party with one of those pins on my lapel, to be greeted by 'Oh, you were in the Tet Offensive too? Did you know so-and-so? Do you remember that night when...?' Instant recognition, immediate belonging, rich brotherhood – it will never be mine, because I did not fight in that war. But I can win my place in another fellowship of suffering: 'those who sow in tears'.

I want that. I want to go to heaven with battle insignia on my chest. I do not want to go to heaven without any war stories to tell. When I go to dinner parties in heaven, I want to run into fellow veterans who wept, fought, and died in the greatest cause on the face of the earth: the glory of the Lord Jesus Christ radiating from his church out into the world with eternally redemptive effect. I want to be one of those who sows now in tears but will reap forever with songs of joy. And I cannot lay hold of the joy then without shedding the tears now. So I throw myself into the effort described in verse 6, and that is how I want to live the rest of my earthly life.

Why would I even try to preserve my life from vulnerability? What do I have to protect? I mean, what is my little life really worth? This year I turn 50. I'm almost dead! I have nothing in myself so valuable that I must cling to it in fear of ultimate loss (Acts 20:24). But here in Psalm 126 God is setting before me the privilege of throwing my all into the labours of his cause. And he promises that the life spent for this purpose will 'return with songs of joy'. The pay-off is there, and it is worth it.

So the devil is lying to us. A life yielded to the cause of Christ does not shrink to a vanishing point. If we give all to Christ and his kingdom, we gain everything *worth* having, whatever else we may lose. But if we coddle and preserve self, we end up with nothing *worth* having, whatever we may retain.

The radical edge of verse 6 is not fully visible in the New International Version. The underlying Hebrew idiom is hinted at more clearly by the New American Standard Bible:

He who *goes to and fro* weeping, carrying his bag of seed,
Shall *indeed* come again with a shout of joy, bringing his
sheaves with him.

The meaning can be grasped with even more precision this way: 'He who (regularly) goes out weeping...'[24] The idea built into the Hebrew is difficult to translate neatly into English, but the idea is something like this: 'The one who *faithfully, persistently, diligently* goes forth into the field weeping, carrying his bag of seed, shall *with infallible necessity* come again with a shout of joy, bringing his sheaves with him.' The *continual* going out with tears is matched by the *certainty* of an abundant harvest coming back in. In other words, 'Whoever sows generously will also reap generously' (2 Cor. 9:6). Therefore, 'Let us not become weary in doing good, for at the proper time we will reap a harvest if we do not give up' (Gal. 6:9). The work of God is seasonal, and we must be 'prepared in season and out of season' (2 Tim. 4:2). 'See how the farmer waits for the land to yield its valuable crop and how patient he is for the autumn and spring rains. You too, be patient and stand firm, because the Lord's coming is near' (Jas. 5:7–8).

In Psalm 126 God is inoculating us against the crippling disease of weak-kneed 'quit-itis', an epidemic among us in these days. We give up too quickly. We tell ourselves that we are working against unprecedented disadvantages, as if the modern world were a uniquely hostile environment for serving the Lord. We tell ourselves that, if only we had lived in the age of the apostles, with all their miracles, the work of God would be easier. I wonder. Romans 16 gives us a keyhole glimpse into their life together:

> I commend to you our sister Phoebe, a *servant of the church* in Cenchrea ... *she has been a great help* to many people, including me. Greet Priscilla and Aquila, *my fellow workers* in Christ Jesus. *They risked their lives* for me ... Greet Mary, who *worked very hard* for you. Greet Andronicus and Junias, my relatives who *have been in prison* with me ... Greet Urbanus, *our fellow-worker* in Christ. Greet Apelles, *tested and approved* in Christ ... Greet Tryphena and Tryphosa, those women who *work hard* in the Lord. Greet my dear friend Persis, another woman who has *worked very hard* in the Lord.
>
> (Rom. 16:1–12)

Think too of the theme of the whole book of Philippians: the 'poured-out life'. Paul is in prison 'for the defence of the gospel' (1:16). But whether by life or by death, his ambition is that Christ should be exalted (v. 20). If he is to go on living, 'this will mean fruitful labour for me' (v. 22). 'For to me, to live is Christ' means, in practical terms, more opportunity to work for him (v. 21). Paul reminds the Philippians that God has given them the privilege not only of believing on Christ but also of suffering for him (v. 29), and thus entering into the fellowship of the suffering (v. 30). Jesus himself is our primary example of selfless outpouring in obedience to God for the blessing of others (2:5–8), for which God highly exalted him (vv. 9–11). Paul himself is being poured out like a drink offering as he serves the faith of the Philippians (v. 17). Timothy, who takes a genuine interest in their welfare (v. 20), is a proven worker (v. 22). Epaphroditus nearly died, he worked so hard to serve Paul (v. 30). Paul has gladly lost everything to gain Christ (3:8). And the Philippians have shared in Paul's troubles through their financial support (4:14), a long-standing pattern of generosity (v. 16).

Were the early Christians powerful because their daily experience was popping with a miracle a minute? Hardly. They rolled up their sleeves and worked. They plodded: right foot, left foot, right foot, left foot. They sweated. They suffered. They locked arms together in shared effort. They cooked meals and swept dusty meeting rooms and ventured into tough neighbourhoods and transported import-ant letters and sat up with sick friends through the night and wrote books and prayed and wept and prayed some more. And they refused to quit. They lived out the beauty of what Charles Simeon said to a friend: 'My dear brother, we must not mind a little suffer-ing.'[25] And what did they get out of it all? They returned with songs of joy, carrying sheaves with them!

God's sovereign miracle of restoration and our dogged efforts in sowing are compatible. Psalm 126 insists that they are compatible. 'Restoring our fortunes' can come to us like streams in the Negev (v. 4). Suddenly, a flash flood of blessing appears out of nowhere. But the harvest of restoration may also emerge as a hard-won crop, after long and faithful sowing with tears (vv. 5–6). God may send us 'streams in the Negev' at any time. We may always be expectant. But if he is pleased to restore Zion through our tearful efforts, it is no less true that 'The Lord has done great things for us.' And we are glad.

We have a hope out beyond the barbed wire of the present moment. We have a sovereign God who is able to restore our fortunes in any way he pleases. Let us strengthen our feeble arms and weak knees (Heb. 12:12). Let us fix our eyes not on what is seen but on what is unseen (2 Cor. 4:18). The One who calls us is faithful and he will do it (1 Thess. 5:24).

> The ransomed of the LORD will return.
> They will enter Zion with singing;
>   everlasting joy will crown their heads.
> Gladness and joy will overtake them,
>   and sorrow and sighing will flee away.
>
> (Isa. 35:10)

Part Two

What we must do

Prologue

When God calls us to sow with tears in Psalm 126, he leads us into the larger question of our role in revival. If revival is God coming down with unexpected power to reinvigorate us, heal us, pour his Spirit out upon us, raise us up, and restore us, then authentic revival goes far beyond all human capacity to produce results. Revival is on a higher plane.[1] And God may, or may not, grant revival in our generation: 'I will have mercy on whom I will have mercy, and I will have compassion on whom I will have compassion' (Exod. 33:19). It is all up to him.

But the freedom of God does not invalidate our participation or release us from responsibility. His surrounding, supporting, nurturing sovereignty is the only thing that renders our efforts fruitful, or even possible. The Westminster Confession of Faith, in the chapter 'Of Good Works', offers us wise counsel:

[Believers'] ability to do good works is not at all of themselves, but wholly from the Spirit of Christ. And that they may be enabled thereunto, besides the graces they have already received, there is required an actual influence of the same Holy Spirit to work in them to will and to do of his good pleasure; *yet they are not hereupon to grow negligent, as if they were not bound to perform any duty unless upon a special motion of the Spirit, but they ought to be diligent in stirring up the grace of God that is in them.*

Our dead hearts are not going to generate the kind of high-intensity spiritual phenomenon that deserves to be called revival. God himself must initiate it 'wholly from the Spirit of Christ'. But that truth does not give us an excuse to wait around, feeling our pulses until we sense 'a special motion of the Spirit' before we act.

We are responsible to engage ourselves energetically by taking full advantage of whatever grace God has already given us. And we should look first and most expectantly to the normal ministries of his church. God ordains the means as well as the end. He is also free to skip over the means and deliver the end on his own. But then that is his part, not ours, is it not?

Revival is nothing but large-scale 'influence of the same Holy Spirit to work in [us] to will and to do of his good pleasure'. It is a mega-miracle of God's sovereign grace. But our part is to declare to God through our words and lives that we are in earnest with him on behalf of his church in our generation. If we are not 'diligent in stirring up the grace of God' that we already have, why should he give us more?[2]

But at this point we pause. We find ourselves standing before the mystery of how God's sovereignty and our responsibility interface with one another. We cannot avoid the mystery, but what are we to make of it? If we handle it clumsily, we risk skewing our understanding of revival, and of many other things! And a skewed understanding can result in frustrated strivings.

Charles Simeon helps us here. He aimed to be thoroughly biblical in his thinking, just as you and I want to be. He affirmed:

I love the simplicity of the Scriptures; and *I wish to receive and inculcate every truth precisely in the way, and to the extent, that it is set forth in the inspired Volume.* Were this the habit of all divines, there would soon be an end of most of the controversies that have agitated and divided the Church of Christ.[3]

This is insightful. Each truth taught in the Bible is taught in a particular way and for a particular purpose. To say 'I believe the Bible' is good, but it's not enough. We must also learn to say, 'I believe all the various truths of the Bible, each according to its own purpose and in its own proportion.' If we handle the diamond-like, multifaceted truth of Scripture in this delicate way, we are protected against lopsided theology – as if, for example, the biblical doctrine of baptism were the be-all, end-all, do-all. Biblical nuance guards us against centring our faith around some pet doctrine. It cultivates in us a sense of proportion and balance. It refines us. It encourages agreement among Christians.

Now, surely, any faithful reading of the Bible will affirm that *both* divine sovereignty *and* human responsibility are *together* operative in the way reality unfolds: 'For the Son of man goes *as it has been determined*; but *woe to that man by whom* he is betrayed!' (Luke 22:22 RSV). The death of Jesus was 'determined' (strong language!), and Judas was also responsible for his role in it ('woe to that man by whom'). The divine and human dynamics are compatible, not contradictory, in the outworkings of reality.

Let me hasten to confess that I cannot explain *how* it all works,[4] but the Scriptures exude confidence that it *is* working. For our practical purpose here, Simeon is a sure guide when he says that 'the truth is not in the middle, and not in one extreme, but in both extremes'.[5] In other words, we should not take the two sides of this question – divine sovereignty and human responsibility – and mush them together in the middle into one indistinguishable blur, robbing each truth of its integrity and power. Neither may we choose one side and reject the other, for both are taught in Scripture. Rather, as we read through the Scriptures from passage to passage, encountering this bipolar truth first on one side and then on the other, we should be 'oscillating (not vacillating) from pole to pole'.[6] And by assembling our theology in this wise way, we hope to be neither neutral nor reductionistic, but *full* and *proportionate* in our thinking. So it is not a matter of either–or but of both–and.

But let us add one further nuance. While both divine sovereignty and human responsibility are operative, are they *equally* significant in the workings of life? Could we think of divine sovereignty and human responsibility as playing *interchangeable* roles? All things considered, God's sovereignty must be the larger truth, the 'wrap-around' truth, the more ultimate explanation for why reality turns one way rather than another at any given moment. Sovereignty *is* supremacy. It *is* ultimacy. We are not on God's level. After all, where did we get the capacity to exercise personal responsibility in the first place? Did God not decide in sovereign freedom to give it to us in our creation? And is he not the one who sustains us in it moment by moment? We must affirm God's supremacy as the *ultimate* insight into life, while we also affirm human responsibility as a *subordinate* truth.

So here is the practical cash value of what I am arguing: we may rest in God's sovereignty as the ground of all our hope, and we must accept our responsibility to roll up our sleeves and get down to work. Each truth has its place and purpose.

A study of biblical revival would lack fullness if it overlooked the subordinate truth (our part) after a reverent affirmation of the ultimate truth (God's part). Rounding things out like this will motivate us to fulfil our responsibility in revival: to prepare the way for the glory of the Lord (Isa. 40:3–5). That is why I have written Part 2 of this book.

7
We return to God

Since 1947 *The Bulletin of the Atomic Scientists* has depicted on its cover the Doomsday Clock. This clock registers how close the world is to nuclear apocalypse, in the opinion of the directors, as its hands are set in relation to midnight. On June 11, 1998, the clock was moved forward five minutes, to nine minutes before midnight, as India and Pakistan were menacing each other with nuclear tests and the larger world failed to contain the spread of nuclear weapons. Only once before, in 1968, had the clock been set forward by so many minutes at once.

But more ominous than any human danger is the unspeakably awesome wrath of God. This is true not only for the truth-suppressing world (Rom. 1:18) but even, in a certain sense, for the people of God as well. We know that at his cross Jesus became a curse for us, removing forever from us the curse of God's law (Gal. 3:13). Because of his amazing love that took him to the cross, the law no longer plays an adversarial role in our lives. We have the righteousness of Jesus covering us, so that we have peace with God and no condemnation (Rom. 5:1; 8:1). But God acts in refining discipline as well as in destroying condemnation. In this sense – refining discipline – judgment begins with the household of God (1 Pet. 4:17).

As the lost world rushes headlong toward a final, destroying judgment at the end of the age, the church endures seasons of remedial judgment in the course of this age. In his great love for us and for his own holy name, the Lord of the church may discipline us with the sting of adversity. Sometimes pain is the only language we'll listen to. Or he may quietly withdraw his presence, until we are so fed up with ourselves and our substitutes for God that we seek him afresh. But however he may choose to deal with any given generation of his church, we know from the letters to the seven churches in chapters 2 and 3 of Revelation that our Lord walks among us, deals directly with us, and sometimes takes unusual steps to refine us.

Our only way through such an occasion of remedial judgment is repentance. Jesus taught repentance as a matter of great urgency (Luke 13:1–9). After all the opportunities God has given and we have wasted, we must *hurry* into repentance. But if we resist repentance, if we ignore the warnings and persist in self-congratulatory complacency, the hands of the divine Doomsday Clock tick forward toward that moment when he comes to remove our lampstand (Rev. 2:5). Jesus said, 'Those whom I love I rebuke and discipline. So be earnest, and repent' (3:19). Our Lord's arsenal is vast. He has more devices for confronting us than we have ways of evading him. His love is even more vast. He would much rather turn the hands of the clock back, if we will only bend our wills around to embrace true repentance. But the clock is ticking in our generation, and we do not have forever to be earnest and repent.

What *is* repentance? How does God want us to *demonstrate* repentance? And what *incentive* do we have to undertake the courageous action required by true repentance? The prophecy of Joel explains all this. In Joel 2:1–11 the Lord threatens his people with armed invasion as a remedial judgment.[1] The attacking army is nearly on them. 'Blow the trumpet in Zion' (v. 1) is like saying 'Turn on the air raid siren!' And why the sudden warning? 'The day of the Lord is coming.' Just over the horizon the wildly destructive enemy is fast approaching, with the Lord himself leading the charge:

> The LORD thunders
>   at the head of his army;

his forces are beyond number,
    and mighty are those who obey his command.

                                 (Joel 2:11)

Now there is a disturbing thought: our own Lord might be the one stirring up our enemies against us. We Christians complain about secular humanism, about postmodern radical subjectivism, about the state schools, overbearing central government, media bias. You name it, we gripe about it. We perceive ourselves as victims and pray for the Lord's protection. In one sense, this is right. We do live in evil days. But how astonishing to realize that maybe, just maybe, our Lord himself is prompting these adversities against us, as he did in Joel's day. Maybe we are not really the victims we think we are. Maybe we are a part of the problem. And maybe we would be wiser to respond to the distress of our historical situation with less defensiveness and more repentance. One reason we see so little repentance in the world is that the world sees so little repentance within the church.

So God turns up the pressure. To quote Matthew Henry, 'God brings us into straits, that he may bring us to repentance and so bring us to himself.'[2] Here in Joel 2:12–17 God gives his people of that generation one last chance to avert disaster. It is late, but not too late. A way of escape still remains open, but only by turning in God's direction via repentance. If his people will return to him, he will cancel the coming invasion and send blessing instead (vv. 18–27), blessing so wonderful it foreshadows the outpouring of the Holy Spirit (vv. 28–32). What easy terms God offers, and what great benefits he promises!

Throughout our passage, Joel 2:12–17, the text breathes with urgency, with intensity. God's wrath is so great, the time so short, our defensive countermoves so utterly futile, God's mercy so rich and free. At this eleventh hour there is just enough time for the people to fall on their faces before their God whom they have offended. But repentance alone can pull them back from the precipice.

Verse 12 declares the word of the Lord. Verses 13–17 apply that message, along with a huge incentive to respond with a full-hearted 'Yes!' to the call of God.

Return to me

'Even now,' declares the LORD,
'return to me with all your heart,
with fasting and weeping and mourning.'

(Joel 2:12)

Serious repentance can avert serious judgment. The door of
mercy is closing. It is still open, but just a crack. The people must
act quickly. 'Even *now*' – not tomorrow when it will be more convenient, when their schedules will be clearer, their finances in order
and personal lives more presentable – 'even now', in the final
seconds before the door closes entirely, the Lord offers one last
opportunity before it is too late for Joel's generation.

But what does God want from us? 'Return to me with all your
heart,' he says. That is the key word in the paragraph: *return*. We
are to return to God (vv. 12 and 13), so that God will return to us
(v. 14).[3] So what does it mean to *return* to God? And how do we
do this with *all our heart*?

The verb 'return' implies that sin is a drifting away from God, a
departure from God, an abandoning of God, an excursion into forbidden regions (Isa. 31:6 NASB). Interestingly, we can turn away
from the Lord (Josh. 22:16; 1 Kgs. 9:6) and we can also turn back
toward him (1 Kgs. 8:33; Ps. 51:13). Within the unchanging
framework of God's grace toward us in Christ, our actual experience of the Lord is not static but dynamic and variable. Our souls
are constantly 'turning' one way or the other. Beneath our outward
social appearances, even beneath our own superficial self-awareness,
we are turning either away from or back toward the Lord at any
given moment. This is true of an individual soul, as it is also true of
the soul of a church, a denomination, a college, or a seminary. And
the tilt or inclination of the soul is more significant in God's eyes
than formal identification as evangelical or any inward self-percep-
tion. The truth of our condition lies deep within, in the drift of our
affections and the bent of our wills. And to *return* to the Lord[4]
means to reorient one's whole being and life to God-centrism:

When all these blessings and curses I have set before you come upon you and you take them to heart wherever the LORD your God disperses you among the nations, and when you and your children *return* to the LORD your God and *obey* him with all your heart and with all your soul according to everything I command you today, then the LORD your God will restore your fortunes and have compassion on you and gather you again from all the nations where he scattered you.

(Deut. 30:1–3)

If you are *returning* to the LORD with all your hearts, then *rid* yourselves of the foreign gods and the Ashtoreths and *commit* yourselves to the LORD and *serve* him only, and he will deliver you out of the hand of the Philistines.

(1 Sam. 7:3)

Seek the LORD while he may be found;
   call on him while he is near.
Let the wicked *forsake* his way
   and the evil man his thoughts.
Let him *return*[5] to the LORD, and he will have mercy on him,
   and to our God, for he will freely pardon.

(Isa. 55:6–7)

Let us *examine* our ways and *test* them,
and let us *return* to the LORD.

(Lam. 3:40)

Returning to the Lord is not a brief shot of emotional adrenaline. It means thoughtfully, courageously setting our lives on a new course, and jettisoning whatever will impede us in our aim. The Heidelberg Catechism of 1563 highlights the life-transforming power of repentance:

Q. What is involved in genuine repentance or conversion?
A. Two things: the dying-away of the old self, and the
   coming-to-life of the new.
Q. What is the dying-away of the old self?
A. It is to be genuinely sorry for sin, to hate it more and more,

and to run away from it.

Q. What is the coming-to-life of the new self?

A. It is wholehearted joy in God through Christ and a delight to do every kind of good as God wants us to.

Running away from sin and back toward God out of joy in him and delight in doing his good will – that is what it means to *return* to God. That is repentance. And it is the first step in our part of authentic revival.

I was disturbed by an article in the *National and International Religion Report* some years ago. A Gallup poll found a record high 74% of adults aged eighteen and older saying they have 'made a commitment to Jesus Christ'. This compares with 66% in 1988 and 60% in 1978. Religion is on the rise, it would seem. But the same article also reported a survey taken by the Roper Organization demonstrating little difference in the actual behaviour of 'born-again Christians' before and after their conversion experience:

> Indeed, the study found that behavior in each of three major categories – use of illegal drugs, driving while intoxicated, and marital infidelity – actually deteriorated after the born-again experience for many people. For example, 4% said they had driven while intoxicated before being born-again, while 12% had done so after their conversion experience. Illegal drugs: 5% before, 9% after; illicit sex: 2% before, 5% after.[6]

How does *this* make sense? Real Christianity is from beginning to end a constant turning toward the Lord. This is why Martin Luther, in the first of his 95 Theses, declared, 'Our Lord and Master Jesus Christ, in saying "Repent," etc., intended that the whole life of believers should be penitence.'[7] And John Calvin called repentance a 'newness' that for the Christian 'ought to extend throughout his life'.[8]

True repentance is not episodic but pervasive. It is not a moment of dewy-eyed sentimentality but a dignifying power lifting us out of the sewers of sin and into joyful nearness to God. It is not superficial, not even behavioural only, but 'searches the inmost emotions'.[9] Repentance is a mentality of brokenness before God's law and desire for God's favour and determination to be faithful to God's Word.[10] The Westminster Shorter Catechism of 1648 asks, 'What is repentance unto life?' And it answers with its usual, tightly packed wisdom:

> Repentance unto life is a saving grace whereby a sinner, out of a true sense of his sin and apprehension of the mercy of God in Christ, doth with grief and hatred of his sin turn from it unto God with full purpose of and endeavour after new obedience.

So repentance does not even ask certain questions. For example, 'Now that I have "fire insurance" against hell, how can I satisfy my appetite for sin to the fullest extent possible without totally discrediting myself as a Christian?' Only hypocrisy asks that question. Repentance asks, 'How can I "lead a life worthy of the Lord, fully pleasing to him" (Col. 1:10 RSV)?' While hypocrisy is restlessly sniffing around at the moral and doctrinal edges, repentance is eagerly pressing into the centre. It is driven by an appetite for God. It hungers and thirsts for righteousness. Repentance says, 'Father, I have sinned ... against you. I am no longer worthy to be called your son; make me like one of your hired men' (Luke 15:18–19). And the true penitent is embraced by the Father.

With all your heart

Joel 2:12 is calling us to deeply genuine repentance. The remarkable phrase *with all your heart* insists upon it, for our natural duplicity is inclined to treat God as if he had the discernment of a child (Jer. 3:10).[11] But God has eyes, he can see if we are withholding a private reserve of self-rule where secret hypocrisies are tucked away. All is laid bare before the One whose eyes are like blazing fire (Heb. 4:13; Rev. 1:14). Thankfully, *with all your heart* does not require sinless perfection. But it does show us that half-hearted repentance counts for nothing with God. In fact it offends God (Jer. 3:6–11). He is in earnest with us, and he calls us to respond to him with 'the entire force of [our] moral purpose'.[12]

Some people have never done anything with all their hearts, and most of us rarely do. We are 'half-hearted creatures, fooling about with drink and sex and ambition when infinite joy is offered us, like an ignorant child who wants to go on making mud pies in a slum because he cannot imagine what is meant by the offer of a holiday at the sea. We are far too easily pleased.'[13] Habituated to the superficiality of modern times, we flit along, just skimming the surface of our souls. But I would venture to propose that, under God, there is nothing in all the universe so vast as the human soul – and nothing, apart from God, so unknown to us. We have depths we ourselves have never seen or felt.

When he calls us to return to him *with all our heart*, God is calling us to extend our conscious grasp into those vast reaches. He is calling us to authenticate our existence with whole-souled earnestness. He is calling us to throw ourselves into the adventure of growing in the knowledge of God, for he alone is great enough to fill the cavernous massiveness of the human soul. And the only way back to him is through repentance with our minds made up, our wills firmly fixed, and our hearts on fire.[14]

With fasting and weeping and mourning

So what should we *do*? How does God want us to *demonstrate* repentance? His instructions given through Joel would never even occur to most Christians today. He says, 'Return to me with all your heart, *with fasting and weeping and mourning*.' Mere emotion alone passes away. But true repentance touches us at such a profound level of our being, it must show. It cannot be contained. Think of the sinful woman who washed Jesus' feet with her tears (Luke 7:36–50). Her heart was too full to do nothing.

To return to the Lord 'with fasting' expels all complacency. We ask new questions of ourselves, such as 'How can I trim my life to obey Christ more fully? How can I "beat my body and make it my slave" (1 Cor. 9:27)? How can I more consistently offer myself as a living sacrifice, holy and pleasing to God (Rom. 12:1)? How can I cleanse myself of silliness and vulgarity and self-indulgence, so that I become "an instrument for noble purposes, made holy, useful to the Master and prepared to do any good work" (2 Tim. 2:21)?' The mentality of fasting asks tough questions and does not spare itself in pursuit of solid answers.

To return to the Lord 'with weeping and mourning' is to grieve over opportunities lost, friends alienated, time wasted, money squandered, sins caressed, offences created, the church troubled, the gospel neglected, the soul starved, the Father's heart wounded. A new spirit wells up in the soul to cry, 'No more triumphalistic self-admiration (Jas. 4:9)! No more blaming of others (Rom. 3:19)! No more giddy worldliness (Titus 2:11–12)!' Instead, a sweet sorrow subdues the nervous chatter of self, the shifty evasiveness of self, the addiction to distraction. We start to care about the right things. We learn to think, to become cautious and even indignant with ourselves (2 Cor. 7:8–11).

Our age, overstuffed with entertainment, nevertheless craves ever more carefree superficiality. This pollutant can seep into the soul of the church. But true repentance fasts, weeps, and mourns. What had once amused us and seemed so natural, even obvious, now shames us. We awaken to the call of God. We resolve to turn around and go hard after him.

This deep repentance speeds our restoration even as it wounds our pride. We may try to save face by preserving an outward countenance of steel, or of jollity. But to be visibly humbled, broken, reduced to tears is a part of our salvation. Worse things could happen to you and me than losing face.

Outward display cannot *substitute* for inward reality, of course. Joel 2:13–17 calls for the practical implementation of verse 12. So what does it *mean* to return to the Lord with all one's heart, with fasting and weeping and mourning? Joel now explains.

Rend your heart

> Rend your heart
>   and not your garments.
> Return to the LORD your God,
>   for 'he is gracious and compassionate,
> slow to anger and abounding in love',[15]
>   and he relents from sending calamity.

(Joel 2:13)

How God loves authenticity! How he despises pretence! One of the marks of Christianity is that it does not settle for outward performance and rote recitation. It goes deeper than manners. It claims the depths of the heart. It is a spiritual dynamic flowing from the inside out, not from the outside in. And this includes Christian repentance.

True repentance throbs in the heart: 'Return to me with all your *heart*'; 'Rend your *heart.*' And in the Bible the word 'heart' covers a good deal of what we are inside. For example, the heart rejoices and mourns (Isa. 65:14). The heart wills (Lam. 3:33, where 'willingly' paraphrases 'from his heart'). The heart thinks (Ezek. 28:2) and understands (Deut. 29:4, where 'mind' translates 'heart'). The heart feels the sting of conscience (1 Sam. 24:5, where 'conscience' translates 'heart'). The heart sums up the whole of one's moral character (Ps. 7:10). So, when we set ourselves on repentance from the heart, it entails more than emotion – not less, but more. It engages *all* that we are, so that we 'cleanse away secret filth in order that an altar may be erected to God in the heart itself'.[16]

Building a clean, new altar within our hearts, where sacrifices pleasing to God through Christ crucified can be offered: that is repentance. Rending our garments is not wrong (2 Kgs. 22:11), but rending our hearts is harder and therefore more significant. It bespeaks deep contrition, tenderness toward God, a new responsiveness. Its opposite is a defiant stubbornness (Zech. 7:12) or a cheap shallowness (Isa. 29:13). But how God loves the spirit of brokenness (Ps. 51:17)! God smiles on the repentance that grabs itself by the scruff of the neck and says, 'No more of that sin for you, self! Get back to God right now!'

We *rend* or tear our hearts when we get tough on ourselves, as tough as the truth must be. We stop excusing our failings. Whining is the voice of hypocritical convenience-religion. If we have disobeyed God's Word, we admit it without equivocating. We reproach ourselves instead of defending ourselves. We assess ourselves with plain honesty. We place ourselves under the judgment of the Word of God, allowing its steady gaze to reveal our faults, scrutinize us, and cleanse us. The ancient Jewish paraphrase called Targum interprets 'Rend your heart' as 'Remove the iniquity of your heart'. Jeremiah uses a different metaphor for the same idea:

'Circumcise yourselves to the Lord, circumcise your hearts, you men of Judah and people of Jerusalem, or my wrath will break out and burn like fire because of the evil you have done – burn with no one to quench it' (Jer. 4:4). And the apostle Paul teaches us to 'mortify' sin in our hearts by the power of the Holy Spirit (Rom. 8:13; Col. 3:5). John Owen put it bluntly: 'Let not that man think he makes any progress in holiness who walks not over the bellies of his lusts.'[17] It is high time for you and me to declare war on our sins.

How unlike the spirit of our age! Today we hear, 'Take it easy on yourself. You can't help these things. Anyway, God loves you. Relax.' God does love us, and passionately too. In fact he loves us too much to dismiss our sins as inconsequential. They clog up his good work in our lives. And Joel's point in his context here is that our sins endanger us by drawing down God's remedial judgments. But repentance can avert them and even prepare the way for the outpouring of the Spirit (Joel 2:28–29).

How can we risk repentance?

If genuine repentance entails a comprehensive reassessment of all of life, a thorough cleansing of our selves and our churches, who can possibly repent? If we were somehow virtuous enough to attain such a high quality of repentance, we would not need to repent in the first place. But we are not virtuous. Our lives are a complex tangle of sins, making repentance expensive, embarrassing, and inconvenient. Where can we find the motivation to sustain us in an undertaking so searching, detailed, and far-reaching? Moreover, repentance risks exposure to a holy God whom we have offended. That is frightening. How can we risk *returning to the Lord our God*?

C. S. Lewis portrays our tension in *The Silver Chair*. Jill bursts into an opening in the forest. She is thirsty. She spies a running stream not far away. But she does not rush forward to throw her face into its refreshing current. She stands still in fear, for a great lion is lying on the ground just this side of the stream. It speaks to her:

> 'Are you not thirsty?' said the Lion.
> 'I'm *dying* of thirst,' said Jill.
> 'Then drink,' said the Lion.

'May I – could I – would you mind going away while I do?' said Jill.

The Lion answered this only by a look and a very low growl. And as Jill gazed at its motionless bulk, she realized that she might as well have asked the whole mountain to move aside for her convenience. The delicious rippling noise of the stream was driving her nearly frantic.

'Will you promise not to – do anything to me, if I do come?' said Jill.

'I make no promise,' said the Lion.

Jill was so thirsty now that, without noticing it, she had come a step nearer.

'*Do* you eat girls?' she said.

'I have swallowed up girls and boys, women and men, kings and emperors, cities and realms,' said the Lion. It didn't say this as if it were boasting, nor as if it were sorry, nor as if it were angry. It just said it.

'I daren't come and drink,' said Jill.

'Then you will die of thirst,' said the Lion.

'Oh, dear!' said Jill, coming another step nearer. 'I suppose I must go and look for another stream then.'

'There is no other stream,' said the Lion.[18]

There we are, yearning to drink from the stream of divine mercy; but the Lion will not move. Can he be trusted if we approach him? Especially in moments of personal moral defeat, what guarantee do we have that returning to God will be to our advantage?

Joel understands our anxiety and offers a satisfying answer. The great encouraging force propelling us forward in the way of repentance is God's own nature. He is merciful to the very depths of his being. The little word 'for' in the middle of verse 13 is our salvation:

Rend your heart
    and not your garments.
Return to the LORD your God,
    for 'he is gracious and compassionate,
slow to anger and abounding in love',
    and he relents from sending calamity.

Repentance is motivated by hope. The assurance of God's *mercy* is what makes repentance conceivable to us. We would be crazy to return to God if he were irreconcilable. But if in fact God is merciful to penitent sinners, then we are crazy *not* to return to him. And the glorious truth is that God is 'rich in mercy' (Eph. 2:4). So remove from your mind all dark, forbidding thoughts of God. Get rid of them all right now. They kill repentance. They harden the heart. A sense of doom, a feeling that God is implacable, that he is impossible to please – that sense of dread sucks us down into despair. And when we give up, we also give in. We slip ever further into the darkness. But a vivid sense of the *mercy* of God is what alone can lift us out of our cynicism and into renewal. 'God's *kindness* leads you toward repentance' (Rom. 2:4).

Ultimate reality

Here in verse 13 Joel is quoting Exodus 34:6. Moses had prayed, 'Show me your glory' (Exod. 33:18). And God did. He drew near to Moses, revealing his glory through carefully chosen words:

> And he passed in front of Moses, proclaiming, 'The LORD, the LORD, the *compassionate and gracious* God, *slow to anger*, *abounding in love* and faithfulness, maintaining love to thousands, and forgiving wickedness, rebellion and sin. Yet he does not leave the guilty unpunished; he punishes the children and their children for the sin of their fathers to the third and fourth generation.'
>
> (Exod. 34:6–7)

The pure essence of God, to the degree that he reveals himself to us in this life – these words distil it for us. Interestingly, we see no mention here of the call of Abraham, no mention of the exodus from Egypt and the crossing of the Red Sea. The Lord disregards for the moment the great historical landmarks of Israel's faith and reveals *himself* in his own essential being and glory. These words are putting us in touch with ultimate reality. What do they say?

He is a God both of mercy and of judgment. He cannot be properly reduced to one or the other quality alone. His very being is marked by tender compassion and terrifying wrath. And the holy Scripture, from Genesis to Revelation, explains to us how to receive his mercy in Christ so that we are protected from his wrath. But God will be merciful and he will also enforce justice. That is who he is, and he will be true to himself.

In Joel 2 the prophet is applying the Exodus 34 vision of God's mercy to all who want to live before him in repentance but who feel overwhelmed by their sinfulness. And Joel's logic, signalled by the pivotal word 'for', is clear: venture forth into vulnerability before God, *trusting him* to deal with you personally as he has declared himself to be objectively. *God is gracious and compassionate, slow to anger, and abounding in love* and he relents from sending calamity. And that is why we can risk returning to the Lord our God.

Do you see how Joel does not even complete his quotation of the entire two verses in Exodus 34? He cites only the first part, affirming God's grace, because God's justice will not crush *returning* sinners. That is not his nature. God's heart is warm toward the penitent: 'The sacrifice *acceptable* to God is a broken spirit; a broken and contrite heart, O God, thou wilt *not despise*' (Ps. 51:17 RSV).

But let us be careful to make an important distinction here. Our brokenness has no meritorious value. Repentance does not *deserve* God's favour. We can never obligate God, as if our repentance were an invoice demanding payment. We can claim nothing from our holy God. Christ did not die to enhance our moralism but to replace it with his own perfect righteousness (Gal. 2:21). Only the obedience of our Saviour *satisfies* the demands of God's holy law. Only his brokenness at the cross actually deserves God's favour. The death of Jesus alone is what brings us back into God's good graces. His merit is freely credited to our accounts in God's database, and we gain access to it personally with the credit card of faith. But, at the same time, it is also true that a tender heart is *acceptable* in Christ.[19] It is far from perfect; but our part is to offer mere acceptability, not meritorious perfection. 'Let the words of my mouth and the meditation of my heart be *acceptable* in thy sight, O LORD, my rock and my redeemer' (Ps. 19:14 RSV). And the remarkable thing is that God does accept, for Christ's sake, the broken and contrite heart. He is not impossible to please. God loves the penitent sinner (Luke 15:20). Richard Sibbes puts it beautifully: 'God takes care of poor weak Christians that are struggling with temptations and corruptions. Christ carries them in his arms. All Christ's sheep are diseased, and therefore he will have a tender care of them.'[20]

So keep your vision of God's mercy brightly clear before your eyes, dwell in the atmosphere of his love for you, and take courageous new steps of repentance. When your heart is fearful, preach a sermon to yourself from Exodus 34:6, just as Joel does to us here. Believing views of the Christ's mercy to sinners do not encourage sin; far from it. They melt the penitent heart; they banish sin; they stoke the fire of consecration. Jonathan Edwards illustrates this from his own personal experience:

> Once, as I rode out into the woods for my health, in 1737, having alighted from my horse in a retired place, as my manner commonly has been, to walk for divine contemplation and prayer, I had a view, that for me was extraordinary, of the glory of the Son of God, as Mediator between God and man, and his wonderful, great, full, pure and sweet grace and love, and meek and gentle condescension. This grace that appeared so calm and sweet, appeared also great above the heavens. The person of Christ appeared ineffably excellent, with an excellency great enough to swallow up all thought and conception – which continued, as near as I can judge, about an hour; which kept me the greater part of the time in a flood of tears, and weeping aloud. I felt an ardency of soul to be, what I know not otherwise how to express, emptied and annihilated; to lie in the dust, and to be full of Christ alone; to love him with a holy and pure love; to trust in him; to live upon him; to serve and follow him; and to be perfectly sanctified and made pure, with a divine and heavenly purity.[21]

Viewing by faith our Lord's 'wonderful, great, full, pure and sweet grace and love, and meek and gentle condescension' cleanses the soul. We are drawn on by his glory. That is what Joel longs for us to understand and experience.

Your God relents

Returning to the Lord makes a difference. When we do, Joel tells us
that it is God's nature to *relent from sending calamity*. God did not
say this to Moses back in Exodus 34, but Joel can see that this is the
obvious point for repentant sinners. So why should we return to the
Lord our God? Our confidence is his mercy, and our incentive is
his relenting. Here is the pay-off for repentance: returning to the
Lord, with our hearts rent for sin and from sin, makes a difference
felt in real life.[22] Repentance is not easy, but it is worth everything
it costs us. I love Robert Burns's line 'They never sought in vain
that sought the Lord aright.'[23]

Some people think it costs too much to obey God. They think
that living life God's way is not worth it. Not so, it costs too much
not to obey God. His judgments are shrewdly effective. We are no
match for him. But through the merit of Christ crucified, returning
to the Lord in repentance opens up to us the smile of God, the nearness of God, the power of God – everything that makes life sweet.

But you may be asking a question here: if God relents from
sending calamity on his penitent people, does our repentance change
God's mind? Do *we* persuade *him* to go from plan A to plan B? The
Revised Standard Version of Joel 2:13 makes the question even more
provocative. It says that God *repents* of calamity. But does God really
repent? Yes. That is what the Bible says. But *in what sense* does God
repent? Remember the wise counsel of St Hilary: 'Our understanding of the [biblical] words is to be taken from the reason why
they were spoken, because the subject [i.e. God] is not subordinated
to the language but the language to the subject.'[24] In other words, we
should not shrink God down to fit inside our little human words.
We should rubberize our words and stretch them out to match the
grandeur of God – or, at least, we should try.

The Bible speaks to us about ultimate reality in terms that we
can understand. God accommodates his Word to our capacities –
not to our ideas, but to our small capacities for understanding great
things.[25] But then, when we interpret biblical language we have to
remember that. And the reason any given biblical author uses ana-
logical language about God is always context-specific. Here in our
passage, Joel is arguing God's readiness to meet repentant people

with his mercy. He wants to encourage us forward into ever more thorough repentance through the prospect of God's own 'repentance'. It is impossible that God will let our repentance go unmet. That is Joel's point. As the Scripture says, 'Draw near to God and he will draw near to you' (Jas. 4:8 RSV).

But I put quotes around the word 'repentance' there ('God's own "repentance"') because, if we push it far enough, 'repent' – that most human of words! – cannot do justice to God.[26] Even at our best, we fallen people make mistakes and then have to back up to take another run at a situation. We struggle to find a better way to proceed. But God is beyond all that.[27] He is orchestrating the unfolding of everything according to his own purpose and he makes no mistakes. His plan requires no mid-course corrections. But not every passage in the Bible troubles itself to speak in these ultimate terms. Scripture is often content to make a valid, if less than final, point. And Joel's message to us is not that God can be deflected from his eternal purpose but rather that true penitents find their sovereign Lord will meet them and reward them. Responsiveness in us discovers a kind of 'responsiveness' in God. Therefore repentance is worth every effort, every difficulty, every adjustment.

He may return

Repentance opens life up again with encouraging new possibilities, as verse 14 explains:

> Who knows? He may return[28] and have pity
> and leave behind a blessing –
> grain offerings and drink offerings
> for the LORD your God.
>
> (Joel 2:14)

Joel protects us from presuming on God when he asks, 'Who knows?' The prophet is not casting doubt on God's unchanging depths of mercy. That was clearly affirmed in verse 13. But he does aim to guard us against deciding for God *how* he will show us his mercy in any given situation. Our repentance is not the bell we ring to call the divine butler; it is his holy gift subduing us to his will.

We must always be confident in God's mercies. But he reserves the right to deal personally with each life, with each church, on a case-by-case basis. And the penitent heart will bow in humility before God's rightful freedom.

Still, Joel has an inkling of what God may have in store: 'He may return and have pity and leave behind a blessing.' The very fact that Joel proposes this hopeful possibility implies something. Does it not imply that returning and having pity and leaving behind a blessing is exactly what God intends to do? Would a prophet mislead us with false expectations? So what does Joel's scenario envision?

If God returns and has pity and leaves behind a blessing, that is the same as saying that he reverses the devastation of 2:3, where Joel describes the approaching invaders: 'Before them fire devours, behind them a flame blazes. Before them the land is like the garden of Eden, behind them, a desert waste – nothing escapes them.'

A scorched earth policy is what God's people must endure if the enemy army passes through. But if they rend their hearts and return to the Lord, he will send the army away and pass through their midst himself. He will intervene ('return') in their lives with solicitous concern ('have pity'), and leave behind his own mark on their experience: not disaster, but blessing.

The hope Joel offers us is meaningful and attractive, if our hearts are broken before God. His words take it for granted that we do not want simply to get out of our present mess, only to return later to our old patterns of God-neglect. His words assume that we want to live new lives. We want to rediscover what it means to honour God at the centre of everything. Is it not striking that the 'blessing' God leaves behind is material for *worship*: 'grain offerings and drink offerings for the LORD your God'? The heartfelt goal of true repentance is that we would get back to putting God first, because only then are we fulfilled.

If the 'blessing', which God 'leaves behind' for us, returns back to him in worship, this gives us an important insight. Think this through with me. God relents and gives us our lives back again. Then the question becomes, what do we do with our new opportunities? The answer is: God's desire for us is not 'foxhole conversions' that do not last but new lives entering joyfully into 'the beautiful cycle of provision and praise'.[29] What God provides for us we return to him in the form of praise. We provide nothing, really; it is all of grace. David understood this when he prayed: 'Everything comes from you, and we have given you only what comes from your hand' (1 Chron. 29:14). Here then is a remarkable insight: the more we end up doing *for* the Lord, the more reasons we have for giving thanks *to* the Lord, because it *all* comes from his 'blessing'. And the penitent understand that living in this way is a privilege to be sought after.

I wonder what the Lord will leave behind for us in our generation. He will be gracious, certainly. But let us be sure that he can see in our hearts a repentant desire to return his blessing in lives and words of praise. Who knows? He may increase our measure of blessing. But one thing is sure: he has no intention of pouring out his blessing in support of our carnal, misplaced affections (Hos. 2:2–13). But if our hearts thrill at the prospect of divine bestowals accelerating our own worship, who knows? Our Lord may return and have pity and leave behind *massive* blessing. Verses 18–27 of Joel 2 go on to show how God was willing to bless the people of Joel's day. And verses 28–32 ('I will pour out my Spirit on all flesh' – see chapter 4 above) describe what he can do for us today. Our part is to keep turning to him.

Now, how might we implement this call to repentance? What could this actually look like in our churches today? Joel concludes by explaining how to follow through on all that he has said.

Call a sacred assembly

> Blow the trumpet in Zion,
>   declare a holy fast,
>   call a sacred assembly.
> Gather the people,
>   consecrate the assembly;
> bring together the elderly,[30]
>   gather the children,
>   those nursing at the breast.
> Let the bridegroom leave his room
>   and the bride her chamber.
>
> (Joel 2:15–16)

With rapid-fire imperatives, Joel urges us to gather for prayer. He is crying out, 'Stop everything! Waste no time! Do this!'[31] Setting our ordinary concerns aside, we assemble for special prayer where our personal repentance amplifies into corporate urgency. No one is excluded. We do not divide into age-groups. (Have we ever shown our children how to repent before God?) No one is exempted. Even the couple on their honeymoon are to put private pleasures aside to seek the Lord at this special prayer meeting – almost inconceivable in our day, when self always comes first! God calls us to gather as his people, not to amass our strength with triumphalistic self-assertion, but to humble ourselves together before our Lord.

Appointing a time for unusual prayer and repentance, creating a special event with a special purpose, is what the Scripture is calling us to do. John Calvin speaks as a pastor to pastors when he says:

> In like manner, the pastors of the church would not be doing ill today if, when they see ruin hanging over the necks of their people, they were to cry out to them to hasten to fasting and weeping; provided – and this is the principal point – they always urge with greater and more intent care and effort that 'they should rend their hearts and not their garments'.[32]

An uninterrupted blur of busy activities is not a convincing response to God. He has no intention of oiling our religious treadmill. He demands that he himself be our great, burning desire, for he loves us with a flamingly intense love. The usual course of events within a church or denomination can slide into complacency toward God, as he becomes the unnoticed backdrop for everything else we do regard as worthy of our intentional focus. We don't mean that to happen, of course, but it does. We must at times go out of our usual way, to show the Lord that we are in earnest with him. We need a sensitivity to our times and seasons, rather than ploughing unthinkingly ahead without variation or nuance or special observance.

So where are the pastors, elders, deacons, and laypeople who will provide this courageous leadership? Where are the prophetic eyes that can see when other events on the church calendar should be cancelled so that the face of God himself may be specially sought? It was Ulrich Zwingli, the Swiss reformer, who put it plainly: 'Do something bold for God's sake!'[33]

Spare your people, O Lord!

Between the temple porch and the altar
    let the priests, who minister before the LORD, weep.[34]
Let them say, 'Spare your people, O LORD.
    Do not make your inheritance an object of scorn,
    a byword among the nations.
Why should they say among the peoples,
    "Where is their God?"''

                                 (Joel 2:17)

The priests link God in heaven above with his people on earth below, so it is right that they lead the way in corporate repentance. Surprisingly, the Hebrew text emphasizes the place where they are to take their stand in ministry: 'between the temple porch and the altar'.[35] We would expect them to be there; it is not unusual. So why does Joel draw attention to their location? He knows that the moment is too critical to be bungled. God must be approached with the proper protocols. Sinners may not stroll into God's presence on their own authority or merit. If they do, they jeopardize everything by offending God at the moment of encounter.

    Today this translates into our need for Christ, the ultimate Mediator.[36] Better than a sinful priest who himself needs forgiveness, we have in our Lord a high priest giving us a perfect entrée into God's holy presence above. In the sacred assembly, therefore, we must deliberately, consciously place ourselves behind Christ as we face God. We must not parade before God our own repentance, as if he should be impressed. Even at our best, we are vile before an infinitely holy God. One man had the insight to put it this way:

I cannot pray, but I sin. I cannot hear or preach a sermon, but I sin. I cannot give an alms or receive the sacrament, but I sin. Nay, I cannot so much as confess my sins, but my confessions are still aggravations of them. My repentance needs to be

repented of, my tears need washing, and the very washing of
my tears needs still be to be washed over again with the blood
of my Redeemer.[37]

This is why we approach God *only* through our sinless high priest,
the Lord Jesus Christ, who intercedes for us at the Father's right
hand. We put all our confidence in him alone.

We should tell God that we are coming to him through the
Mediator. We should make it explicit to ourselves and to God. Let
us never take Jesus for granted but openly declare our radical
dependence on his all-sufficiency for us.

And at a human level, Joel is calling the leaders of God's people
to step forward and minister in repentance: 'Let the priests weep.
Let them say...' We ministers are to set a tone of deeply moving
repentance in our churches. If we are cool about this, if we say in
our hearts, 'The people need this, but I don't,' how can we expect
them to be touched? Sometimes it's the leaders who are the most
unyielding and the last to break. We fear losing face. But that pride
is itself one of the provoking sins pulling down God's displeasure. It
is 'God's most stubborn enemy'.[38] It is the first sin we need to
repent of.

But when we ministers are released from the prison of professional pride, *how* are we to pour out hearts at the sacred assembly?
God gives us the words he wants to hear: 'Spare your people, O
LORD.' The verb 'spare' means to look on someone with concern,
with tender regard (Deut. 7:16; Isa. 13:18). Then that meaning
extends to refusing to inflict harm (1 Sam. 24:10). So the word
unites feelings with actions. 'Spare your people' is a way of saying,
'Look on us with *pity*, and let your love for us *show* in deliverance.'
And because we are reading this word in the Bible, we can add a
theological dimension: 'Do not view us as we are in ourselves. View
us as we are in Christ. Let your heart be prompted by all that *he* is
to us. Own us as your inheritance and *act*, O Lord!'

Where is their God?

But what will become of us, if God leaves us to the foolishness of
our own brainy ideas? According to verse 17, his church will

degenerate into 'an object of scorn, a byword among the nations'. God is very shrewd. He has many ways of disciplining us. One of his devices is simply to let the church sink into laughable irrelevance, so that we become a joke in the eyes of the world.[39] People look on and shake their heads: 'What a bunch of losers they are!'

But that does not have to happen. God does not want it to. We are *his* people. We are *his* inheritance, as verse 17 claims. He has chosen us; claimed us; adopted us; put his own holy name on us. We are his personal property, his problem, his project, his responsibility. He has a vested interest in our success. Joel urges us to cry out to him: 'Protect your investment! Grant unmistakable attestation of your presence with us in the eyes of the nations! Hallow your name before the world through us, *even through us!*'

Joel's prophetic heart cannot endure the prospect of the ungodly nations throwing their heads back in uproarious laughter and sneering ridicule ('Where is their God?'). But the fortunes of the church do reflect on God. The inner logic of verse 17 demands the connection ('your people … your inheritance … their God'). *We are the currency with which God buys credibility in the eyes of the world.*[40] The church is the earthly platform on which God displays his saving glory. If we fall into contemptuous ineffectiveness, it casts doubt on the power of our Lord, as if he could do nothing but look helplessly on. So Joel leads us to pray, in effect, 'For your own name's sake, do not devalue us! Do not let the world blaspheme you by disparaging us!'

Is it not significant that God has tethered his own honour in the world firmly to our welfare? We are truly his people. This gives us a strong argument to deploy in prayer. Why indeed should the nations say, 'Where is their God? Where is this "power" they talk about in their gospel? Where is the cogency of their principles? Where is their ability to sustain lifelong marriages? Where is their moral courage in the face of adversity? Where is their willingness to suffer cheerfully for their beliefs? Where is the racial reconciliation they talk about? Where is their unbending moral integrity under temptation? *Where is their God?*'

We live in a blaspheming, God-trivializing world. The natural human heart delights in every pretext for disregarding the majesty of God. So if his church sinks into absurdity, that is all the excuse some need for rubbishing everything holy, which then reinforces their godless lifestyles. A church in decline encourages public sin and dishonours God, but a vibrant church is a living reproach to sin and demands the world's recognition that Jesus is a glorious Lord. And that should be our ultimate aim, for it is God's ultimate aim:

> Turn to me and be saved,
>> all you ends of the earth;
>> for I am God, and there is no other.
> By myself I have sworn,
>> my mouth has uttered in all integrity
>> a word that will not be revoked:
> Before me every knee will bow;
>> by me every tongue will swear.
> They will say of me, 'In the LORD alone
>> are righteousness and strength.'
> All who have raged against him
>> will come to him and be put to shame.
> But in the LORD all the descendants of Israel
>> will be found righteous and will exult.
>
> (Isa. 45:22–25)

Advertising the Lord's saving all-sufficiency is what human history is all about. Is there not enough glory in him to move us to repent of our half-hearted repentance? Our generation of the church either will be confronted with our Lord's remedial judgment or will return to him with all its heart. But there is no escaping the choice. And the only way forward, toward everything we long for, is to bow at the feet of Jesus in genuine, whole-hearted repentance. Will we trust him enough? We cannot trust him perfectly; but will we trust his mercies *enough* to receive a fresh work of repentance and transformation here in our time?

8

We seek God

When Aleksandr Solzhenitsyn received the Templeton Award in 1983, he began his address with these words:

> Over half a century ago, while I was still a child, I recall hearing a number of older people offer the following explanation for the great disasters that had befallen Russia: 'Men have forgotten God; that's why all this has happened.' Since then I have spent well-nigh fifty years working on the history of our revolution; in the process I have read hundreds of books, collected hundreds of personal testimonies, and have already contributed eight volumes of my own toward the effort of clearing away the rubble left by that upheaval. But if I were asked today to formulate as concisely as possible the main cause of the ruinous revolution that swallowed up some sixty million of our people, I could not put it more accurately than to repeat: 'Men have forgotten God; that's why all this has happened.'[1]

When we forget God, bad things happen. Even Christians can forget God. We forget him whenever we lose sight of the fact that he himself, mediated to us by his Spirit and declared from his

Word – he is the power and attraction and genius of the church. When we forget him and run off to other secrets to success, bad things happen. But when we seek him, good things happen: good things like revival.

Whether we are forgetting God or seeking God is the pivot on which all else turns in the life of the church. Francis Schaeffer makes the point salient:

> The *central* problem of our age is not liberalism or modernism, nor the old Roman Catholicism or the new Roman Catholicism, nor the threat of communism, nor even the threat of rationalism and the monolithic consensus which surrounds us [nor, I would add, postmodernism, consumerism, and other more contemporary '-isms']. The real problem is this: the church of the Lord Jesus Christ, individually or corporately, tending to do the Lord's work in the power of the flesh rather than of the Spirit. The central problem is always in the midst of the people of God, not in the circumstances surrounding them.[2]

The most important word in that statement is the simple word 'tending' – just *tending* to serve God in the flesh. What great consequences fall from our mere tendencies! We are not heretics or apostates. We mean well. We are merely *prone* to wander, *prone* to leave the God we love. And that tendency, the mere tilt of the soul away from God and toward self-reliance and self-exaltation and self-seeking, even as we do the Lord's work – if it goes unchallenged – is in God's sight a forgetting of him, a forsaking of him, with heavy consequences.

It is time to seek the Lord

If the prophet Hosea were to rise up among us today, he would say again what he said to his own generation, 'it is time to seek the LORD' (Hos. 10:12). We have tried everything else. We have tried to reinvent church to attract the entertainment-addicted public and we are left with not much of a message to that public. We have tried signs and wonders, self-esteem and emotional healing, health

and wealth. We are highly motivated, well-equipped, results-orien-
ted, smart people, and we have tried everything. After all this, still
the church languishes in mediocrity and still the world potters on
its way into hell. Is it not time now to seek the Lord?

Seeking the Lord is the opposite of forgetting him. It is a key
that opens up a new future for God's people. Second Chronicles
15:1–4 declares that, if we will seek the Lord, it will make a real-life
difference very much to our advantage.

The Chronicler lived in the post-exilic period, 'a day of small
things' (Zech. 4:10), an easily discouraging time. Returning from
Babylonian exile, his generation was struggling to reassemble a
viable witness to God back home in the promised land. They had
to start all over again. They were tempted to see themselves as
deprived, stripped of all the advantages that their forefathers had
enjoyed, victims of history. How they must have looked back on
the glory days of David and Solomon with wistful longing, with a
sense of having been born out of time, of having missed it, as we
might look back on the Great Awakening. 'If only we had lived
back then, what we might have achieved! But here we are, stuck in
this utterly fifth-rate age.' Nothing is so demoralizing as to see ourselves as having been passed by. They felt like that, and so too can
we.

Enter the Chronicler. 'Not so,' he insists. He would say, 'We
today have, in principle, all the same advantages that made them
great in the past. True, we do not have the money, the manpower,
or the political clout they had. But we have *God*, just as much as
they did. And if we will only seek him as they did, we too will find
God to be our all-sufficiency today, just as they did back then. And
we will achieve greatness in our own time as they did in theirs. Do
not tell yourself that life has passed you by. That is false and self-
defeating and dishonouring to God. The opportunity of life lies
gloriously before you. Exploit the moment by seeking God, and
watch him do a new work in our generation today.'

The Chronicler sees through the God-concealing appearances
of life. He sees with deep insight into the God-inhabited truth
of life. He understands that the basic issue we face is the same in
all ages, once we scratch beneath the surface of things. He lays
bare what that turning point is and how we can do the Lord's work

triumphantly in our own place and time, irrespective of outward variables. It seems so obvious, but it all depends, at bottom, on our relationship with God. Yes, there is a valid place for the wise use of the best means.[3] God himself has fashioned human nature in such a way that we respond differently to different ways of presenting the gospel. So we ministers would be foolish to sneer at the use of means as unworthy of our thoughtful consideration and strategic deployment. But our generation *tends* to make much of means and methods, and little of Almighty God himself.

The Chronicler would not have fitted in today. Banking on the reality of God was the whole burden of his inspired message.[4] Here follows just a sample of his out-of-date, simplistic, impractical theology:

> Saul died because he was unfaithful to the LORD; he did not keep the word of the LORD and even consulted a medium for guidance, and did not inquire of the LORD. So the LORD put him to death and turned the kingdom over to David son of Jesse.
>
> (1 Chron. 10:13–14)

> And you, my son Solomon, acknowledge the God of your father, and serve him with wholehearted devotion and with a willing mind, for the LORD searches every heart and understands every motive behind the thoughts. If you seek him, he will be found by you; but if you forsake him, he will reject you forever.
>
> (1 Chron. 28:9)

> If my people, who are called by my name, will humble themselves and pray and seek my face and turn from their wicked ways, then will I hear from heaven and will forgive their sin and will heal their land.
>
> (2 Chron. 7:14)

> For the eyes of the LORD range throughout the earth to strengthen those whose hearts are fully committed to him.
>
> (2 Chron. 16:9)

The Chronicler believed literally that seeking God would make a difference, *the* difference.

So, as the post-exilic generation of God's people surveys the ruins of the once great theocracy and settles into the work of rebuilding, overwhelmed by the task lying before them, wondering, 'What can *we* do?' the Chronicler retells the story of their national greatness. He inspires his contemporaries through the voices and achievements of their heroes of the past. He warns them through the failures of the past. He reminds them that the secret to greatness has always been this one thing: the blessing of God. They may expect his blessing again if they will seek him again. And through the Chronicler, God is saying to us today, 'Let me *show* you the difference I can make.'[5]

The prospects for our generation hinge on our confidence in God's offer. We cannot and would not do some things that previous generations have done. As conditions change, new strategies must be employed. But *if we want the touch of God on us*, the Chronicler calls us to follow again the course that made the church great at her greatest moments in the past: seek God through worship and prayer, obey his Word courageously, advance boldly against the opposition, to see his cause triumph. And our confidence lies in God's promise that he will *show* himself to be our all-sufficiency. If we will put God first by seeking him in these tried-and-true ways, he will smile on us again.

I have chosen 2 Chronicles 15:1–4 as our study because verse 2 declares so clearly the essence of the Chronicler's message. His theology, in turn, flows out of the Deuteronomic covenant, which stands at the foundation of the entire Old Testament. And since the Old Testament is consummated in the New Testament, this one remarkable verse, 2 Chronicles 15:2, takes us close to the heart of God's Word to his servants in every generation.[6]

Here is the immediate context. Asa, king of Judah, was attacked by Zerah the Cushite and his vast army. Outnumbered, Asa fell to his knees in prayer: 'Help us, O LORD our God, for we rely on you' (14:11). And God did help them. 'The LORD struck down the Cushites before Asa and Judah' (v. 12). '[The Cushites] were crushed before the LORD and his forces' (v. 13). The improbable victory was not a human achievement. God himself intervened, honouring Asa's prayer of faith. But, while Asa and his army did not save the day by their own skill and cleverness, they did walk away with 'a large amount of plunder' (v. 13). Flushed with victory, enriched with prizes of war, Asa and his army returned to Jerusalem rejoicing. As they were approaching the city, someone stepped forward to greet them with a message from God:

> The Spirit of God came upon Azariah son of Oded. He went out to meet Asa and said to him, 'Listen to me, Asa and all Judah and Benjamin. The LORD is with you when you are with him. If you seek him, he will be found by you, but if you forsake him, he will forsake you.'
>
> (2 Chron. 15:1–2)

Our experiences have meaning. Every day we are proving the truth of principles we may not even comprehend. Following the events of chapter 14, Azariah the prophet makes explicit the deeper meaning of the victory Asa and Judah have just won. And that meaning is summed up in the phrase 'The Lord is with you when you are with him.'

How simple, and how profound. Let us open it up by asking two questions. First, what does it mean for the Lord to be 'with us'? Secondly, what does it mean for us to be 'with him'?

The Lord is with you . . .

First, then, how is the Lord 'with us'? What *kind* of divine presence is this? In a wonderful way, God is present everywhere all the time. '"Do not I fill heaven and earth?" declares the LORD' (Jer. 23:24). He is omnipresent in his very nature. After all, he is no local, tribal deity. He is the absolute Spirit. And his gracious omnipresence envelops, as in an atmosphere, each one of us personally: 'Where can I go from your Spirit? Where can I flee from your presence?' (Ps. 139:7). But Azariah does not have this kind of divine presence in mind.

There is another way in which our Lord is 'with us'. He promises, 'Never will I leave you; never will I forsake you' (Heb. 13:5, echoing Deut. 31:6). God does not make this promise to everyone, but only to his adopted children. None but his own walk through the constantly shifting scenes of life with this divine nearness always attending their way. God promises to lead us through this earthly pilgrimage, all the way, and he will never abandon us. We may not always *feel* him near, but he *is* near, for nothing can separate us from the love of God in Christ Jesus our Lord. But Azariah does not have this kind of divine presence in mind, either.

The promise of this divine presence is conditional: 'The LORD is with you *when you are with him.*' We may experience God in this way or we may not. It depends. So what is the Bible saying?

The contextual connection with the victory Asa has just won argues that this divine presence is God's active support of his people, his grace empowering their efforts, his intervention in their struggles. Remember that Azariah's declaration here in verse 2 interprets the meaning of what happened on that battlefield in chapter 14. God was 'with' Asa when he fought for Asa, overturning the superior odds stacked against him. When 'the LORD struck down the Cushites before Asa and Judah', he was *with* Asa and Judah. Here is the point: the spring of all our true prosperity is *the manifest presence of God* with us. That is the kind of divine presence Azariah has in mind.

The remarkable thing about belonging to God is that we are connecting with ultimate reality. We are making contact, to his glory and our own advantage, with no one less than *God*. He is there for us, ready to meet us and work among us. Does that not open up new possibilities? Should this not be the church's most conspicuous distinction? Moses pleaded with God:

> If your Presence does not go with us, do not send us up from here. How will anyone know that you are pleased with me and with your people unless you go with us? What else will distinguish me and your people from all the other people on the face of the earth?
>
> (Exod. 33:15–16)

This kind of divine presence can be *sensed*. Later in our passage, in verse 9, the Chronicler tells us:

Then he [Asa] assembled all Judah and Benjamin and the people from Ephraim, Manasseh and Simeon who had settled among them, for large numbers had come over to him from Israel when they *saw* that the LORD his God was with him.

When God draws near to his church with divine attestation of his smile on us, people can see it. And they are attracted to it.

This truth is so exciting that you would think that everyone would love it. But not everyone does. Talk of God's manifest presence makes some Christians nervous. They think that God's work should be silent and unseen. They feel comfortable with doctrinal cognition. And doctrinal understanding is essential! We die without it. But still, some people break out in a rash at the thought of God's immediacy *as a felt experience.* They may not know that the sensible presence of God is itself a biblical doctrine, pervasive in the work of the Chronicler and other biblical authors. But this anti-experience bias is nothing new. Responding to similar criticisms in his time, Jonathan Edwards lamented: 'How greatly has the doctrine of the inward experience or sensible perceiving of the immediate power and operation of the Spirit of God been reproached and ridiculed by many of late!'[7] Edwards went on to argue from Scripture for the following general truth:

It is God's manner in the great works of his power and mercy *to make his hand visible and his power conspicuous* and men's dependence on him most evident, that no flesh should glory in his presence, that God alone might be exalted and that the excellency of the power might be of God and not of man, and that Christ's power might be manifested in our weakness and none might say, mine own hand hath saved me.[8]

The manifest presence of God is real, it is our inheritance in Christ, and it brings honour to God. God's felt nearness is one of the primary marks of revival, distinguishing the church as the habitation of the living God. He is able to add a special X-factor to our obedient initiatives that outperforms the best of human devices.

...when you are with him

We have seen that this divine presence goes with us on a condition. 'The Lord is with you *when you are with him.*' Secondly, then, what does it mean for us to be 'with God'? That's a striking thought, isn't it? We are accustomed to thinking of God being with us. But here the Scripture says that *we* are to be *with God.* What does that mean?

The prophet explains his message by adding two corollary declarations. Positively, 'If you seek him, he will be found by you.' And negatively, 'But if you forsake him, he will forsake you.' In the coherence of our passage, *seeking* the Lord is equivalent to *being with* the Lord. Forsaking the Lord is the opposite: abandoning him for (supposedly) superior resources elsewhere. Seeking the Lord or forsaking the Lord – those are the only alternatives offered to us here. Every one of us is doing either the one or the other. So if we are not seeking the Lord, we are not in neutral; in his sight, we are forsaking him, even if we think we are living admirable Christian lives. How then do we 'seek' the Lord, so as to be 'with him'?

If you seek him

Seeking God is not easy to define.[9] But at the least, it means to live an intentionally Godward life. By analogy, the Lord commanded the Jewish exiles in Babylon, 'Seek the peace and prosperity of the city to which I have carried you into exile' (Jer. 29:7). They were to live intentionally for the peace and prosperity of Babylon. To seek the Lord, then, is more than a general bias in God's favour. It's more than a pro-God default setting in our mental software. To seek him is to live an intentionally Godward life. We make God himself our aim and goal.[10]

Truly seeking God is a complex convergence of yearnings to live near to God, to experience his favour and win his intervention, and to live solely for him. The Bible teaches us that true seeking includes prayer:

I sought the LORD, and *he answered me.*

(Ps. 34:4)

> *Seek* the LORD while he may be found;
>   *call on* him while he is near.

(Isa. 55:6)

> Then you will *call upon* me and come and *pray* to me, and I will listen to you. You will *seek* me and find me.

(Jer. 29:12–13a)

The conviction that drives God-seeking prayer is that all true accomplishments in doing the work of God are really the accomplishments of God himself. When we pursue him in prayer, we are admitting that the real answers and the real joy and the real breakthroughs lie with God. Seeking him humbles us to compliant obedience to his Word and ways, for seekers must approach him on his terms. We learn patience and self-discipline. We flatten ourselves before God in radical dependence, crying out that he would make his blessing real to us.

God-seeking prayer is persistent, tenacious. We reach out to him, and we refuse to let go: 'In the day of my trouble I seek the Lord; in the night my hand is stretched out without wearying; my soul refuses to be comforted' (Ps. 77:2 RSV). When we are seeking the Lord, we do not settle for trite, easy answers. We want truth. We want reality. And we do not give up until we find God truly and really. Nothing but God himself will satisfy. C. S. Lewis describes this mentality as 'an appetite for God',[11] a kind of gnawing hunger that defines satisfaction only in terms of God: 'The lions may *grow weak and hungry*, but those who *seek* the Lord lack no good thing' (Ps. 34:10). As lions prowl for food, ravenous with hunger, and may find no relief, so we seek the Lord, driven by a kind of hunger as well. But true seekers 'lack no good thing'.

Maybe this explains why we do not see more earnest seeking of God in our churches. We are satisfied with less than the treasures that God has to give. Maybe we do not even want God – or not *that* much of God. A little bit of him will do: enough to keep us out of trouble with him but not enough to break our pride and remake our whole lives. Christians sitting in church week after week whose hearts do not pant after God, and probably do not pant after much of anything, are forsaking the Lord, however blameless they may appear to be outwardly. Remember that 'seeking' and 'forsaking' are the only two categories here. And this prophetic word is addressed to believers.

Seeking is also loving (Ps. 4:2), asking (Ps. 27:4), pursuing (Ps. 34:14), and hoping (Ps. 69:6). When we seek the Lord, we stop 'playing church' and engage with him earnestly. We have no intention of manipulating him to obey our will. Our aim is to lay ourselves out before him as *his* servants ready to do *his* will, joyfully accepting whatever terms *he* sets for our service (Acts 5:41). To seek the Lord is to fix the purpose of our souls on him alone. We cannot be satisfied with less than all he will give us, according to the gospel. The very word 'seek' implies uncommon intensity, thoughtful inquiry, and earnest devotion. It reminds us that authentic Christianity is not a static state but a dynamic relationship with the living God.

Think of it in this way. In 1 Kings 10:24 we read that 'the whole earth *sought* the presence of Solomon to hear his wisdom' (RSV). In our terms, Solomon had celebrity status. Both sages and ordinary people ('the whole earth') mobbed Solomon to listen to him, to admire him, to enjoy him, and to learn from him. Should we not seek God's presence at least as avidly as the ancient world sought Solomon's, and as fans today seek the objects of their devotion? Should we not be eager to have his autograph, as it were, inscribed on every aspect of our lives and our churches?

The fact is that we are all seekers, more than we realize. Whenever we turn to someone for help, we seek that person, whoever it may be. Our seeking may not be recognizable as a form of prayer. But we are constantly seeking someone or something, if not God: 'In the thirty-ninth year of his reign Asa was afflicted with a disease in his feet. Though his disease was severe, even in his illness he did not seek help from the LORD, but only from the physicians' (2 Chron. 16:12).

It was not wrong for Asa to go to his doctors. His folly was to push God out to the margin of his confidence. Whomever or whatever we resort to for wholeness, success, effectiveness, happiness – that person or thing is what we are seeking. That is where our confidence really lies. And God calls us not only to confess his all-sufficiency in credal affirmation, but also to honour his all-sufficiency with practical demonstration. Otherwise, we stand in danger of turning to some inferior substitute:

> When Amaziah returned from slaughtering the Edomites, he brought back the gods of the people of Seir. He set them up as his own gods, bowed down to them and burned sacrifices to them. The anger of the LORD burned against Amaziah, and he sent a prophet to him, who said, 'Why do you consult [literally, 'seek'] this people's gods, which could not save their own people from your hand?'
>
> (2 Chron. 25:14–15)

You and I *are* seeking, every day in many ways. But are we seeking *God?* Seeking is more than praying. It is not less than praying, but it is more. Seeking God through prayer is meaningful and convincing if it gives voice to an intentionally Godward life, consecrated to him, excluding the idols of the world.

An obvious follow-up question now presents itself. Assuming that we are seeking the Lord alone, are we seeking him properly? We may be exclusively fixed on the one true God alone. Hopefully, we are. Now let us take it a step further. How may we seek the Lord in a way that *he* regards as acceptable? His Word is clear. Successful seeking is unconditional seeking:

> But if from there you seek the LORD your God, you will find him if you look for him with all your heart and with all your soul.
>
> (Deut. 4:29)

> You will seek me and find me when you seek me with all your heart.
>
> (Jer. 29:13)

> And without faith it is impossible to please God, because anyone who comes to him must believe that he exists and that he rewards those who earnestly seek him.
>
> (Heb. 11:6)

True seeking is more than a devotional feeling. It includes that, for it engages '*all* your heart'. But it is more. True seeking is a morally cleansing power touching all of life. True seeking makes a statement to God: 'I mean business with you. When I am on my knees in prayer; when I am driving to work; when I am having dinner with my family; when I am out on a date; when I am at school; when I am on the Internet; when I am alone; in my most private thoughts; wherever I am, whatever I am doing, I am living with you as my aim, Lord. I want to lead a life *fully pleasing* to you (Col. 1:10 RSV). I do not want to offend you in any way at all. I want no tension between us. I want you to see here in my life solid evidences that I am sincere in seeking you.'

But wait a minute. Is this legalism? Have we now begun to smuggle in some kind of pious self-improvement under the biblical banner of seeking the Lord? It depends. If by our seeking we are declaring to God, 'Receive my devotion to assuage your wrath, to fulfil your law, to buy your blessing,' then yes, it is legalism. We then dishonour Christ crucified, for he *alone* is meritorious, and he is *fully* meritorious, on our behalf. We then violate the sacred truth of justification by grace alone through faith alone in Christ alone. We cannot buy God's love, because it is not for sale (Isa. 55:1). He loves us freely (Hos. 14:4). We receive his love as an unearned and undeserved gift with the empty hands of faith.

But faith is a mentality that seeks God. By our seeking we are declaring to God, 'Nothing I can do establishes, secures, or maintains my position in your favour. Christ alone is my legitimacy before you. But you are calling me through Christ to turn away from my own poverty and live and labour out of the vastness of your all-sufficiency, and I want to answer your call with all my heart.' If our seeking gives outward expression to this spirit of faith, then no, it is not legalism. After all, real faith does not do nothing. Real faith seeks God. And under Christ, our fruitfulness depends on it.

Within an unconditional framework (God says to us, 'I will, because I will'), grace also contains a dimension of conditionality (God says to us, 'I will, if you will'). And seeking the Lord is our way of accepting God's 'if you will', in order to lay hold of God's 'I will'. Our seeking does not *deserve* God's favour. Only Jesus deserves anything good from God. Our seeking does not guarantee any particular response from God. We are not telling God what to do or venturing any predictions. He alone decides what is best for us. But God does promise to prove his nearness in ways we do not deserve and cannot predict or control, as we seek him. And we who lay hold of that promise long for his presence and for the triumph of his gospel as outcomes so desirable that we are willing to do whatever it takes to seek him acceptably, confident that he will keep his promise.[12] He himself has put that longing in our hearts and he will bring our desire to consummation.

Seeking the Lord, therefore, is neither for the legalistic nor for the listless. God will not allow us to trivialize him in either way. But if, through the merit of Christ, we will seek him alone and seek him aright, then he *will* be found by us. He will be with us. That is the promise of 2 Chronicles 15:2. And this verse is not limited to the Old Testament but applies universally to the people of God who are doing his work in his way with his results. 'If you seek him, he will be found by you.'

But if you forsake him

'The Lord is with you when you are with him' spins off a second corollary. We do not always respond well to God's overtures, so we need to understand what it means *not* to seek the Lord. 'If you forsake him, he will forsake you,' the Bible warns us. Again, is this legalism? Does Romans 8 not assure us that nothing will ever separate us from the love of God in Christ Jesus our Lord? In what sense might our Lord of inseparable love also forsake us? Somehow *both* can be true. But how?

In a final sense, no Christian will ever be forsaken by God. If he set his love on us when we were his enemies, does it make sense that he would drop us now that he has made us his friends (Rom. 5:5–10)? At no point will God ever say to one of his children, 'That's it. I'm fed up. The deal's off. I can put up with a lot but I never agreed to go *this* far with you and your problems.' Our Father will never say that to us. He knew ahead of time what a hassle we would be. He anticipated and compensated for all our failings through the cross of Christ atoning for us and through the Holy Spirit sanctifying us.

But in a less-than-final sense, we may indeed be forsaken by God. Asa himself was. This man of God, a man to whom the assurances of Romans 8 infallibly applied, was forsaken, in a duly qualified sense, by his faithful God. We read of it in 2 Chronicles 16. It happened when Asa transferred his security from the God of Israel to foreign military muscle. He no longer treated God as if God were all-sufficient. He forsook God for a political alliance, and God forsook him. Hanani the seer told him: 'Because you relied on the king of Aram and not on the LORD your God, the army of the king of Aram has escaped from your hand' (2 Chron. 16:7).

How life's opportunities are lost when we forsake the Lord! Oh, what could have been! We cannot push 'rewind' to recover those moments that have slipped by for ever. But we can get back on track with God by seeking him afresh. Tragically, Asa did not. When Hanani confronted him he only became defensive; he threw the prophet into jail. Asa closed his mind to the truth when he closed the prison door on the truth-teller. The Chronicler also records that 'at the same time Asa brutally oppressed some of the people' (v. 10). He turned sour. He hardened his heart. When affliction struck Asa personally (he contracted a disease in his feet), 'even in his illness he did not seek help from the LORD, but only from the physicians' (v. 12). Step by step, Asa forsook God, and God withdrew his hand of blessing from Asa.

Asa's own life proved the truth of Azariah's prophetic message. When Asa sought the Lord (2 Chron. 14 – 15), the Lord was found by him. But when he forsook the Lord (2 Chron. 16), the Lord forsook him. His life spiralled down into political diminution and physical decrepitude. And if we who belong eternally to Christ forsake him by diverting our practical confidence to other objects of trust, he will forsake us as well. We will discover how bitter life can be without the nearness of God, for no one dishonours God and finds honour for himself. The Lord never promised to support our carnality and worldliness. We too are living illustrations of 2 Chronicles 15:2, one way or the other.

The alternatives before us are clear. Either we are seeking God or we are forsaking God. We are tending one way or the other. Interestingly, when Asa stopped seeking the Lord and started to forsake him, he did not become an atheist. He was still a Bible-believer.

But he allowed his vision of God's all-sufficiency so to dim that he no longer held fast to God. He found other ways to cope. Faith in God seemed an impracticable policy for the hard business of everyday life, while other approaches seemed more realistic.

Asa should have known better. He did know better, as chapters 14 and 15 prove. But we do not always make decisions on the basis of truth. Sin confuses our thinking. Fear can make us irrational. We can forget. But the degree to which you and I are not adhering firmly to God with a practical faith is the degree to which we are abandoning him. And, to that degree, he will abandon us.

We all know what it is like personally when God withdraws his gracious presence. We may carry on in our Christian routines, but without the vivid personal reality of God attending our way. We are left to our weary and wearisome selves, struggling along, ungladdened by his nearness and unsupported by his providences. To live and work under the blank stare of God, as it were, is unbearable. He makes sure of that.

It can happen to a church as well, although it may not be obvious at first. The church machinery may continue to tick, its institutional momentum running along, money in the bank, and so on. But when the Lord removes a church's lampstand (Rev. 2:5), that church's radiance fades. Its credibility as a spiritual force is no longer taken seriously. The children of that church grow up and leave, never to return, for there is nothing to return to. The church's witness counts for nothing. It has become bored and boring. A vaguely defined restlessness enters the soul of such a church. The offers arriving in the mail for various gimmicks to liven up the church programme become attractive. 'Could this – could that – be our answer?' a pastor may wonder. But fads cannot replace the departed Glory. Only a prophetic analysis understands the real problem and only spiritual leadership points the way to the real answer.

Here is a solemn truth: no church has a secure and permanent place in God's kingdom. Every church is under divine inspection (Rev. 1:12–13, 20). Our Lord is looking to see whether we will seek him or forsake him. And if we do disappoint him, he may well pull the plug. He has the right; he has the power. And will the last one to leave please turn out the lights?

In 2 Chronicles 15:3–4 the prophet Azariah continues to speak as the voice of the Holy Spirit. He shows us a scenario of the people of God forsaken by him, and what they did about it.

He was found by them

For a long time Israel was without the true God, without a priest to teach and without the law. But in their distress they turned to the LORD, the God of Israel, and sought him, and he was found by them.

(2 Chron. 15:3–4)

What makes life really unbearable is the absence of God. 'Without the true God' in verse 3 translates into 'their distress' in verse 4. 'Without the true God' in our lives today translates into the *distress* of discredited ministers and restless, conformist churches, plundered by the world.

Through the words of Azariah, the Chronicler takes us back into the history of Israel, to validate the theology affirmed in verse 2 ('The LORD is with you when you are with him'). That principle is not a naked abstraction, hanging in mid-air, to be bandied about by idle talkers. It expresses how God shapes our daily lives. And the tragic eras of Israel's history prove its power.

Let verse 3 register its full force: 'Israel was without the true God.' Israel? The Assyrians, yes; the Egyptians, yes. But *Israel* without the true God? How could that be so? When they treated God as less than ultimate, less than all-sufficient, less than fully satisfying, when in their perception of reality God was no longer the primary factor to be considered, when he became to them ornamental rather than essential, when they began to operate as if he were irrelevant, he made himself irrelevant. He withdrew his means of grace: *a priest to teach* and *the law*. The delivery systems of divine mercy shut down. He pulled the plug. It is possible for the church to carry on with banners flying and drums beating and crowds cheering but without the God of truth and the truth of God. It has happened before. Why can it not happen again? Is it not happening now in some of our denominations?

But the burden of the Chronicler is not merely to threaten us with misery, although there is no greater misery than to be 'Israel without the true God'. The Chronicler's burden is to show us that, when the church suffers weakness and chaos and ineffectiveness, *there is a reason*. The deepest root of our difficulties is not a mystery. It can be explained. It is explained right here. We have forsaken God, and God has forsaken us. But the Chronicler also wants to show us that *there is a way back*. There is hope for a forsaken church, because God's offer remains in force: 'If you seek him, he will be found by you.'

God can be sought and he can be found. He offers himself to us today. Maybe your church is 'without the true God' right now. The church programme may be charging ahead with great sound and fury but without the felt presence of God. The Chronicler wants us to know that God's discipline can be lifted. His presence can return. He can be found. What would be the Chronicler's point in telling us about Israel's rediscovery of God in the past (v. 4) if the same confidence did not belong to us today? This is God's word to our generation: 'If you seek him, he *will* be found by you ... In their distress they turned to the LORD, the God of Israel, and sought him, and he *was* found by them.' God was within reach then and he is within reach now.

The message of the Chronicler is this: *God will be with us in visible manifestations of his favour, when we are with him in convincing demonstrations of our seeking.*[13] If we are willing to push the question back far enough, we will eventually discover our need of the Lord's gracious initiative in the first place. Only he can prompt us even to seek him. But the prophetic burden of the Chronicler is no less true. His message is simpler and more immediately pressing: if you seek him, he will be found by you. But if you forsake him, he will forsake you.

John Newton, in a letter dated 1 June 1761, wrote to a young friend describing what it is like to live with a God-seeking mentality:

We know from experience how little reading and hearing and resolving can do for us, when the Lord is absent and our hearts in a hard and stupid frame. Alas! how can we render, unless we first receive? But oh, when his Spirit and power are with us, what a delightful surprising change! Then old things become new, hard things easy, and out of weakness we are made strong! Then our enemies attempt in vain to find and ensnare us. He enables us to run through their troops, to leap over their walls, to esteem their darts and swords as straw and rotten wood and to go forth in his strength conquering and to conquer. I hope my letter will find you in this experience, with your bow abiding in force and your enemies under your feet, and may it long continue. This is a privileged, glorious state indeed. But it calls for much watchfulness and prayer. The Lord expects a particular closeness and obedience from those whom he thus delights to honour, and Satan watches with envy and rage to find an opening by which to assault such a soul. I hope you will remember that all your comfort and prosperity depends upon keeping near to him who is the sun, the shield, the life of his poor children, and that neither experiences, knowledge nor attainments can support us, or maintain themselves, without a continual supply from the Fountain. This supply is kept up by constant prayer, and prayer will languish without continual watchfulness.[14]

The Lord is with us when we are with him. If we seek him, he will be found by us. But if we forsake him, he will forsake us. This is the Word of God, and we will either prosper or wither according to our response to it. The promise of his presence is glorious. The threat of his absence is ominous. How we respond in our generation will show either how real or how theoretical God is to us, how precious or how incidental he is to us. We are not his favourites, his pets, that we can trample his Word underfoot and get away with it. Our Father does not run his household like that. Whatever we may do, one thing is certain. God will keep his Word.

Second Chronicles 15 forces the issue of personal engagement with God himself. Is it not significant that the Chronicler does not call us to *serve* the Lord or even to *obey* the Lord but to *be with* the Lord by *seeking* the Lord? He is calling us into the very heart of authentic Christian experience, underlying and energizing our serving and obeying and everything else. Each of us needs to think this through: *how can I make my life today, amid all my duties, a platform for being with God? How can I take the raw materials of this day and dignify them with the underlying purpose of seeking the face of God? How can I live out the Chronicler's message right here, right now?*

If we set our souls to this tune, we will sing. And our music will resonate with the beauty of the cross, for we will live in yieldedness and surrender to God. We will leave behind all brash self-display, all swagger, and learn what it means to seek first God's kingdom and his righteousness. We will ask new questions, like, 'How can I rid my life of whatever displeases the Lord?' We will *think* about how we live, and we will *think for ourselves*. It does not matter what some other Christian family or some other church is doing. What will matter to us primarily is one thing only: that we would seek the nearness of God, whatever it takes, and whatever else others may do.

God is not far away in some distant corner of the universe. He is right here, right now, ready to meet us again. Is it even conceivable that we could find some persuasive reason *not* to answer his gracious summons?

9
We humble ourselves

I bought a copy of *Self* magazine at the grocery store today. I hope you did not. But I wanted to see what the other side is up to. In any case, that brash title – *Self* – should not shock us. *Self* is not unusual as an indicator of our corporate character today. It is representative. The features in this month's issue hover around the predictable themes of food ('When "Healthy" Eating Isn't Healthy'), sex ('Women Who Won't Take *No* for an Answer'), the body ('Don't Waste Your Workout: 10 Fitness Do's and Don'ts'), money and romance ('How to Manage Money and Love'). The mood throughout is an amoral, hedonistic breeziness, not exactly fertile soil for producing heroic souls who will stand up to change the course of history. *Self*'s ethos is visceral, superficial, commercial. The title itself is a sign of the times, as is the motto inscribed on the subscription postcard insert: 'Make yourSELF a priority!' Oh, how we do! How we dote on ourselves, pamper ourselves, protect our space! And we would not think of endangering our precious health for anything. After all, if you do not have your health, what do you have? Or so they say.

I was struck by the following observation in a recent issue of the *New York Times Book Review*:

Of the many differences between the movie 'Titanic' and history, one in particular is telling. In the movie, as the ship is sinking the first-class passengers (all third-class human beings) scramble to climb into the small number of lifeboats. Only the determination of the hardy seamen – who use guns to keep the grasping men at bay – gets the women and children into the boats. In fact, according to survivors' accounts, the 'women and children first' convention was observed with almost no dissension, particularly among the upper classes ... The men on the first-class list of the Titanic virtually made up the Forbes 400 of the time. John Jacob Astor, reputedly the richest man of his day, is said to have fought his way to a boat, put his wife in it and then stepped back and waved her good-bye. Benjamin Guggenheim similarly refused to take a seat, saying: 'Tell my wife ... I played the game out straight and to the end. No woman shall be left aboard this ship because Ben Guggenheim was a coward.' In other words, some of the most powerful men in the world adhered to an unwritten code of honor – even though it meant certain death for them. The movie makers altered the story for good reason: no one would believe it today.[1]

I cite this not to make a statement about class, but because I think the reviewer's instincts about us today are on target. 'Me-first-ism' has come to feel so normal that we may have difficulty in believing that real people could live in any other way, especially when it costs.

Having thrown off the Victorian yoke of duty and virtue through self-mastery, the modern world has sunk into an orgy of pandering to the appetites of the masterful Self. Advertisers promote selfism, psychotherapists and educators reinforce it, and religion legitimates it.[2] Self is the great idol standing at the centre of our conceptual world, to which all bow low. We even have a duty-to-self ethic, as if self-denial were harmful, immoral, and deviant. 'I *owe* it to myself to be happy, to grow as a person, to discover myself, to fulfil my potential, to caress my victimhood, to get in touch with my feelings, *even if it hurts you*. I am drowning in my duties. If I don't break free, I'll die.' For the Christian, whatever happened to the all-sufficiency of Christ?

Thanks to selfism, we now labour under a cruel tyranny: an ideal of physical beauty, youthful health, effortless wealth, and autonomous personal control, all quite impossible to realize. But the pursuit of the ideal is very really destructive. We may thank the beloved idol Self for today's neglected children, divorces, broken hearts, our widespread cynicism and disillusionment and sense of emptiness.

Even more, we may thank selfism for the malaise infecting the church. The church, which ought to be exposing the idol's vicious pretence, has in some cases agreed to service the claims of Self as chaplain to an alien spirit. But, most significantly for our purpose here, self-absorption hinders revival, because self-absorption is self-exaltation. Revival thrives in an atmosphere of self-humbling. So we have to choose between selfism and revival. We cannot have both.

In Isaiah 57:14–16 the prophet reveals one of the secrets of heaven. To whom does God draw near with renewing mercies? Not to the proud, the self-admiring, the self-centred. They have their reward – the idol, with its harsh demands and bitter miseries. But our God draws near to 'him who is contrite and lowly in spirit'.

Remove the obstacles

And it will be said:
'Build up, build up, prepare the road!
Remove the obstacles out of the way of my people.'

(Isa. 57:14)

God has not abandoned us. He has sworn to put on display before this whole world, infested with selfism, his own beautiful supremacy (Isa. 40:3–5). Every knee will bow and every tongue will confess, when the adoration of Another replaces the worship of Self (45:22–25). We who believe cherish God's solemn oath as our assurance of liberation from slavery on the plantation of Master Self. We will not always grovel at the feet of the idol. Our Saviour has promised to release us into the dignifying and satisfying worship of God. We savour a truth that our world does not understand: the key to our future, the *summum bonum* for the human person, is not self-esteem but Christ-esteem. We can never think too well of him. We can never do too much for him.

Moreover, God has already begun to fulfil his oath. His glory rose on us with spiritual radiance in the first advent of our Lord (Luke 3:1–6; John 1:14) and it will burst forth with stunning finality at his second advent (1 Pet. 4:12–13). So the divine glory has already shone on us, but not yet in its fullness. Between our Lord's first and second comings, we live in a kind of historical twilight – the tension of promised glory already glimpsed but not yet fully unveiled (1 John 3:2).

We have a long way to go before the world is flooded with the glory of Christ. Many obstacles stand in the way before the magazines at the checkout counters of our supermarkets exalt Christ rather than self. Isaiah 57:3–13 illustrates the ugly moral chaos dominating the world as it is now, reminding us that evil can charm the fancies even of the people of God. We create our own impediments, making our progress in the ways of God the more difficult. But that does not stop our Lord.

He is able at any time to activate among us his word of promise, lifting our eyes from ourselves to his own glory. His decisive intervention is a present reality, not only a future hope. Verse 14 simmers with the warmth of God's declared will for us here and now: 'Build up, build up, prepare the road! Remove the obstacles out of the way of my people.'[3] If we drive God to it by our stubborn disobedience, he may hide his face from us (v. 17). But he is also able to clear away the sins clogging up his good work in our lives. He is able to speed us forward into scenes of blessing so God-filled they may seem nearly eschatological. And it's encouraging to see that God is *disposed* to create new paths for us, as the *command* form of the verse implies: 'Build up ... prepare ... remove!'

Do you see how an air of mystery hangs over verse 14? 'And it will be said'; but by whom? 'Build up, build up, prepare, remove.' These commands are all in the plural, but addressed to whom? Isaiah does not explain who is speaking or who is being spoken to. Out of nowhere, an unidentified voice cries out to unseen hearers. In a way, the very ambiguity of the verse is helpful. The fact that no particular agents or means are identified implies that agents and means are less than primary in importance. Our almighty Lord, whose will must be speaking through the anonymous voice – the message is on behalf of 'my people' – is never at a loss for instruments to accomplish his purpose. He is all he needs, and therefore he is all we need. And how is that significant? It means that *this word from the Throne is always ready to be actualized.*[4] Whenever God is pleased to implement this divine declaration, a way forward opens up before us with new clarity, enlarged access, and unanticipated success.[5] God is able to act suddenly, unexpectedly, without waiting for conditions favourable to our progress. He is the One who creates those conditions ('Remove the obstacles').

How then can we ever give up and quit? We are always one inch away from heaven-sent revival. Our Lord has only to say this word and the church breaks through to spectacular new gains. Worn-out ideas and stale experiences dissolve into newness at his command; we are released from our compromises into brave principles; the races come together in peace; marriages are renewed; churches are reunited; the Word of God is believed without quibbling; missionaries go forth into hard places with powerful success. Our own deepest intentions, which set us on the way of the Lord to begin with but now are too often frustrated, find new satisfaction. This is all so close to us, dependent not on favourable circumstances but only on the merest decree of God.

As long as these words shall stand in the Book of God – 'Remove the obstacles out of the way of my people' – we will not have exhausted the possibilities of the Christian life or the potential of our present situation. All God has to do is move his little finger, and the limitations binding us and blinding us fall away. But to whom is such access to grace opened up?

To revive the spirit of the lowly

For this is what the high and lofty One says –
    he who lives forever, whose name is holy:
'I live in a high and holy place,
    but also with him who is contrite and lowly in spirit,
to revive the spirit of the lowly
    and to revive the heart of the contrite.'

(Isa. 57:15)

We must come to terms with who God really is and who we really are. John Calvin introduces his *Institutes* by affirming that we must know two things, God and ourselves, if we are to make meaningful contact with reality.[6] This verse in Isaiah 57 brings us very close to reality, for it shows us who God is and who we are in relation to God. It gives us hope that we, even we, might experience the living God.

Is it not significant that we know who we are only in relation to God? This is the opposite perspective of Descartes (1596–1650), who in his quest for certainty doubted everything he could possibly doubt until only he, the doubter, was left. 'I think [i.e. doubt], therefore I am.'[7] Having whittled away at everything he ever thought was true, having challenged every authority and doubted every verity, he was left alone with himself. He then aimed to re-assemble his knowledge of reality based on the adequacy of his doubting, inquiring self. He thought that realism could be achieved only by thinking his way from the self outward. But Isaiah takes a different view. His beginning point is not self down here but God out there in a high and holy place. Everything starts with God. Everything depends on him. 'God is, therefore I am.' And if that is so, then what we need above all is not keenness of Cartesian scepticism, or any other merely human approach to life, but lowliness of heart. God himself insists that we may have no knowledge of God, or of anything, without humility before God.[8]

Authentic Christianity is marked throughout by humility. Jonathan Edwards, writing out of the experience of revival, explains how pride clogs up the work of God in the soul and in the church:

> [Spiritual pride] is the main door by which the devil comes into the hearts of those who are zealous for the advancement of religion ... This is the main handle by which the devil has hold of religious persons and the chief source of all the mischief that he introduces, to clog and hinder a work of God ... Spiritual pride disposes [one] to speak of other persons' sins, their enmity against God and his people, the miserable delusion of hypocrites and their enmity against vital piety and the deadness of some saints, with bitterness or with laughter and

levity and an air of contempt; whereas pure Christian humility rather disposes [one] either to be silent about them or to speak of them with grief and pity. Spiritual pride is very apt to suspect others; whereas an humble saint is most jealous of himself; he is so suspicious of nothing in the world as he is of his own heart. The spiritually proud person is apt to find fault with other saints, that they are low in grace, and to be much in observing how cold and dead they are, and being quick to discern and take notice of their deficiencies. But the eminently humble Christian has so much to do at home, and sees so much evil in his own heart, and is so concerned about it, that he is not apt to be very busy with other hearts; he complains most of himself, and complains of his own coldness and lowness in grace. He is apt to esteem others better than himself.[9]

And Calvin prizes humility as the merest basic to our faith:

A saying of Chrysostom's has always pleased me very much, that the foundation of our philosophy is humility. But that of Augustine pleases me even more: '... so if you ask me concerning the precepts of the Christian religion, first, second and third, and always I would answer "Humility." '[10]

And Charles Simeon, responding to a letter of brotherly admonition from a friend, confessed:

Another observation, in a former letter of yours, has not escaped my remembrance – the three lessons which a minister has to learn: 1. Humility. 2. Humility. 3. Humility. How long are we learning the true nature of Christianity![11]

And C. S. Lewis explains the centrality of pride in our moral psychology:

According to Christian teachers, the essential vice, the utmost evil, is Pride. Unchastity, anger, greed, drunkenness, and all that, are mere fleabites in comparison: it was through Pride

that the devil became the devil: Pride leads to every other vice:
it is the complete anti-God state of mind.[12]

Now why does Simeon assert that humility is nothing less than
'the true nature of Christianity'? Why does Lewis condemn pride as
'the complete anti-God state of mind'? Because from *Him* and
through *Him* and to *Him* are all things; to *Him* be the glory forever
(Rom. 11:36). This is the design, the inner logic, and the intention
of all of reality.

Verse 15 moves forward, from its beginning to its end, with
solemn dignity and increasing force. It begins with a royal pro-
nouncement: 'For this is what the high and lofty One says – he who
lives forever, whose name is holy.' Isaiah presents our Lord to us in
his infinite superiority. How do we see him?

First, he is exalted, supreme, sovereign ('high and lofty'). As long
as our eyes are fixed downward on the earth and our own achievements, we tend toward self-exaltation. We remain content with ourselves and our churches. We feel generally comfortable, even
worthy. But lifting our eyes to the high and lofty One, our complacency dissolves. To quote Calvin:

> Hence that dread and wonder with which Scripture com-
> monly represents the saints as stricken and overcome whenever
> they felt the presence of God. Thus it comes about that we see
> men who in his absence normally remained firm and constant,
> but who, when he manifests his glory, are so shaken and
> struck dumb as to be laid low by the dread of death – are in
> fact overwhelmed by it and almost annihilated. As a con-
> sequence, we must infer that man is never sufficiently touched
> and affected by the awareness of his lowly state until he has
> compared himself with God's majesty.[13]

Beholding God in his exalted majesty and seeing ourselves in our
sinful vileness, here in this moment of insight, humility – that is to
say, realism – is reborn in our hearts.

Secondly, God is eternal ('he who lives forever'). You and I will
not last long. We are even now fading. The acids of age and decay
are eating away at us, and there is nothing we can do about it.

Every day that passes leaves us with one *less* day to live. I look at myself with astonishment. Whatever happened to that eighteen-year-old I used to see in the mirror? Truly, the wages of sin is middle age! Our hopes and purposes are vulnerable, for we ourselves are dying a little bit more every day. We alter course as we become better informed or our mood swings around. But God dwells in sublime eternality, unchanged and unchanging, fixed in purpose, steady in resolve, ever fresh, ever alert, ever able. He has never sighed in discouragement. He has never yawned in weariness, being ever sufficient within his own exuberant inexhaustibility.

Third, God is in another category from us ('whose name is holy'). The word 'holy' does not reveal what God is as much as it declares what he is not. He is not down on our level. He is superior. We are not in his league. No one is.[14] The term 'holy' alerts us to the distance between God and ourselves. The word distinguishes more than it describes. Moreover, his 'name' is holy. In all God does to make himself known, he preserves his uniqueness. Therefore God cannot be understood except as one who is *un*like us. If we want God at all, we must accept him as he is, on his terms. We must adjust to him, for he will never 'ungod' himself.

Having been introduced by his herald Isaiah, now this awesome King himself speaks: 'I live in a high and holy place' – and (as Matthew Henry puts it) 'I will have all the world to know it.' No apologies, no back-pedalling, no hesitation, no self-doubt: this is the God who 'dwells in unapproachable light' (1 Tim. 6:16 RSV). Not very democratic and inclusive, is he? There he is on high, in total inaccessibility, radiating out of himself an intensity of light that is to us totally unapproachable. We could as easily dance on the blazing surface of the sun as swagger nonchalantly into God's presence.

Here then are powerful truths about God, clearly taught in holy Scripture but too often overlooked in our giddy Christianity of today. We have too little sense of the loftiness of God and we think too well of ourselves. We think we know him better than we really do. So it is good for us to be confronted again with the incomparable grandeur of God. But this is important: Isaiah does not lift up before us these views of the majesty of God to slap us down. Quite the opposite. We do need to be humbled before God, but only because the posture of humility brings us under his blessing. Frederick

William Faber (1814–1863) mingles eloquently these two dimensions making up the fullness of our relationship with the living God:

My God, how wonderful thou art,
   Thy majesty how bright!
How beautiful thy mercy-seat
   In depths of burning light!

How dread are thine eternal years,
   O everlasting Lord,
By prostrate spirits day and night
   Incessantly adored!

O how I fear thee, living God,
   With deepest, tenderest fears,
And worship thee with trembling hope
   And penitential tears!

Yet I may love thee too, O Lord,
   Almighty as thou art,
For thou has stooped to ask of me
   The love of my poor heart.

No earthly father loves like thee;
   No mother, e'er so mild,
Bears and forbears as thou hast done
   With me, thy sinful child.

How beautiful, how beautiful
   The sight of thee must be,
Thine endless wisdom, boundless power,
   And awful purity!

Once we have been released from the delusion of casual familiarity with God by seeing him truly as 'the high and lofty One', we might, unlike Faber or Isaiah, rush to the opposite error. We might begin to feel that God is so far removed from us in his 'high and holy place' that we do not matter to him. We might even feel that he despises us. We might despair. But verse 15 announces to us the gospel: God's terrible grandeur is matched by his gracious nearness.

I live in a high and holy place,
> *but also* with him who is contrite and lowly in spirit,
to revive the spirit of the lowly
> and to revive the heart of the contrite.

Now there is a thought. Such a one as *God* drawing near to the likes of us with reviving power, and not compromising himself!

However much we may recite the trendy creed of self-esteem, the truth is that we feel very small in our complex, impersonal world. Maybe that is *why* we recite it so devoutly. Andy Warhol's quip about 'fifteen minutes of fame' for each of us resonates with ironic and melancholy force. What is my little life really worth, anyway? What is yours? Not much, judging by our pop culture of throw-away fads and last week's passé rock stars.

How much more are we to God above! The lofty One comes down to live and linger with the crushed of spirit. (In v. 19 he calls them 'mourners'.) These are the ones God favours. Regarding them as his intimates, he draws near with reviving mercies. God has a special place in his heart for those who feel their sinfulness most keenly. How different he is from earthly rulers and worldly celebrities!

The LORD is close to the broken-hearted
> and saves those who are crushed in spirit.

> (Ps. 34:18)

The LORD is exalted over all the nations,
> his glory above the heavens.
Who is like the LORD our God,
> the One who sits enthroned on high,
who stoops down to look
> on the heavens and the earth?

He raises the poor from the dust
> and lifts the needy from the ash heap;
he seats them with princes,
> with the princes of their people.

He settles the barren woman in her home
    as a happy mother of children.

Praise the LORD

(Ps. 113:4–9)

Though the LORD is on high, he looks upon the lowly,
    but the proud he knows from afar.

(Ps. 138:6)

This is the one I esteem:
    he who is humble and contrite in spirit,
    and trembles at my word.

(Isa. 66:2)

God opposes the proud but gives grace to the humble.

(Jas. 4:6)

The dwelling of God with the lowly was most remarkably revealed in the descent of the Son of God down to our level, incarnate as one of us, and even beneath us as a condemned slave on a cross (Phil. 2:6–8). The Word of God says, 'Do not be proud, but be willing to associate with people of low position' (Rom. 12:16), and God himself practises what he preaches. Almighty God on high loves nobodies. He is not insecure and grasping, as we may be, impressed by worldly symbols of success. He does not value upward mobility: 'that which is highly esteemed among men is abomination in the sight of God' (Luke 16:15 AV). Disregarding self-concern, yet in doing so not violating himself but honouring himself, the all-glorious God associated with us lowly sinners in Jesus of Nazareth. And he continues to do so through his Spirit, who brings to us the living presence of Jesus.

The reviving nearness of God can come to any church that is willing to rediscover what it means to be 'contrite and lowly in spirit'. One church, for example, may be privileged financially and socially, while another is less favoured. But that means nothing to God. If that poor church will humble itself and tremble at his word, the high and lofty One will dwell with them, to revive them. They will stand out as a God-inhabited congregation, radiant with a Presence that the rich church cannot imitate out of its own resources. And, if that rich church will humble itself, God will dwell with them as well. What a merciful God, who 'descends even to the lifeless, that he may breathe new life into them and form them anew'![15] Our Saviour preaches good news to the poor, binding up the brokenhearted, proclaiming freedom for the captives and the year of the Lord's favour (Isa. 61:1–2; Luke 4:14–21). We must get real with God: '... your heart was tender and you humbled yourself before the LORD ...' (2 Kgs. 22:19 NASB).

This is why it works to our advantage not to become defensive when God disciplines us. We so readily think dark thoughts of God when confronted with his holiness and our sinfulness. How wildly we swing from self-admiring complacency to God-denying despair! Our highs are inflated with empty wind, and our lows can sink us down into blathering irrationality (1 Kgs. 19:10, 14). And so in Isaiah 57:16 God comes to stabilize us with still more encouragement. We may need patient preparation before a divine visitation is suitable. He may hide his face from us for a time, even a long time. But God knows when we have been subdued to lowliness. He knows when we are ready and he will delay not a moment longer.

The spirit of man would grow faint

> I will not accuse forever,
>   nor will I always be angry,
> for then the spirit of man would grow faint before me:
>   the breath of man that I have created.
>
> (Isa. 57:16)

God goes on record with a promise. We are no match for his withering anger, true enough. But he will not grind us down into the dust, never to rise again. Why? Unrelenting discipline would counteract his own intention in creating us to begin with. The emphatic word in the last line of verse 16 is the pronoun: 'the breath of man that *I* have created'. God cannot be so recklessly overbearing as to unmake what he has lovingly made. He does not treat us as our sins deserve (Ps. 103:10). He remembers that we are dust (Ps. 103:14). So what are we implying by our depressing thoughts of God? That divine creation is brought to consummation in divine annihilation? Ridiculous! The contrite and lowly in spirit find that God does not accuse forever nor is he always angry. Discipline is never his final word to his own (Isa. 54:7).

Or we could put it another way. Did God create us? Yes. Do we still exist? Yes. So how is it significant that God has chosen not to uncreate us? It means that he has more mercy yet in store for us. There in the church's future Mercy stands, beckoning, welcoming our arrival. Our best days still lie ahead, for we are God's personal project. So we must not give up, as if God intended the worst. The very thought is blasphemous. His discipline may be needed, but it will never go too far. He wants us, to whom he has given new life, to *live*:

> Endure hardship as discipline; God is treating you as sons ... We have all had human fathers who disciplined us and we respected them for it. How much more should we submit to *the Father of our spirits* and live!
>
> (Heb. 12:7, 9)

The Lord will answer

So God condescends to the broken. He understands how fragile we are. But if that is so, why does he not grant his people revival whenever they cry out to him for it? You and I may be seeking him with deeply earnest sincerity, yet God seems unyielding, silent, remote. Why? Is the humility he requires all that complex? Isaiah shows us, in chapter 58, verses 1–12, the courageous practicality of true humility. It is more searching than we might have thought. Humility is more than the occasional spasm of remorse or word of self-deprecation. It is a whole way of life marked by practical self-forgetfulness out of generous concern for others. So the prophet dwells on this one point for twelve hard-hitting verses, lest we miss the message. Here is a prophetic description of the humility God looks for:

Shout it aloud, do not hold back.
    Raise your voice like a trumpet.
Declare to my people their rebellion
    and to the house of Jacob their sins.
For day after day they seek me out;
    they seem eager to know my ways,
as if they were a nation that does what is right
    and has not forsaken the commands of its God.
They ask me for just decisions
    and seem eager for God to come near them.
'Why have we fasted,' they say,
    'and you have not seen it?
Why have we humbled ourselves,
    and you have not noticed?'

Yet on the day of your fasting, you do as you please
    and exploit all your workers.
Your fasting ends in quarrelling and strife,
    and in striking each other with wicked fists.
You cannot fast as you do today
    and expect your voice to be heard on high.
Is this the kind of fast I have chosen,
    only a day for a man to humble himself?
Is it only for bowing one's head like a reed
    and for lying on sackcloth and ashes?
Is that what you call a fast,
    a day acceptable to the LORD?

Is not this the kind of fasting I have chosen:
to loose the chains of injustice
    and untie the cords of the yoke,
to set the oppressed free
    and break every yoke?
Is it not to share your food with the hungry
    and to provide the poor wanderer with shelter –
when you see the naked, to clothe him,
    and not to turn away from your own flesh and blood?
Then your light will break forth like the dawn,

and your healing will quickly appear;
then your righteousness will go before you,
    and the glory of the LORD will be your rear guard.
Then you will call, and the LORD will answer;
    you will cry for help, and he will say: Here am I.

If you do away with the yoke of oppression,
    with the pointing finger and malicious talk,
and if you spend yourselves on behalf of the hungry
    and satisfy the needs of the oppressed,
then your light will rise in the darkness,
    and your night will become like the noonday.
The LORD will guide you always;
    he will satisfy your needs in a sun-scorched land
    and will strengthen your frame.
You will be like a well-watered garden,
    like a spring whose waters never fail.
Your people will rebuild the ancient ruins
    and will raise up the age-old foundations;
you will be called Repairer of Broken Walls,
    Restorer of Streets with Dwellings.

So what does real humility look like in actual experience? *The humility that counts with God reshapes a life into a pattern of practical initiatives for the sake of others.* This is helpful. We need this. We are self-centred in ways we cannot even see, and true humility is a more rugged exercise than we might have thought. It is not a matter of disparaging oneself, of a morose long face and tedious religious services and the occasional good deed. True humility rolls up its sleeves and gets down to work serving others. Humility fasts, but not merely from food. The humble fast from their lifestyles of self-indulgent heedlessness to the human needs close by.

God is addressing people who are in earnest with him ('day after day they seek me out', v. 2). There we are in our churches, Bibles open on our laps, eagerly listening to our preachers ('they seem eager to know my ways'), heads bowed in prayer, crying out for national renewal ('They ask me for just decisions') and for spiritual revival ('they seem eager for God to come near them'). Now, what is wrong with this picture? Our nation shows no sign of turning back from its rush into self-destruction as our binge on stylish Me-ism tears down more and more restraints on our recklessness. Our country is a selfocracy, *and the church is little different*. That is what is wrong with this picture. We disapprove of much in our society today, and so we should. But we have not subjected our own selfism to a radical critique. We are less Christian than we think we are, and all too content with what we are. Then we wonder why God does not answer our prayers and step in with reviving intervention!

Isaiah 58 gives us an insight into the ways of God that we might not have thought of. The impediment to revival is not God's unwillingness to bless, but our own unpreparedness for blessing. Self-absorption is the mark of our age. Think about it. What if God *were* to grant revival today? What would we do with it? We would probably use the energy and joy of revival to reinforce the very privatization of Christianity that renders us unconvincing to begin with. So here in Isaiah 58 God shows us how we can demonstrate to him that we *are* ready for revival. He calls us to humble ourselves in practical self-forgetfulness.

The prayer attributed to St Francis of Assisi (1181–1226) expressed the spirit of true humility:

> Lord, make me an instrument of your peace. Where there is hatred, let me sow love; where there is injury, pardon; where there is doubt, faith; where there is despair, hope; where there is darkness, light; where there is sadness, joy. O divine Master, grant that I may not so much seek to be consoled, as to console; to be understood, as to understand; to be loved, as to love. For it is in giving that we receive; it is in pardoning that we are pardoned; and it is in dying that we are born to eternal life.[16]

That is the spirit of Isaiah 58. That is the spirit of humility. *And that is the spirit God promises to greet with 'Here am I'* (v. 9).

We must not sentimentalize Christian humility as a mood, a posture, a tone of voice, or a personality type. It is more rigorous. It is a divine instrument of peace in consoling, understanding, loving, giving, pardoning, and dying. It is cheerful hard work. It is thinking first of the other person. It is lifting my head from my own depressing self-concern to look around and care for others.

Isaiah helps us to see that our humility can be morally hypocritical even as it is psychologically sincere. We mean well. But if we isolate self-humbling, contrition, lowliness, and fasting – Isaiah interchanges his wording – into a narrow religious piety without heroic initiatives of love toward others, we cast doubt on the real-life moral value of our humility. A humility that afflicts itself with fasting, but indulges itself with the gains of injustice, means nothing to God. It is, in fact, stubborn self-exaltation under the mask of meek self-humbling, and God is not deceived. Should we be surprised that revival stands far off?

We would not idealize the early church. They had their problems. But they were still made of the stuff that enabled them to Christianize their world. What about us today?

In the Old Testament they called it Baal. Today we call it lifestyle. And that is just another name for Self. When Self is exalted over Jesus, we are morally enfeebled. We are held captive to the world. And compromise becomes very thinkable.

The logic may run something like this: my lifestyle is necessary to my happiness. Obeying Jesus is important, too, of course – within the religious component of my total lifestyle package, anyway. So while Jesus reigns within that religious area, he must win approval from the rest of my lifestyle values whenever he wants to exercise influence beyond the narrow range of religion. Sorry, Jesus. You lose.

Not that we actually think this way, of course. But it does not have to be intentional. Self-exaltation just runs in our veins. Let us face it. We are not really selfless, humble people. We just like to think that we are. It feels better. But if our Christian living is not a matter of conviction, then it's just a matter of convenience. If we *are* obeying Jesus at any given point, we are doing so not because he is Lord but because obedience at that point happily coincides with the rest of our lifestyle. And there is a word for that: *hypocrisy.*

Revival would not change the face of our country today by advancing a conservative political platform. Revival would transform our nation by the courageous and beautiful example of

Christians who demonstrate before the watching world the lordship of Jesus over the whole of life, rather than the overall domination of Baal with Sunday morning stop-offs at church. Our country will remain impervious to the transforming power of the gospel as long as the church remains impervious to the transforming power of the gospel. Our nation needs to see an alternative: churches full of Christians for whom Jesus is Lord, no matter what personal sacrifice has to be made to exalt his lordship in our lives and families and communities. The triumph of the gospel in the world awaits the triumph of the gospel in the church. But as things stand now, the nation cannot see an alternative to Self, because there is none to be seen.

Humility will bring us back to the foot of the cross. Humility will fix our course on the way of the cross. When we look at Jesus dying there on that cross, we see a man who was so humble before God that he was willing to *go anywhere* and *do anything* for our sakes in obedience to the will of the Father. That is humility. That is Christianity. That is what our country needs to see in you and me today. And that is what Isaiah 58 is calling us to. But as long as we continue to adjust our principles from one moment to the next on the basis of how we feel or what is most comfortable or least disruptive to our comfort zones, we will remain in bondage, prostrate before the same idols others worship; we will know nothing of Isaiah 58, the cross, and revival.[17]

The example of Jesus proves that true humility is a comprehensive motivating principle, not a selective ornamental preference. It is an energy for helpfulness, not an excuse for introversion. Authentic humility is a total mentality of self-disregard, an outlook on all of life – in the family, at work, driving down the highway, talking on the telephone, negotiating a deal, making a decision. But it is not a religious gesture for a special occasion.

The reason we do not see Christian humility in this comprehensive way is that we do not see all of Christian sanctification in this way. We must understand that biblical holiness is not selective but pervasive. I might prefer to obey God in some areas of my life while I knowingly disregard his imperatives in other areas, but God 'connects the dots' in a way that my hypocrisy is too blind to see. Sometimes, when he disciplines us, we are bewildered, even offended. We wonder, 'Why is God doing this to me? I am trying to live for him. I've made some hard decisions for him.' And that may well be true – within a certain range of (to me) acceptable divine commands. But there may be something out at the edge of our discipleship that we find just too difficult to obey, something that appears to us so demanding, so unreasonable, so impossible, so expensive, so inconvenient, so embarrassing, so frightening, so disappointing, that we turn away. We disregard it. We focus on the manageable commandments of holy Scripture, hoping that God will understand and accept our terms. But he will not. He demands all. And he should. He is God. He is actually expecting us to think of him and treat him as if he were literally and really *God*. And One such as God deserves nothing less than whole-life sanctification, not a selective menu-religion.

You and I are moral and spiritual 'supersystems'.[18] That is to say, there are links and connections between the various aspects of your soul (and of mine) tying your being together into a coherent unity. Everything within you is interconnected. This linkage is not always obvious, but it is still there. If you wilfully disregard God's will in one area of your life, you weaken the integrity of all your obedience elsewhere in your life. If the obedience that you do manage does not arise out of a principial commitment to Jesus as Lord, you show him that, where you do obey him, you do so not because he is Lord but because that aspect of obedience happens to fall within the range of what you regard as reasonable, affordable, convenient, and so on. You expose your obedience as, not real obedience, but merely a deal you think you can strike with the Lord, to fob him off. True humility is not sinless perfection, thankfully. But true humility is prepared in principle to say yes to God wherever, whenever, however he calls for obedience, just because he is our God (Gen. 22:1–19). But when we jerry-build our own manageable version of Christianity, so that we cut and paste our own convenience religion and call it the way of the cross, God is offended. He withdraws. No matter how many tears we may shed, no matter how many days we may fast, why should revival ever come?

The message of Isaiah 58 is obvious, and the contextual connection with 57:14–16 is significant. It shows us that heaven refuses to listen to empty cant:

You cannot fast as you do today
and expect your voice to be heard on high.

(Isa. 58:4)

If prayer is a *substitute* for humble obedience to the practical implications of the gospel, it is a waste of time. Prayer is a high and holy privilege, and we do not live deeply enough in prayer. But *just* praying for revival is not what God is asking for. Our prayers may even antagonize him: 'O LORD God Almighty, how long will your anger smoulder against the prayers of your people?' (Ps. 80:4).[19] But the prayer God does listen to is couched in concrete, lived-out humility, dying to self and living to God by giving to others. 'Then you will call, and the LORD will answer; you will cry for help, and he will say: Here am I' (v. 9).[20]

So let us stop licking our wounds and caressing our victimhood and protecting our space and pampering the flesh while, at the same time, offering to God a pious face. Let us so humble ourselves that we do a very, very radical thing. We actually, literally *obey God*, as he reveals his will in holy Scripture, in daring new ways. And that will happen when we start loosing the chains of injustice, setting the oppressed free, sharing our food with the hungry, and clothing the naked, for all that means in our families, churches, and communities. And I am convinced that God means this both in the obvious literal sense and also in a profoundly spiritual sense – the sufferings of both body and soul. Nothing less will match the actual human needs right around us, for which God cares so deeply.

History records the liberating power of true humility.[21] In chapter 2 we looked back to the revival of 1742 in the parish of Cambuslang, Scotland. The minister of the parish, Mr M'Culloch, noted the difference in his people:

The formerly covetous and worldly-minded and selfish have got a public spirit and zealous concern for promoting the kingdom and glory of Christ in the conversion and salvation of souls; and for this end, are careful not only to live inoffensively themselves but usefully to others, so as all about them may be the better for them.[22]

Moreover, during this season of blessing:

[s]everal people bore witness that freedom in prayer came only
when they ceased to be self-regarding and preoccupied about
their own concerns; like Job, they found that the Lord turned
their captivity when they prayed for their friends.[23] ... One
account ended: ... 'Oftimes I find myself inhibited when I
would pray for blessings to myself; but when I begin to pray
for others, and for the Advancing of the Kingdom of Christ, I
get much liberty and enlargement of heart.'[24]

My wife and I attended our college reunion several years ago. We
sat near our classmates, Stephen and Carol Montgomery, soon to
leave Evanston, Illinois, for Galmi, Niger, Africa, to work under
difficult conditions in a mission hospital ministering to the diseased
poor. Since then we have been receiving periodic e-mails from the
Montgomerys. They conclude each one with this statement from
Pascal: 'All the precepts have been written. It only remains to put
them into practice.' Stephen and Carol are practising quiet obedience to the precepts of gospel humility. And Isaiah 58 argues that
their prayers, through the merit of Christ crucified, have credibility
in heaven.

What outpouring of grace would God grant if we overfed, self-
absorbed, navel-gazing, thumb-sucking developed-world Christians
were to follow, in a thousand different ways, the Montgomerys'
example, Pascal's maxim, and Isaiah's sermon? To the extent that
you and I take new, courageous steps of obedience to God, validat-
ing the authenticity of our humility – to that extent we may look
expectantly for our Lord to declare anew to our generation, 'Here
am I.'

A prayer

Our Father, here at the end of this book, I ask for your reviving touch on every reader. Unless you add your blessing, that is all the book can be – a book, words, paper, all of little lasting worth. But you are able to animate your Word. You are able to quicken our dull hearts. You are able to impart to us such a sense of your goodness that we hunger and thirst for you above all else. Would it not bring honour to you for this generation of your people – for this reader here and now – to break through to new depth and reality with you? Did Jesus not die to bring us life? Send your Spirit, Father, to make your Word reverberate with living power in our hearts. Release us from the sins that hold us back. Help every one of us to move forward by faith, taking new steps of bold obedience, for your greater glory, our richer happiness, and the salvation of the nations. Bring your presence down upon us, we pray. Revive your church. Let the Lamb receive the reward of his suffering. In the holy name of Christ. Amen.

Appendix

As a student at Wheaton College in 1968, I heard Dr Francis Schaeffer deliver the lectures that became his book *Death in the City*.[1] From the life of Jeremiah, Dr Schaeffer called us to a courageous faith in hard times. His message remains compelling to this day.

What if, after all, God does *not* send revival in our time? What if we slide into irreversible mediocrity, compromise, and inconsequentiality, so that our generation of the church becomes useless to God (Matt. 5:13)? The purpose of God will still triumph. A mere remnant can serve as a bridge into the next, more faithful generation. But God *will* rebuild. He remains committed to the glory of his own holy name in this world.

This appendix counsels us in how to think, how to feel, how to live, when we seem to stand alone, like Jeremiah. We must not become strident and shrill. We must not give up, either. We must keep on and must do so with compassion. I will never forget Dr Schaeffer's final words ringing in Edman Chapel as he concluded his lecture: 'Keep on, keep on, keep on, keep on, and then *keep on!*' As long as God exists, we must keep on declaring his truth, no matter what hardship we may face. And we must do so with compassion (2 Tim. 2:24–26). It is this rugged gentleness that God

210

might just use to precipitate the great spiritual breakthrough we all long for. But whatever God ordains for our generation, 'The persistence of compassion' will always be timely.

I leave you with Dr Schaeffer's prophetic words.

The Persistence of Compassion

Francis Schaeffer

We have already had a glimpse of the personal results to Jeremiah that the preaching of judgment brings. In Anathoth, the people said, 'Keep quiet or we're going to kill you.' The threats to his liberty were not idle for we read in Jeremiah 20:2, 'Then Pashur smote Jeremiah the prophet, and put him in the stocks that were in the high gate of Benjamin, which was by the house of the Lord.' The first thing they did was to fasten him in the stocks. Poor Jeremiah, who has been preaching faithfully in the midst of this 'post-Christian' culture, finds himself in the stocks. But his punishment didn't end there.

The stocks were not enough for him, so they put him in prison. 'For then the king of Babylon's army besieged Jerusalem: and Jeremiah the prophet was shut up in the court of the prison, which was in the king of Judah's house' (Jer. 32:2). Just as his prophecy is coming true, just as the king of Babylon is at the doors, just as the false prophets are being proven wrong, Jeremiah is put into prison, the prison that is in the king's house. Those who know the Doge's palace in Venice can picture this, because that palace contained the most important prison. Apparently it was the same here.

Later on, in 33:1, Jeremiah is still in prison: 'Moreover the word of the Lord came unto Jeremiah the second time, while he was yet shut up in the court of the prison.' But even that was not the end. In Jeremiah 37:15–16, we read, 'Wherefore the princes were wroth with Jeremiah, and smote him, and put him in prison in the house of Jonathan the scribe: for they had made that the prison. When Jeremiah was entered into the dungeon and into the cells, and Jeremiah had remained there many days...' So they gradually increased the punishment – from stocks, to a prison, to a dungeon. Finally, as we read Jeremiah 38:4 and 6, every one of us must be moved. For here is a man of flesh and blood, like ourselves, in a historic space-time situation with his own aspirations, and he is carted off and put into a dungeon. And now his very life is threatened: 'Therefore the princes said unto the king, We beseech thee, let this man be put to death: for thus he weakeneth the hands of the men of war that remain in this city.' That is, Jeremiah is not giving an optimistic answer; he isn't saying everything is going to turn out well. He isn't saying there is an easy solution; all we need is a little more technical advance to make the grade. He is cutting down their humanistic optimism, saying that they are under the judgment of God, and thereby weakening the people, undercutting their morale. 'For this man seeketh not the welfare of this people, but the hurt.' Of course it is not true. Jeremiah is wanting their real welfare. He is saying, 'You must be healed of the real disease, which is your revolt against God, and not merely of some superficial, external wound.' But that didn't please the dignitaries.

So we read, 'Then Zedekiah the king said, Behold, he is in your hand: for the king is not he that can do any thing against you. Then took they Jeremiah, and cast him into the dungeon ... that was in the court of the prison: and they let down Jeremiah with cords. And in the dungeon there was no water, but mire: so Jeremiah sunk in the mire.' The story would make vivid drama, but it is not merely a piece of theatre. Jeremiah, a man like yourself, was put into the innermost dungeon, where they put a rope around his arms and lowered him down into the mire. As he went down, he must have wondered: 'What are my feet going to touch?' He wasn't going to drown, but there was mud at the bottom, and as they let him down, he sunk, and he sunk, and he sunk to his knees, to his waist, to his arm-pits? We do not know, but he was there, there as a result of his faithful preaching of God's judgment to a 'post-Christian' world.

It's no small thing to stick with the message. It's easy to opt out. Both hippies and evangelicals easily can opt out into their own little ghetto, saying nice things to themselves and closing their eyes to the real situation that surrounds them. One can opt out in many ways. But if one really preaches the Word of God to a post-Christian world, he must understand that he is likely to end up like Jeremiah.

We must not think that Jeremiah's trials were merely physical. They were psychological as well, for Jeremiah never saw any change in his own lifetime. He knew that seventy years later the people would return, but he didn't live to see it. Jeremiah, like every man, lived existentially on the knife-edge of time, moment by moment; and like all of us, he lived day by day within the confines of his own lifetime.

Jeremiah was not just a piece of cardboard; he had a psychological life just as you and I have. How then was he affected? There were times when Jeremiah stood in discouragement, overwhelmed by preaching the message of God faithfully to this culture and ending up in the stocks, the prison, and the dungeon.

In Jeremiah 15:10 we read, 'Woe is me, my mother, that thou hast borne me a man of strife and a man of contention to the whole earth! I have neither lent on usury, nor men have lent to me on usury; yet every one of them doth curse me.' I am glad Jeremiah said that, because I get discouraged too. And if you are being faithful in your preaching and not just opting out, in a culture like ours you too will experience times of discouragement.

And you say, how can a man of God be discouraged? Anybody who asks that has never been in the midst of the battle; he understands nothing about a real struggle for God. We are real men. We are on this side of the fall. We are not perfect. We have our dreams, our psychological needs, and we want to be fulfilled. There are times of heroism as we stand firm and are faithful in preaching to men who will not listen. But there are also times when we feel overwhelmed.

In Jeremiah 20:14–18, we read of one of the great cries of discouragement in the Bible, parallel to some of the cries of Job. But the intriguing thing is that neither Job, nor Jeremiah, nor David in the Psalms (where David often cried out to God, saying, 'Have you turned away your face forever, O God? Where are you?') – in none of these cases does God reprove His people as long as they do not turn from Him, nor blaspheme Him, nor give up their integrity in their attitude toward Him. There is no contradiction here. It is possible to be faithful to God and yet to be overwhelmed with discouragement as we face the world. In fact, if we are never overwhelmed, I wonder if we are fighting the battle with compassion and reality, or whether we are jousting with paper swords against paper windmills.

So Jeremiah says in 20:14–18, 'Cursed be the day wherein I was born: let not the day wherein my mother bare me be blessed. Cursed be the man who brought tidings to my father, saying, A man child is born unto thee; making him very glad. And let that man be as the cities which the Lord overthrew, and repented not: and let him hear the cry in the morning, and the shouting at noontide; because he slew me not from the womb; or that my mother might have been my grave, and her womb to be always great with me. Wherefore came I forth out of the womb to see labor and sorrow, that my days should be consumed with shame?' Jeremiah was discouraged because he was a man standing against a flood. And I want to say to you that nobody who is fighting the battle in our own generation can float on a Beauty Rest mattress. If you love God and love men and have compassion for them, you will pay a real price psychologically.

So many people seem to think that if the Holy Spirit is working, then the work is easy. Don't believe it! As the Holy Spirit works, a man is consumed. This is the record of the revivals; it is the record of those places in which God has really done something. It is not easy!

As I stand and try to give a message out into the world – at the cafe tables and in the universities, publicly and privately – it costs a price. Often there is discouragement. Many times I say, 'I can't go up the hill once more. I can't do it again.' And what is God's answer? Well, first it is important to know that God doesn't scold a man when his tiredness comes from his battles and his tears from compassion.

Jeremiah, we recall, was the weeping prophet. This has psychological depth as well as historic meaning. He is really *the man weeping*. But what does God expect of Jeremiah? What does God expect of every man who preaches into a lost age like ours? I'll tell you what God expects. He simply expects a man to go right on. He doesn't scold a man for being tired, but neither does He expect him to stop his message because people are against him. Jeremiah proclaimed the message to the very end. He was always against going down to Egypt for help. And, as the captivity came, he could have escaped to Babylon. Instead he stayed with the people of God to keep preaching the message even after the judgment had fallen. His people dragged him down to Egypt, and even there he continued to preach the same message, down in Egypt where he never, never wanted to go.

Jeremiah, then, provides us with an extended study of an era like our own, where men have turned away from God and society has become post-Christian. Now, before returning to the book of Romans with which these lectures began, we should tie together the exposition of Jeremiah.

First, we may say that there is a time, and ours is such a time, when a negative message is needed before anything positive can begin. There must first be the message of judgment, the tearing down. There are times, and Jeremiah's day and ours are such times, when we cannot expect a constructive revolution if we begin by overemphasizing the positive message. People often say to me, What would you do if you met a really modern man on a train and you had just an hour to talk to him about the gospel? And I've said over and over, I would spend forty-five or fifty minutes on the negative, to really show him his dilemma – to show him that he is more dead than even he thinks he is; that he is not just dead in the twentieth-century meaning of dead (not having significance in this life) but that he is morally dead because he is separated from the God who exists. Then I'd take ten or fifteen minutes to preach the gospel. And I believe this usually is the right way for the truly modern man, for often it takes a long time to bring a man to the place where he understands the negative. And unless he understands what's wrong, he will not be ready to listen to and understand the positive. I believe that much of our evangelistic and personal work today is not clear simply because we are too anxious to get to the answer without having a man realize the real cause of his sickness, which is true moral guilt (and not just psychological guilt feelings) in the presence of God. But the same is true in a culture. If I am going to speak to a culture, such as my culture, the message must be the message of Jeremiah. It must be the same in both private and public discourse.

Secondly, with love we must face squarely the fact that our culture really is under the judgment of God. We must not heal the sickness lightly. We must emphasize the reality. We must proclaim the message with tears and give it with love. Through the work of the Holy Spirit there must be a simultaneous exhibition of God's holiness and His love, as we speak. We cannot shout at them or scream down upon them. They must feel that we are with them, that we are saying that we are both sinners, and they must know these are not just God-words but that we mean what we say. They must feel in our own attitudes that we know we too are sinners, that we are not innately good because we have been born into an evangelical home, attend an evangelical church or an evangelical school, or take some external sacraments.

There is in all of this a time for tears. It will not do to say these things coldly. Jeremiah cried, and we must cry for the poor, lost world, for we are all of one kind. There is of course a sense in which there are two humanities, one saved, one lost. But the Bible also tells us that there is only one humanity; we all have a common ancestor and all have been made in the image of God. So I *must* have tears for my kind. But with the tears the message must be clear: our culture, our country, our churches have walked upon what God has given us, and thus all these are under the judgment of God.

It is my experience that giving the realistic message does not turn people off – if they feel compassion in you. As a matter of fact, it is the other way. The real thinkers, the artists understand the scream of modern man: 'There's something wrong with my culture. It is a dead end.'

Take, for example, the picture by Edvard Munch in which a man is screaming. Or listen to young people crying, 'It's plastic. Our culture is plastic.' The artists, the poets, the hippies, and the yippies are screaming, 'Something's wrong.' Modern man knows this, but no one tells him why. It is up to Christians to do so: to point out what is wrong and to show modern man why he is hung up and why his culture is plastic.

Often Christians, young and old alike, have not faced the facts about their own countries – that they are under the judgment of God. Perhaps that explains why they are often without enthusiasm in their proclamation of the gospel, why they just give the crumbling wall a coat of paint.

Third, we must say that if we believe in truth, we must practise truth. We live in an age of Hegelian synthesis and relativism; men don't believe truth exists. How do we expect a world to take us seriously when we say we believe truth exists and then live in a relativistic way?

I would like to quote from the last appendix in my book, *The God Who Is There*. It repeats in a shorter form, 'The Practice of Truth', the speech I gave in Berlin at the Congress on Evangelism. 'In regard to the first of the principles of which we spoke at the beginning of Appendix A: *The full doctrinal position of historic Christianity must be clearly maintained*, it would seem to me that the central problem of evangelical orthodoxy in the second half of the twentieth century is the problem of the *practice* of this principle. This is especially so when we take into account the spiritual and intellectual mentality which is dominant in our century ... The unity of orthodox or evangelical Christianity should be centred around this emphasis on *truth*. It is always important, but doubly so when we are surrounded by so many for whom the concept of truth, in the sense of antithesis, is considered to be totally unthinkable ... Moreover, in an age of synthesis men will not take our protestations of truth seriously unless they see by our actions that we seriously *practise* truth and antithesis in the unity we try to establish and in our activities ... Both a clear comprehension of the importance of truth and a clear practice of it, even when it is costly to do so, are imperative if our witness and our evangelism are to be significant in our generation and in the flow of history ... In an age of relativity the *practice* of truth when it is costly is the only way to cause the world to take seriously our protestations concerning truth. Cooperation and unity that do not lead to purity of life and purity of doctrine are just as faulty and incomplete as an orthodoxy which does not lead to a concern for, and a reaching out towards, those who are lost ... All too often the only antithesis we have exhibited to the world and to our own children has been *talking* about holiness *or* our *talking* about love; rather than the consideration and practice of holiness and love together as truth, in antithesis to what is false in theology, in the church, and the surrounding culture.'

I want to ask you something. Remember the false prophets in Jeremiah's dark day saying, 'Peace, peace.' Can you imagine

Jeremiah saying to them, 'We're all in one group because we all wear ecclesiastical coloured ties'? I can't. He didn't do it. And I firmly believe that this is one of the things we must understand in our days of desperate need when men no longer believe in truth. We cannot expect them to take seriously our belief in objective truth, if in our practice we indicate only a quantitative difference between all men who are in ecclesiastical structures or who use theological language. I do not mean that we should not have open dialogue with men; my words and practice emphasize that I believe love demands that. But I do mean that we should not give the impression in our practice that just because they are expressed in traditional Christian terminology all religious concepts are on a graduated, quantitative spectrum, that in regard to central doctrine no chasm exists between right and wrong.

Fourth, we must realize that to know the truth and to practise it will be costly. At times the price will be high in your individual family. Often there is a tremendous pressure upon young Christians as they face their non-Christian families. But the price is also high in society. You may not get the honour which you covet in the scholastic world, in the artistic world, in the professional world or even in the business world. The price may be high indeed.

Fifth, we must keep on preaching even if the price is high. There is nothing in the Bible that says we are to stop. The Bible rather says, keep on, keep on. We may think of Paul as he writes in 2 Corinthians 11:24–28 (paraphrase): 'I've been beaten by the Jews, I've been beaten by the Gentiles, I've battled the seas, I've known the wrath of men, and I've known the force of Satan.' Did Paul stop? Paul said, 'No, I want to come to Rome and preach the gospel there as well.'

Perhaps you know the story of Martin Luther. When he had begun his preaching, he received word about the first Protestant martyrs. Some monks had read Martin Luther's work, turned to this way of thinking, and were burned alive in the Grand Place in Brussels. There is now a marker in the Grand Place where they were burned. And the story is that when Martin Luther heard that, he began to walk the floor and he said, 'I can't go on. I can't do it any more. Because of me other men are being killed. I can't go on!' Then as he wrestled with it, he understood that because it was truth, no matter what the cost to himself or anybody else, he must go on. Thank God, Martin Luther marched straight forward, and we had the Reformation.

Christianity is not a modern success story. It is to be preached with love and tears into the teeth of men, preached without compromise, without regard to the world's concept of success. If there seem to be no results, remember that Jeremiah did not see the results in his day. They came later. If there seem to be no results, it does not change God's imperative. It is simply up to you and me to go on, go on, go on, go on, whether we see the results or whether we don't. *Go on.*

We in L'Abri Fellowship have seen many results and we have much to be thankful for. Even since we have been here at Wheaton College, we have had several parents come to us telling us what it means to them that their children have come back to Christianity. We have seen many things to encourage us, but there are also discouragements. And even if there were only discouragements, God's Word is still the message of Jeremiah: go on and preach, preach the truth of the revelation of God no matter what the cost; go on, go on, go on. If you are not willing to go on, you have to ask yourself the question: do I really believe Christianity is true or is my Christianity only an 'upper-storey' religious concept?

Our day is not totally unique. Time after time Christian cultures have thrown themselves away. Take, for example, the church of the apostle Thomas in India. It began to whittle away at the truth. So the church largely died. There are two ways to bring about such death: one is to compromise the truth and the other to have a dead orthodoxy. Both can equally grind down and destroy the message of a church in a generation, especially if the generation is hard. Do we realize that in China at about the year AD 800 there were Christian churches in almost every single great city? Do we realize that there were hundreds of Christians in the Arabian peninsula just before Mohammed in AD 550? Why was it that Mohammedanism was able to rush over that country? Because of military force? No. When Mohammed came forward and looked at the Christians he said, 'There's nothing here.' And he was largely right. Mohammedanism started and it swept that portion of the world. The same thing was true with the church in North Africa, and the primitive church in

Armenia, in Georgia, in Gaul. In each of these places there was a Christian church and a growing Christian culture but the church collapsed. The pattern is clear: defection and destruction.

And we as Christians today, what are we saying? We are saying that we want reformation and we want revival, but still we are not preaching down into this generation, stating the negative things that are necessary. If there is to be a constructive revolution in the orthodox, evangelical church, then like Jeremiah we must speak of the judgment of individual men great and small, of the church, the state, and the culture, for they have known the truth of God and have turned away from Him and His propositional revelation. God exists, He is holy, and we must know that there will be judgment. And like Jeremiah we must keep on so speaking regardless of the cost to ourselves.

My last sentence is simply this: The world is lost, the God of the Bible does exist; the world is *lost*, but truth is truth, keep on! And for how long? I'll tell you. Keep on, Keep on, Keep on, Keep on, and then KEEP ON!

Notes

Preface

1. It is important to emphasize the normality of revival. If revival were by nature different from the normal work of the gospel, then we would have to allow for a two-tiered church. At the lower level would be the believers who have the merit of Christ and the indwelling of the Spirit. They would be the drones of the church. At the higher level would be the super-Christians who have the merit of Christ and the indwelling of the Spirit *plus* another layer of hyperblessing, different in nature from what God gives his ordinary children. Such a two-tiered view of the church would distort the gospel and invite self-admiration. Revived churches do not possess anything different from what all other true churches possess. They have the normal blessing of God, but it is operating with unusually quickening spiritual power.
2. Note how the outpouring of the Holy Spirit upon the Gentiles in Acts 10:44–48 follows and resembles the Spirit's outpouring upon the covenant people in Acts 2.
3. The word 'revive' is echoed in the RSV (and NRSV), NASB, and NIV at Psalm 85:6.
4. Cf. *Oxford English Dictionary*, s.v. 'revive'. Listed there is usage dated 1440: 'God ... mortifieth and *reviveth*, smiteth and healeth.' This represents the sense of the English verb in its native force, consistent with the Piel of *hyh* in the Hebrew text of Psalm 85:6. The REB paraphrases the sense: 'Will you not *give us new life* that your people may rejoice in you?' Psalm 85:6 is discussed further in chapter 2 below.

5. Iain H. Murray, *Pentecost – Today? The Biblical Basis for Understanding Revival* (Edinburgh: The Banner of Truth Trust, 1998), 3; *Revival and Revivalism: The Making and Marring of American Evangelicalism, 1750–1858* (Edinburgh: The Banner of Truth Trust, 1994), 374. Cf. *Oxford English Dictionary*, s.v. 'revival'.
6. Shel Silverstein, *Where the Sidewalk Ends* (New York: HarperCollins, 1974), 35.
7. C. S. Lewis, *A Preface to Paradise Lost* (London: Oxford University Press, 1961), v.

Introduction

1. C. S. Lewis, *The Abolition of Man* (New York: Macmillan, 1965), 24.
2. Francis A. Schaeffer, 'How Heresy Should Be Met', *Reformation Review* (July 1954), 8–10.

Part One: What God Can Do

Prologue

1. The word *merely* is the operative one. Revivals should be subjected to historical study. But the ministry of George Whitefield, for example, deserves more searching reflection than to be explained away in terms of his alleged theatrical persona. Cf. Arnold Dallimore, review of Harry S. Stout, *The Divine Dramatist: George Whitefield and the Rise of Modern Evangelicalism*, in *Reformation and Revival Journal* (autumn 1992), 125–128.
2. Because I understand revival to be a heightened form of normal Christian experience, I could not treat revival as a merely human event without also undercutting the whole of authentic Christianity.
3. No one has helped us to think more searchingly about revival experience than Jonathan Edwards. See especially his 'Religious Affections', 'Thoughts on the Revival', and 'The Distinguishing Marks of a Work of the Spirit of God', all contained in the two-volume Banner of Truth reprint of *The Works of Jonathan Edwards* (1834; reprint, 1979).
4. See, for example, Isaiah 40:5, 9; 41:17–20; 49:25–26; 52:10; 60:1–3; 62:1–5; 66:14.

Chapter 1: God comes down to us

1. John Calvin, in his *Commentary on the Book of the Prophet Isaiah*, vol. 4 (Grand Rapids: Eerdmans, n.d.), 352, identifies this kind of faith as a

mark of true believers: 'Believers must differ from unbelievers in acknowledging a powerful and kind God, even when they perceive no tokens of his power or kindness; and thus, even when he is at a great distance, they nevertheless call on him; for God never ceases to care about his people (1 Pet. 5:7) since he governs unceasingly every part of the world.'

2. C. S. Lewis, *The Screwtape Letters* (New York: Macmillan, 1970), 39.

3. Cf. John Owen, 'God's Withdrawing His Presence, the Correction of His Church', in William H. Goold (ed.), *The Works of John Owen*, vol. 9 (1850–53; reprint, Edinburgh: The Banner of Truth Trust, 1982), 296–307.

4. A. Skevington Wood, 'The Mystery of Revival', *Heartcry! A Journal on Revival and Spiritual Awakening* (spring 1997), 22.

5. Calvin, *Isaiah*, 361.

6. See Martyn Lloyd-Jones, *Revival* (Westchester: Crossway, 1987), 306.

7. The realism of the prophet finds an echo in David Wells's words to our generation in *God in the Wasteland: The Reality of Truth in a World of Fading Dreams* (Grand Rapids: Eerdmans, 1994), 117: 'I believe that the church has lost the transcendent truth and goodness of God, and I believe that if it fails to recover this truth and goodness, Christianity will buckle completely under the strains that are being exerted upon it by modernity. I do not mean to suggest that this recovery will be anything other than dangerous, however, for there is an unyielding flintiness to the purposes of God. His redemptive presence, in truth and holiness, is found only on his terms, and these are very different from what comes most immediately and most naturally to modern minds. He stands resolute and unmovable between the meaning he provides of himself and of life's purposes and the caprices of private intuition and consumer appetite by which these would be taken captive. If we grasp the reality of God, it will be on his terms and not on our own.'

8. Henri Blocher, *Original Sin: Illuminating the Riddle*, ed. D. A. Carson (Grand Rapids: Eerdmans, 1997), 11.

9. With the same hope David prays in Psalm 51:18–19 that God would restore the institutional wreckage his personal sins have caused.

10. Calvin, *Isaiah*, 374.

11. Edwards, *The Works of Jonathan Edwards*, vol. 2, 291.

12. *The Revival of Religion: Addresses by Scottish Evangelical Leaders Delivered in Glasgow in 1840* (1840; reprint, Edinburgh: The Banner of Truth Trust, 1984), 316–317, records this from the Isle of Skye: 'It was a common thing [during this season of renewal], as soon as the Bible was opened ... and just as the reader began, for great meltings to come upon the hearers. The deepest attention was paid to every

word as the sacred verses were slowly and solemnly enunciated. Then the silent tear might be seen stealing down the rugged but expressive countenances turned upon the reader ... The word of the Lord was precious in those days; and personal inconvenience was little thought of when the hungering soul sought to be satisfied.'

13. This and the following quotations are taken from the displays at The Billy Graham Center, Wheaton, Illinois.

Chapter 2: God reinvigorates us

1. George Smeaton, *The Doctrine of the Holy Spirit* (Edinburgh: The Banner of Truth Trust, 1974), 288–289.

2. Abraham Kuyper recalls the revival of a church in Holland: 'it brought to the Cross not a wild and worldly population, but a company of strictly orthodox and outwardly blameless parishioners'. Murray, *Pentecost – Today?*, 27.

3. Cf. Ezra 1:5; 3:10–11; 6:14–22; Haggai 1:2–15.

4. See, for example, Genesis 33:10; 1 Chronicles 28:4; 29:17; Psalm 147:10–11; Ecclesiastes 9:7.

5. Cf. John Donne, 'God's Mercies', in *Donne's Sermons*, ed. Logan Pearsall Smith (Oxford: Clarendon Press, 1919), 136, 139: 'When we fix ourselves upon the meditation and modulation of the mercy of God, even his judgements cannot put us out of tune, but we shall sing and be cheerful even in them ... If some king of the earth have so large an extent of dominion in north and south that he hath winter and summer together in his dominions, so large an extent east and west that he hath day and night together in his dominions, much more hath God mercy and judgement together. He brought light out of darkness, not out of a lesser light. He can bring thy summer out of winter, though thou have no spring. Though in the ways of fortune or understanding or conscience thou have been benighted till now, wintered and frozen, clouded and eclipsed, damped and benumbed, smothered and stupefied till now, now God comes to thee, not as in the dawning of the day, not as in the bud of the spring, but as the sun at noon to illuminate all shadows, as the sheaves in harvest to fill all penuries. All occasions invite his mercies, and all times are his seasons.'

6. Romans 3:21–26 fills the crucial gap in the moral equation. God's holy wrath is ultimately satisfied – not just deferred, but positively assuaged – at the cross of Jesus. This is the hope of all the ages. Without his cross, we could not be finally certain that God's mercies toward us sinners at any particular moment were not arbitrary and changeable. All revival flows to us through Christ crucified.

7. Job uses this word to describe the unbearably bitter provocation of the 'comfort' of his three companions in Job 6:2. In the parallelism of Proverbs 12:16 this word is logically equivalent to the irritation of a personal insult. And in Proverbs 27:3 this word is used to describe the intolerable strain of a fool's annoying company.

8. This verb is used, for example, for breaking a covenant in 1 Kings 15:19 and for breaking a vow in Numbers 30:8 [in Hebrew 30:9].

9. God does not treat bane and blessing with equanimity. On Romans 9–11, C. E. B. Cranfield, in *A Critical and Exegetical Commentary on the Epistle to the Romans*, vol. 2 (Edinburgh: T. & T. Clark, 1979), 448, writes: 'We shall misunderstand these chapters, if we fail to recognize that their keyword is "mercy". Mercy throbs at the profoundest depths of God's being.' Cf. Anselm, *Proslogion*, chapter 9.

10. The Tanakh version of the Jewish Publication Society (1985) takes the liberty of paraphrasing the sense: 'Surely You will revive us again.'

11. See Psalm 36:9 ('With you is the fountain of life'); 42:2 ('My soul thirsts for God, for the living God'); 145:16 ('You open your hand and satisfy the desires of every living thing'). But 'those who are far from you will perish' (Ps. 73:27).

12. Cf. Deuteronomy 30:16 ('For I command you today to love the Lord your God, to walk in his ways, and to keep his commands, decrees and laws; then you will live and increase, and the Lord your God will bless you in the land you are entering to possess'); Psalm 16:11 ('You have made known to me the path of life; you will fill me with joy in your presence, with eternal pleasures at your right hand').

13. See E. Kautzsch (ed.), *Gesenius' Hebrew Grammar*, rev. A. E. Cowley, 2nd English ed. (1910; reprint, Oxford: Clarendon Press, 1988), § 135, although they do not cite this particular instance. Bruce K. Waltke and M. O'Connor, *An Introduction to Biblical Hebrew Syntax* (Winona Lake, Ind.: Eisenbrauns, 1990), 16.3.2e, define the nature of such emphasis as 'psychological focus' or 'strongly focused attention'.

14. Jonathan Edwards, 'A Faithful Narrative of the Surprising Work of God', in *The Works of Jonathan Edwards*, vol. 1, 344–364.

15. Ibid., 350. This understanding of revival differs from that taught by Finney, who believed that 'a revival of religion is not a miracle' but 'the result of the right use of the appropriate means'. See Charles Grandison Finney, *Lectures on Revivals of Religion*, ed. William G. McLoughlin (Cambridge: Harvard University Press, 1960), 12–13.

16. See Tom Utley, 'Christ Simply Did Not Give a Jot about Politics', *Daily Telegraph*, 8 January 1999, at website www.dailytelegraph.co.uk.

17. Arthur Fawcett, *The Cambuslang Revival: The Scottish Evangelical Revival of the Eighteenth Century* (London: The Banner of Truth Trust, 1971), 113.

18. Cf. Exodus 32:11–14; Numbers 14:13–16; Deuteronomy 9:27–29; 1 Samuel 12:22; 1 Kings 8:41–43; 2 Kings 19:34; 20:6; Psalm 23:3; 106:6–8; Isaiah 43:7; 48:9–11; Ezekiel 20:8–22; 36:22–32.

19. John Owen, 'Of Communion with the Holy Ghost', in William H. Goold (ed.), *The Works of John Owen*, vol. 2 (1850–53; reprint, Edinburgh: The Banner of Truth Trust, 1980), 253. Owen's wording is slightly altered for clarity.

20. Calvin comments, 'In supplicating that mercy may be extended to them, and deliverance granted them, they confess that they are deprived of all *sense* of both these blessings' (italics added). John Calvin, *Commentary on the Book of Psalms*, vol. 3 (Grand Rapids: Eerdmans, 1949), 372.

21. Edwards, *The Works of Jonathan Edwards*, vol. 1, 376.

22. Commenting on verse 5, Calvin's realism is refreshing: 'Our corrupt nature is ever relapsing into the wanton indulgence of its native propensities.' Calvin, *Commentary on the Book of Psalms*, vol. 3, 371.

23. D. Martyn Lloyd-Jones, *What Is an Evangelical?* (Edinburgh: The Banner of Truth Trust, 1992), 9–10.

24. Cf. Gerhard von Rad, *Old Testament Theology*, vol. 1, trans. D. M. G. Stalker (New York: Harper & Row, 1962), 239–241.

25. Martyn Lloyd-Jones, *Joy Unspeakable: Power and Renewal in the Holy Spirit* (Wheaton: Harold Shaw, 1984), 276.

26. Cf. Hans-Joachim Kraus, *Theology of the Psalms*, trans. Keith Crim (Minneapolis: Augsburg, 1986), 42–43.

27. Derek Kidner, *Psalms 73–150: A Commentary on Books III–V of the Psalms* (London: InterVarsity Press, 1975), 311.

28. Jonathan Edwards describes redemptive history similarly in *The Works of Jonathan Edwards*, vol. 1, 539: 'It may be here observed that from the fall of man to our day the work of redemption in its effect has mainly been carried on by remarkable communications of the Spirit of God. Though there be a more constant influence of God's Spirit always in some degree attending his ordinances, yet the way in which the greatest things have been done towards carrying on this work always have been by remarkable effusions, at special seasons of mercy...'

29. See, for example, Isaiah 45:8; 46:13; 51:5; 52:7; 56:1.

Chapter 3: God heals us

1. These verses anticipate our study of repentance in chapter 7.

2. The verb *šûḇ* construed with '*el* suggests a turning toward someone, a moving in that person's direction, as in verse 2. But here the verb is

construed with '*ad*, suggesting a returning all the way to that person. Cf. J. C. L. Gibson, *Davidson's Introductory Hebrew Grammar: Syntax* (Edinburgh: T. & T. Clark, 1994), § 118, Rem. 1. Thomas Edward McComiskey (ed.), *The Minor Prophets: An Exegetical and Expository Commentary*, vol. 1 (Grand Rapids: Baker, 1992), 229, comments: 'Hosea calls his people not only to turn toward God, but to make him the termination of their return. This is complete repentance. They are to reenter the sphere of Yahweh's dominion.'

3. Cf. Alexander B. Grosart (ed.), *The Works of Richard Sibbes*, vol. 2 (1862–64; reprint, Edinburgh: The Banner of Truth Trust, 1983), 254–255: 'The best provision for preventing destruction is spiritual means. God himself is a spirit, and spiritual means reach unto him who is the first mover of the great wheel of all affairs of this world. It is preposterous to begin at the second cause. We trouble ourselves in vain there, when we neglect the first. We should therefore begin the work in heaven, and first of all take up that quarrel which is between God and our souls. If this be done first, we need not fear the carriage of second things, all which God, out of his good providence and gracious care, will frame to work for good to his own (Romans 8:28), for whose sakes, rather than help should fail, he will create new helps (Isaiah 4:5). Wherefore, in all things it is best to begin with God.'

4. Cf. Raymond C. Ortlund Jr., *Whoredom: God's Unfaithful Wife in Biblical Theology*, ed. D. A. Carson (Grand Rapids: Eerdmans, 1996).

5. Grosart (ed.), *The Works of Richard Sibbes*, vol. 2, 265, with slight rewording.

6. I interpret this ambiguous Hebrew form with the RSV and NRSV, *pace* the NIV ('Our gods').

7. 'We will not mount war-horses' may allude to *matériel* imported from Egypt. Cf. Isaiah 31:1–3.

8. Cf. Grosart (ed.), *The Works of Richard Sibbes*, vol. 2, 303, with slight rewording: 'Sin is a disease and a wound; for what is pride but a swelling? What is anger but an intemperate heat of the soul, like an ague, as it were? What is revenge but a wildfire in the soul? What is lust but a spreading canker in the soul, tending to a consumption? What is covetousness but a sword, a perpetual wounder of the soul, piercing it through with many sorrows? What is apathy but, as it were, the lethargy and apoplexy of the soul? And so we might go on in other resemblances.'

9. James Luther Mays, *Hosea: A Commentary* (Philadelphia: Westminster, 1969), 187, italics added.

10. See chapter 2, note 9 above.

11. Derek Kidner, 'The Way Home: An Exposition of Hosea 14', *Themelios* (spring 1976), 35.

12. *Pace* the NIV, I accept the emendation of the third person suffix to second person in the Hebrew text, with the RSV, NASB, and NRSV.

13. Grosart (ed.), *The Works of Richard Sibbes*, vol. 2, 308–309, with slight rewording for clarity.

Chapter 4: God pours out his Spirit upon us

1. A. W. Tozer, 'Power in Action', *Heartcry! A Journal on Revival and Spiritual Awakening* (summer 1997), 7.

2. Ibid., 8–9.

3. The NIV reads 'people'. I prefer the literal rendering 'flesh', however, to preserve the contrast between *Spirit* and *flesh*.

4. The NIV reads 'my servants', presumably because of the wording in Acts 2:18, which in turn echoes witnesses in the Septuagint tradition. It is invalid, however, to allow this New Testament text, *qua* text, to be read back into the Old Testament. Moreover, the NIV's wording alters the meaning of the line.

5. Rabbinic tradition took it further. 'The Shekinah rests only on a wise man, a strong man, a wealthy man and a tall man,' such as Moses, according to the Talmud, 'Shabbath', 92a.

6. Joel's emphasis lies on the universal spirituality of God's people. The structure and offices of the church are a separate question. The apostle who affirmed Galatians 3:28 with all his heart is the same one who also affirmed, for example, 1 Timothy 2:12. The Spirit's fullness does not necessarily translate into formally recognized church leadership. If it did, then, in principle, regenerate children could be qualified for pastoral leadership over their parents. Cf. Acts 20:28; 1 Timothy 3:1–7.

7. Thomas J. Finley, *Joel, Amos, Obadiah* (Chicago: Moody Press, 1990), 75, represents one line of interpretation when he writes, 'The sun could be darkened by eclipse, but heavy smoke in the atmosphere may be what turns the moon to blood-red. Perhaps the smoke will derive from volcanic and tectonic activity on the earth as well as through war.' From another point of view, John Calvin, *Joel, Amos and Obadiah* (Edinburgh: The Banner of Truth Trust, 1986), 100–101, proposes what is (to me) a more convincing approach to these verses: 'What [Joel] says of blood and darkness is no doubt to be taken metaphorically for a disordered state of things ... It is the same as though he said, "So great will be the succession of evils that the whole order of nature will seem to be subverted ... [T]he calamities which shall come will take away every token of God's kindness.' ... As God, then, would take away all tokens of his favour, so the prophet, by blood, by

darkness and by dark clouds sets forth metaphorically that sorrow by which the minds of men would necessarily be possessed.'

8. Matthew Henry, in his *Commentary on the Whole Bible*, vol. 4, 1217, enlarges our understanding of what it means to call on the name of the Lord: 'This calling on God supposes knowledge of him, faith in him, desire towards him, dependence on him, and, as an evidence of the sincerity of all this, a conscientious obedience to him; for, without that, crying Lord, Lord, will not stand us in any stead. Note, It is the praying remnant that shall be the saved remnant. And it will aggravate the ruin of those who perish that they might have been saved on such easy terms.'

9. C. S. Lewis, *The Silver Chair* (New York: Collier, 1972), 19. An anonymous hymn-writer (c. 1878) put it this way:

> I sought the Lord, and afterward I knew
> He moved my heart to seek him, seeking me.
> It was not I that found, O Saviour true;
> No, I was found of thee.
>
> Thou didst reach forth thy hand and mine enfold.
> I walked and sank not on the storm-vexed sea.
> 'Twas not so much that I on thee took hold
> As thou, dear Lord, on me.
>
> I find, I walk, I love, but O the whole
> Of love is but my answer, Lord, to thee,
> For thou wert long beforehand with my soul;
> Always thou lovedst me.

10. The map in *The NIV Study Bible* at Acts 2 shows how extensive an area of the ancient world was represented by the Jewish pilgrims visiting Jerusalem for the feast of Pentecost (Acts 2:5).

11. I apologize for the rudeness of this translation, but the NIV smoothes over the presence of the partitive preposition in Peter's quotation of the Septuagint. The Greek tradition does not read, 'I will pour out my Spirit' (NIV), but 'I will pour out *from* my Spirit'. This is why the AV (1611) translates Acts 2:17 'I will pour out of my Spirit', the NEB (1970) 'I will pour out ... a portion of my spirit', and the NASB (1971) 'I will pour forth of My Spirit'.

12. See note 3 above.

13. See note 11 above.

14. See Acts 1:15; 2:41; 4:4; 5:14; 6:7; 9:31; 11:21; 12:24; 13:49; 14:1; 16:5; 19:20; 28:31.

15. See note 11 above.

16. Edwards, 'Faithful Narrative', in *The Works of Jonathan Edwards*, vol. 1, 344.
17. The Westminster Confession of Faith, XVI, 3. John G. Lorimer, 'Encouragements from the Promises and Prophecies of Scripture', in *The Revival of Religion*, 231–232, counsels us in a wise response to the promises of Scripture: 'In conclusion, let me exhort Christians to be comforted and animated. None can enjoy greater sources of satisfaction and hope; other causes may fail – theirs is sure of ultimate triumph; come what will of present difficulty or trial, they are on the winning side: let them be persuaded of this, and exercise lively faith in the promises of God. Such faith will impart cheerfulness and joy to all their prayers and labours ... They will be ever expecting good, and good will be ever flowing in upon them. Not that they are to reason with themselves in this manner: "Revivals, and ultimate and universal success are promised; they shall come of themselves; let us resign ourselves to the ease of a dreaming expectation." No: this would be a gross perversion of the Scripture doctrine of promises and predictions – of the same character with a prostitution of the doctrine of the perseverance of the saints. Promises are not intended to supersede prayer or labour, but to give cheerfulness and support under the discharge of their duties. Such perversions would be unfit for present obedience, and would even prevent Christians availing themselves of the advantages of revivals when they came.'
18. Anne Ortlund, 'Macedonia' (1966).
19. H. C. G. Moule, *Charles Simeon* (London: Inter-Varsity Fellowship, 1965), 108.

Chapter 5: God raises us up

1. See R. Kent Hughes, *Ephesians: The Mystery of the Body of Christ* (Wheaton: Crossway, 1990), 66; *The Dictionary of National Biography*, vol. 2 (Oxford: Oxford University Press, 1960), 276.
2. A. W. Tozer, *The Pursuit of Man* (Camp Hill: Christian Publications, 1978), 91–92.
3. This was his remark on hearing of the death of Alexander, Earl of Galloway.
4. Cf. Thomas Chalmers' (1780–1847) famous sermon, 'The Expulsive Power of a New Affection'.
5. Ezra 1:1 – 6:22 and Haggai 1:1–15 tell the story of the returnees, their struggles to rebuild the work of God in the promised land, and God's interventions on their behalf.
6. Walther Eichrodt, *Theology of the Old Testament*, vol. 1 (Philadelphia: Westminster, 1961), 191. See Exodus 3:13–15.

7. William Greenhill, *An Exposition of the Prophet Ezekiel* (reprint, London: Henry Bohn, 1846), 741.

8. C. S. Lewis, *The Lion, the Witch and the Wardrobe* (New York: Macmillan, 1972), 165–166, italics his.

9. See Bruce Waltke, 'The Valley of Dry Bones', *Reformed Quarterly* (spring 1998), 3.

10. Edwards, 'Christian Knowledge, or, The Importance and Advantage of a Thorough Knowledge of Divine Truth', in *The Works of Jonathan Edwards*, vol. 2, 158.

11. Jim Elliff, 'Reformation or Revival?' *Heartcry! A Journal on Revival and Spiritual Awakening* (autumn 1997), 23–24.

12. Walther Eichrodt, *Ezekiel: A Commentary* (Philadelphia: Westminster, 1970), 509.

13. See Finney, *Lectures on Revivals of Religion*, 13: 'There is nothing in religion beyond the ordinary power of nature. It consists entirely in the right exercise of the powers of nature. It is just that, and nothing more.' Given his theology, Finney could never have written Ezekiel 37 – nor, for that matter, Romans 8, etc.

14. A. B. Simpson, *The Holy Spirit, or, Power from on High: An Unfolding of the Doctrine of the Holy Spirit in the Old and New Testaments*, vol. 1 (Harrisburg: Christian Publications, n.d.), 248.

15. See Gerald A. Larue, *Babylon and the Bible* (Grand Rapids: Baker, 1969), 54.

16. Cf. Isaiah 41:4; 43:10, 13, 25; 46:4; 48:12; 51:12.

17. Modern confusion about the meaning of authentic spirituality is discussed insightfully by D. A. Carson, 'When Is Spirituality Spiritual? Reflections on Some Problems of Definition', in *The Gagging of God: Christianity Confronts Pluralism* (Grand Rapids: Zondervan, 1996), 555–569.

18. Cf. Waltke, 'The Valley of Dry Bones' (note 9 above), 16: 'And let us pray that the Church will ask for and embrace the fullness of God's Spirit.' Both verbs there are important: *ask for* and *embrace*.

19. C. H. Spurgeon, quoted in Erroll Hulse, *The Great Invitation* (Welwyn, Hertfordshire: Evangelical Press, 1986), 179.

Chapter 6: God restores us

1. Viktor A. Frankl, *Man's Search for Meaning* (New York: Washington Square Press, 1969), 117–118.

2. The translation of Psalm 126 offered here adapts the NIV to the interpretation in Walter Beyerlin, *We Are Like Dreamers: Studies in Psalm 126* (Edinburgh: T. & T. Clark, 1982). Beyerlin's proposal is subjected to a critique in Allan M. Harman, 'The Setting and

Interpretation of Psalm 126', *The Reformed Theological Review* 44 (1985), 74–80. But each of Harman's points can be rebutted. Moreover, his interpretation does not alleviate the difficulties that prompted Beyerlin's proposal in the first place.

3. The NIV reads, 'When the Lord brought back the captives to Zion...' The historical referent may well have been the return of the Jewish captives from Babylon, but the meaning of the Hebrew wording here is a separate question. I consider it more likely that the language means what the RSV and NRSV interpret it to mean, as reflected above, for technical philological reasons, because of the parallel in verse 4 which the NIV does construe in terms of 'restoring fortunes', and because the imagery of verses 5 and 6 is of a more general nature than 'bringing back captives'. The RSV/NRSV wording, however, is properly qualified by H. C. Leupold, *Exposition of the Psalms* (Grand Rapids: Baker, 1969), 889: '"Restore our fortunes" is readily understood but is a bit unfortunate in that it brings the heathen goddess of good luck, Fortuna, into the picture. More to the point would be an expression like, "Work a total change in our situation," as a translation of the unique Hebrew expression...'

4. The word 'men' remains useful as shorthand for human beings, and its usage can even be elegant. But the NIV's 'men who dreamed' here might give the impression that there is something particularly male about the dreaming, which there is not.

5. With the RSV/NRSV, the Hebrew particle should be made visible in English.

6. The NIV translates 'and we are filled with joy'. But this verse does not include the verb 'to be filled'. Verse 2 does use that verb. Moreover, it seems preferable to show in English that verse 3 registers the presence of a third word for happiness, in addition to 'laughter' and 'songs of joy' in verse 2. I have, therefore, followed the RSV at this point.

7. Because verse 5 takes the form of a proverb, I prefer to translate with a timeless English present tense rather than with the NIV's future tense ('will reap').

8. The passage goes on to contemplate the possibility that the prophet or dreamer could be false, for not all dreams are revelatory. But the passage assumes that a dream *could* convey prophetic revelation.

9. 'Zion' is to be equated with the people because of the parallel in verse 4: 'Restore *our* fortunes.'

10. Calvin, *Commentary on the Book of Psalms*, vol. 5, 97.

11. I intend this word in its plain, non-technical sense. In the past, 'enthusiasm' was synonymous with 'fanaticism'. But that usage is now regarded as archaic.

12. Edwards, *The Works of Jonathan Edwards*, vol. 1, 380.

13. Ibid.
14. Ibid., 381.
15. Ibid., 397.
16. Ibid., 412, italics added.
17. Jonathan Edwards ventured the proposal that revival is the device God uses when he wills for his great work to surge forward in this world. See his 'History of the Work of Redemption', in *The Works of Jonathan Edwards*, vol. 1, 539: 'It may here be observed, that from the fall of man to our day, the work of redemption in its effect has mainly been carried on by remarkable communications of the Spirit of God. Though there be a more constant influence of God's Spirit always in some degree attending his ordinances, yet the way in which the greatest things have been done towards carrying on this work always have been by remarkable effusions, at special seasons of mercy, as may fully appear hereafter in our further prosecution of our subject.'
18. Barry J. Beitzel, *The Moody Atlas of Bible Lands* (Chicago: Moody, 1985), 36. As he notes there, the very name 'Negev' may connote dryness. Cf. Syriac *ngb*, to dry up, become dry.
19. Willem A. VanGemeren, 'The Psalms', in *The Expositor's Bible Commentary*, ed. Frank E. Gaebelein, vol. 5 (Grand Rapids: Zondervan, 1991), 791.
20. See Kidner, *Psalms 73–150* (chap. 2, note 27, above), 439.
21. Finney uses the agricultural metaphor as well, but within a different theological framework. He argues (astonishingly) that revival 'is not a miracle, or dependent on a miracle, in any sense'. He contends that revival 'is the result of the right use of the appropriate means'. And although he allows that the blessing of God is needed, he claims explicitly that revival operates by 'the ordinary rules of cause and effect'. And then he draws in the metaphor of sowing seed to misrepresent the view of revival that Edwards and others teach, as if divine sovereignty discouraged human labour. On this point, Finney's thinking is reductionistic and unbiblical. His triumphalistic theory leaves no room for the sower's tears and necessarily diminishes the reaper's joy. Our psalmist would never have argued along Finney's line. A law of God can be analogous to a law of nature, to encourage our confidence in God's faithfulness to his Word, without excluding the mystery of God's sovereign ultimacy as to how and when he may fulfil his Word. See Finney, *Lectures on Revivals of Religion*, 12–15.
22. Henry, *Commentary on the Whole Bible*, vol. 3, 734.
23. Ibid., edited for clarity.
24. Cf. Waltke and O'Connor, *Biblical Hebrew Syntax* (chap. 2, note 13, above), 35.3.2c.
25. Moule, *Charles Simeon* (chap. 4, note 19, above), 155.

Part Two: What We Must Do

Prologue

1. Revival is not different in nature from the normal work of the gospel. It is an extraordinary work of the biblical gospel. So revival is not on a higher plane than the gospel; revival is on a higher plane than all *human* capacity to produce results. When the gospel is not 'working', modern evangelicalism too often resorts to human devices. But we must not humiliate the gospel by igniting our own back-up power systems. Without the power of God, we are out of business. See Exodus 33:15.

2. Jonathan Edwards affirms the importance of our place in God's work of revival in his 'Thoughts on the Revival', in *The Works of Jonathan Edwards*, vol. 1, 390: 'This work [of revival], which has lately been carried on in the land, is the work of God, and not the work of man. Its beginning has not been of man's power or device, and its being carried on depends not on our strength or wisdom; but yet God expects of all, that they should use their utmost endeavours to promote it, and that the hearts of all should be greatly engaged in this affair. We should improve our utmost strength in it, however vain human strength is without the power of God; and so he no less requires that we should improve our utmost care, wisdom, and prudence, though human wisdom of itself be as vain as human strength. Though God is wont to carry on such a work in such a manner as many ways to show the weakness and vanity of means and human endeavours in themselves, yet, at the same time, he carries it on in such a manner as to encourage diligence and vigilance in the use of proper means and endeavours, and to punish the neglect of them. Therefore, in our endeavours to promote this great work, we ought to use the utmost caution, vigilance, and skill, in the measures we take in order to it. A great affair should be managed with great prudence.'

3. Moule, *Charles Simeon*, 77, italics added.

4. I do offer some preliminary, biblical reflections on this question in 'The Sovereignty of God: Case Studies in the Old Testament', in Thomas B. Schreiner and Bruce A. Ware (eds.), *Still Sovereign: Contemporary Perspectives on Election, Foreknowledge and Grace* (Grand Rapids: Baker, 2000), 25–46.

5. Moule, *Charles Simeon*, 77.

6. Ibid.

Chapter 7: We return to God

1. Scholars debate whether the 'large and mighty army' of chapter 2 is a metaphor for a locust plague, as in chapter 1, or whether it is a literal human army. Cf. Hans Walter Wolff, *Joel and Amos* (Philadelphia: Fortress, 1977), 41ff.
2. Henry, *Commentary on the Whole Bible*, vol. 4, 1210.
3. Cf. Zechariah 1:3; Malachi 3:7; James 4:8.
4. Here in Joel 2:12–13 we find the same distinction in Hebrew idiom observed at Hosea 14:1 in chapter 3, 62–65. In verse 12 Joel calls us to return *unto* the Lord, and in verse 13 *toward* the Lord.
5. NIV: 'turn'; RSV/NRSV: 'return'; NASB: 'return'.
6. *National and International Religion Report* (8 October 1990), 8. The trenchant analyses of David Wells give depth and texture to our interpretation of such data. Cf. *God in the Wasteland* (Grand Rapids: Eerdmans, 1994) and *Losing Our Virtue: Why the Church Must Recover Its Moral Vision* (Grand Rapids: Eerdmans, 1998).
7. See Philip Schaff, *History of the Christian Church*, vol. 7 (1910; reprint, Grand Rapids: Eerdmans, 1970), 160.
8. John Calvin, *Institutes*, 3.3.1–2.
9. Ibid., 3.3.6.
10. Doctrinal fidelity is not the primary subject of this book, but neither may it be overlooked. Faithfulness to the gospel cannot *ultimately* be enforced in our Christian institutions by external devices; it must flow out of an abiding spirit of repentance within. Faithfulness flourishes wherever God's servants love the gospel because they love the Lord of the gospel more than they love acclaim from the world. But when this spirit wanes, a Christian institution must expect theological restlessness soon to appear, eroding faithfulness and weakening the integrity of the institution. Therefore, along with the necessity of requiring good-faith subscription to its doctrinal standard, a Christian institution must also cultivate in its soul a compelling *love* for the Lord and his Word. Those members of the institution who fail to evidence such a spirit cannot be allowed to set the tone for the rest and may need to move on. But that takes us into the subject of reformation, rather than revival.
11. Cf. Calvin, *Joel, Amos and Obadiah*, 59.
12. John Merlin Powis Smith, William Hayes Ward, and Julius A. Bewer, *A Critical and Exegetical Commentary on Micah, Zephaniah, Nahum, Habakkuk, Obadiah and Joel* (1911; reprint, Edinburgh: T. & T. Clark, 1965), 105.
13. C. S. Lewis, *The Weight of Glory and Other Addresses* (1949; reprint, Grand Rapids: Eerdmans, 1974), 2.

14. Cf. Deuteronomy 4:25–31; 30:1–10; 1 Kings 8:46–51.
15. Because these phrases draw heavily on Exodus 34:6, I have inserted quotation marks to make explicit that another source underlies the words of Joel. Cf. Wolff, *Joel and Amos*, 39.
16. Calvin, *Institutes*, 3.3.16.
17. John Owen, 'Of the Mortification of Sin in Believers', in Goold (ed.), *The Works of John Owen* (chap. 2, note 19, above), vol. 6, 14.
18. Lewis, *The Silver Chair*, 16–17, italics his.
19. Cf. Calvin, *Institutes*, 3.17.5.
20. Grosart (ed.), *The Works of Richard Sibbes*, vol. 7, 185.
21. Edwards, 'Memoirs', in *The Works of Jonathan Edwards*, vol. 1, xlvii.
22. Cf. Jeremiah 18:7–10; 26:3, 13, 19; Jonah 3:9 – 4:2.
23. Robert Burns, 'The Cotter's Saturday Night', verse 6.
24. St Hilary, *De Trinitate*, IV.14.
25. Cf. Calvin, *Institutes*, 1.17.12–13.
26. Cf. Numbers 23:19; 1 Samuel 15:29; Malachi 3:6.
27. For recent discussions of the preposterous notion that God is limited in his capacities of knowledge and control, see Douglas F. Kelly, 'Afraid of Infinitude', and Timothy George, 'A Transcendence-Starved Deity', *Christianity Today* (9 January 1995), 32–34; D. A. Carson, 'God, the Bible and Spiritual Warfare: A Review Article', *Journal of the Evangelical Theological Society* 42 (1999), 251–269; and *Modern Reformation* (September/October 1999).
28. The NIV reads, 'He may turn ...' But Joel is deliberately using the Hebrew root *šûḇ* for the third time, matching his calls that we *return* to God (vv. 12, 13). His wording implies God's readiness to meet our returning to him with his own 'returning' to us.
29. Leslie C. Allen, *The Books of Joel, Obadiah, Jonah and Micah* (Grand Rapids: Eerdmans, 1976), 82.
30. The NIV reads, 'Bring together the elders'. But the parallel ('children, those nursing at the breast') implies that elderly or aged people are in view. The NIV's wording might suggest to the mind the office of elder rather than aged people in a more general sense.
31. Cf. Douglas Stuart, *Hosea–Jonah* (Waco: Word, 1987), 253.
32. Calvin, *Institutes*, 3.3.17.
33. See Timothy George, *Theology of the Reformers* (Nashville: Broadman, 1988), 160.
34. The NIV reads, 'Let the priests, who minister before the LORD, weep between the temple porch and the altar.' But the RSV/NRSV show the emphasis in the Hebrew word order, which is reflected in the adjustment of the NIV in the text.
35. See *The NIV Study Bible*, under 1 Kings 6, for an artist's depiction of this area of the temple.

36. See Hebrews 4:14–16; 10:19–22.
37. William Beveridge (1638–1708), as quoted in J. C. Ryle, *Old Paths, Being Plain Statements on Some of the Weightier Matters of Christianity* (reprint, London: James Clarke, 1972), 130, note 2.
38. Edwards, *The Works of Jonathan Edwards*, vol. 1, 399.
39. Cf. Deuteronomy 28:37; Psalm 44:14; 79:4; Jeremiah 18:16; 19:8.
40. Cf. Exodus 32:11–12; Numbers 14:13–16; Deuteronomy 9:26–29.

Chapter 8: We seek God

1. Aleksandr Solzhenitsyn, 'Men Have Forgotten God', *Religion in Communist Dominated Areas* 22 (1983), 54.
2. Francis A. Schaeffer, 'The Lord's Work in the Lord's Way', in *No Little People* (Downers Grove, Ill.: InterVarsity Press, 1974), 64, italics his.
3. Cf. Jonathan Edwards, 'The Religious Affections', in *The Works of Jonathan Edwards*, vol. 1, 244: 'If true religion lies much in the affections, we may infer that such means are to be desired as have much tendency to move the affections. Such books, and such a way of preaching the Word and the administration of the ordinances, and such a way of worshiping God in prayer and praises, as has a tendency deeply to affect the hearts of those who attend these means, is much to be desired.'

   In his 'Thoughts on the Revival', 391, he applies this principle to his own methods of preaching the gospel: 'I should think myself in the way of my duty to raise the affections of my hearers as high as possibly I can, provided that they are affected with nothing but truth, and with affections that are not disagreeable to the nature of the subject.'

   Means are God's usual way in ministry. But means are not ultimate. God alone is ultimate, causative, creative and powerful. Therefore, above all else, we must have the favour of God upon us!
4. Cf. Christopher Begg, ' "Seeking Yahweh" and the Purpose of Chronicles', *Louvain Studies* 9 (1982–83), 128–141.
5. Cf. Raymond B. Dillard, 'Reward and Punishment in Chronicles: The Theology of Immediate Retribution', *Westminster Theological Journal* 46 (1984), 164–172.
6. Cf. Deuteronomy 4:29; Jeremiah 29:13; Hebrews 11:6.
7. Edwards, *The Works of Jonathan Edwards*, vol. 1, 248.
8. Ibid., italics added.
9. Verse 4 uses another Hebrew word for seeking God, but the two words seem broadly synonymous. Cf. the parallelism in 1 Chronicles 16:11; Psalm 38:12; 105:4. And in our passage, both forms of

'seeking' are rewarded with the same 'finding': 'he will be found by you' (v. 2), 'he was found by them' (v. 4).

10. Cf. Sibbes, 'The Successful Seeker', in *Works of Richard Sibbes*, vol. 6, 109–132.

11. C. S. Lewis, *Reflections on the Psalms* (New York: Harcourt, Brace & World, 1958), 51.

12. Cf. John Piper, *Future Grace* (Sisters, Oreg.: Multnomah, 1995), section VI, 'Unmerited, Conditional Future Grace', 229–271.

13. Cf. John Owen, 'God's Presence with a People the Spring of their Prosperity', in Goold (ed.), *The Works of John Owen*, vol. 8, 431–452.

14. *The Works of John Newton*, vol. 6 (1820; reprint, Edinburgh: The Banner of Truth Trust, 1988), 15–16, edited slightly for clarity.

Chapter 9: We humble ourselves

1. Fareed Zakaria, 'To Hell in a Handbasket', *New York Times Book Review*, 19 April 1998, 17.

2. See Philip Cushman, 'Why the Self Is Empty', *American Psychologist* 45 (1990), 599–611. While this article contains keen insights into our corporate mentality today, I do not agree with some of its underlying premises.

3. Since nothing else in the passage encourages us to construe the 'road' and 'way' as literal, we take these to refer figuratively to the moral and spiritual direction of our lives. Cf. verses 17–18: 'his wilful ways', 'his ways'.

4. These 'blind' imperatives, addressing non-existent persons, are a function of the poet's sensitive imagination perceiving this purpose of God as somehow operative by itself in the natural order of things. So the verbs may be taken as expressive of a general divine purpose, capable of being realized in various historical situations. Cf. S. R. Driver, *A Treatise on the Use of the Tenses in Hebrew* (Oxford: Clarendon Press, 1892), §§ 56–57; Waltke and O'Connor, *Biblical Hebrew Syntax*, 34.3d.

5. J. A. Alexander, *Commentary on the Prophecies of Isaiah*, vol. 2 (Grand Rapids: Zondervan, 1974), 349, calls this 'a prophecy which, in design as well as fact, is perfectly unlimited to any one event or period, yet perfectly defined as a description of God's mode of dealing with his church and with those who although in it are not of it'.

6. Calvin, *Institutes*, 1.1.1–3.

7. René Descartes, *Discourse on Method* (New York: The Liberal Arts Press, 1956), 21.

8. See Proverbs 1:7; 9:10; Gerhard von Rad, *Wisdom in Israel* (Nashville: Abingdon, 1972), 65–68.

9. Edwards, *The Works of Jonathan Edwards*, vol. 1, 398–99.
10. Calvin, *Institutes*, 2.2.11.
11. Moule, *Charles Simeon*, 65.
12. C. S. Lewis, *Mere Christianity* (New York: Macmillan, 1958), 94.
13. Calvin, *Institutes*, 1.1.3.
14. See Exodus 15:11; 1 Samuel 2:2; Isaiah 40:25.
15. Calvin, *Commentary on the Book of the Prophet Isaiah*, vol. 4, 214.
16. Horton Davies (ed.), *The Communion of Saints* (Grand Rapids: Eerdmans, 1990), 73.
17. Cf. Os Guinness and John Seel (eds.), *No God but God: Breaking with the Idols of Our Age* (Chicago: Moody, 1992), 10: 'Modernity represents a special challenge to revival: Quite simply, the church of Christ has not experienced revival under the conditions of advanced modernity. On the one hand, modernity undercuts true dependence on God's sovereign awakening by fostering the notion that we can effect revival by human means. On the other hand, modernity makes many people satisfied with privatized, individualistic, and subjective experiences that are pale counterfeits of true revival. While many Christians no longer have a practical expectation of revival, those who count on God's sovereignty over modernity have every reason to look to God for revival once again.'
18. See Harold O. J. Brown, *The Sensate Culture* (Dallas: Word, 1996), 8.
19. Cf. Isaiah 1:10–17; Ezekiel 8:17–18.
20. Jonathan Edwards discusses the value of active concern for others in his 'Thoughts on the Revival', in *The Works of Jonathan Edwards*, vol. 1, 428–429.
21. See J. Edwin Orr, 'Revival and Social Change', *Fides et Historia* 6 (1974), 1–12.
22. Fawcett, *The Cambuslang Revival*, 210.
23. See Job 42:10 AV.
24. Fawcett, *The Cambuslang Revival*, 211–212, edited slightly for clarity.

Appendix

1. Francis A. Schaeffer, *Death in the City* (Downers Grove, Ill.: Inter-Varsity Press, 1969). Biblical quotations in Dr Schaeffer's text are from AV.

Scripture index